The Myth of 'Roo

By

Deon le Roux

To my wife Elizna and my daughter Isabella.
You are my heroes and this book, like everything else in my life is for you.
I love you.

To Darryl and Otto... well enough said.

To Janine "J-bird" Williams, thanks for repairing the tenses in my language used.

Contact Information
Website: *http://www.facebook.com/#!/pages/The-Myth-of-Roo/215858558475924*
Email: *the.myth.of.roo@gmail.com*

ISBN 978-0-473-19770-4

Copyright © Deon le Roux, 2011

All rights reserved.

Table of Contents

Part 1 – The Journey to the Journey 2

    Chapter 1 – Double shot long black... 2

    Chapter 2 – The early years 4

    Chapter 3 - Trippy idea 14

    Chapter 4 – Preparation H 22

    Chapter 5 – Dry runs 28

Part 2 – Aotearoa, Land of the long white cloud. 32

    Chapter 7 – The West Coast, rain and John Cleese 40

    Chapter 8 – Best made plans 65

PART 3 – The Myth of 'Roo 67

    Chapter 9 – Going down under to the big smoke 71

    Chapter 10 – Debbie does Victoria 79

    Chapter 11 – Waltzing South Australia 91

    Chapter 11 – Really far Outback in the Northern Territories 123

    Chapter 13 - Queensland, Banana bender country 189

Part 1 – The Journey to the Journey

Chapter 1 – Double shot long black...

History books are filled with stories of ordinary people achieving extraordinary things. This pioneering drive of the human race has allowed us to progress from hairless monkeys living in caves to interplanetary travel. Spend any time reading these books and you find many stories of epic adventures, each with their own unique challenges and seemingly insurmountable obstacles that had to be overcome.

Excellent examples that readily come to mind are the adventures of Edmund Hillary climbing that huge bloody mountain; Einstein who had the not so smart people misquoting the $M=EC^2$ formula and Columbus finding the rastas in Jamaica instead of the US of A. Even the spaceship Apollo 13 had a (Whitney) Houston problem.

Much like the brave people in these epic adventures facing many hurdles along the way, so too did our little adventure have its greatest challenge. I admit that ours was nothing like climbing Everest or building an atomic bomb, but at least it was better than sitting on a couch having chocolate-covered peanuts eating competitions.

Our adventure takes us over approximately nine and a half thousand kilometres through some of the hottest and most desolate places on earth. Places known to have the highest density of poisonous creatures per capita and the lowest density of human beings per square mile. Our route will expose us to extremes of everything from traffic, to animals, to weather, to people of dubious character. The sum total of our kit we can hold in our arms. We will have no support crew or backup plans, limited water and food supplies, certainly no common sense and all this for twenty three days.

So with all that said; what, you might ask is our greatest challenge?

Well, simply put, it is coffee.

Hi, my name is Deon and I am a coffee snob.

Chapter 2 – The early years

As I had just mentioned, I am Deon le Roux, born during the crazy seventies in the capital city of South Africa, Pretoria. After moving to the Western Cape briefly, I ended up in the Eastern Cape where I grew up. I then moved around a bit and found myself in the capital city of New Zealand, Wellington. This story is not about my life and certainly not about me moving around the world so enough of that.

This story is my experience of realising a dream. There are a few characters in this book that will pop up often so I thought I would introduce them to you now. Before I do, I want to get back to the point just made, that this book is my experience of this amazing adventure. I am sure a few things might have looked or felt different from the view point of the other aforementioned characters and if you are interested to hear their experience of the events detailed here, please read the books they wrote about it. If you can't find those books, well, then you will just have to take my word for it that this is how it all went down.

The other thing I need to make clear upfront is that even though I give both the New Zealanders and the Australians some stick, I am a great fan of both countries and respect their culture and people. In fact, I love both countries so much I have taken on New Zealand citizenship and now live in Australia. I am well aware of the fact that my sense of humour sometimes sounds a bit off, but that is just how I roll. I apologise if I offend anyone, it is certainly not my intention.

With the disclaimers out of the way, I want to start off by thanking the main characters. They made this bucket list experience possible and shared the adventure with me to make it the life changing adventure it was.

So let's get on with it! Please meet my lovely wife Elizna. We met when we were nine years old. Our families attended the same church and her older brother and my older brother were in the same class in school and were pretty good mates back in the day. Her younger brother and my younger brother are also the same age, so there were many excuses for us to all see each other. This suited me well as I was utterly and completely in love with her from the first time I saw her.

I was a bit of a nerdy kid and it took me fifteen years to actually ask her out and start the relationship that became our marriage. We have been married for a number of years now and still very happy together. Without her support this adventure would never have happened so I am eternally grateful for her understanding and patience with my little obsession.

The other main protagonist is Darryl Godwin. Firstly, I must stress that it is Darryl, not Darrell, not Darren and please never, ever Goodwin. This is a sore point, so please get it right. Darryl Godwin. Now that we have that settled, we met in Wellington, New Zealand in 2007. I had been working for Deloitte for a few months when he also joined, fresh from Ireland, although he is originally from South Africa. We quickly became good mates and soon became the driving force behind each other's bike obsession. It was largely due to his eagerness to go on this trip that we managed to go, so I am in debt to him for helping me turning this dream into a reality.

It is also worth introducing now our third amigo, Otto, who joined us for the New Zealand leg of this adventure. Otto is a good mate of mine who, if I had to sum him up in a sentence it would go something like this: "Come on Otto, we are all ready and waiting for you." Good luck though, as he will not be rushed, but he will probably laugh, so that's all good. Otto made the trip down South even more enjoyable and I am still giving him stick for not joining us for the trip to Australia.

You will come to know the other characters as the story unfolds, but there is one other important introduction still to be made………..the motorbikes, our obsession!

Motorbikes are strange machines which some people love and others hate. Getting on a motorbike, especially a big one is a serious commitment. It's like a cowboy getting on a bull and telling the clowns to get the hell out of the way or something like jumping into the sea for a swim with some sharks. It can also loosely be compared to deciding who to vote for in the national elections based on politicians' election promises. You have to know what you are doing or you could end up in trouble. A bike can turn on you if you do not pay it the proper respect, but if you treat it well, it will turn you on.

My love for motorbikes goes back many, many moons. I cannot rightly tell you the exact moment I started liking bikes. I think it might have been two, maybe three minutes after conception. However it wasn't till much later that I would actually start riding them.

I had a few moments on bikes in my very young years, but my first real experience with them started on a particular weekend about half way through high school. Leslie, my best friend from school managed to convince his father it was a good idea that we take his two motorcycles to my Dad's farm for the weekend. We had been "borrowing" the bikes in the evenings when I slept over at his house, usually sometime between 1:00 a.m. and 3:00 a.m. when no one would know, so getting approval to borrow the bikes was a bit of a surprise.

I couldn't believe he managed to convince his dad that this was ok, as we were sixteen and always in trouble. Basically, we were not the kind of kids that you would trust with motorbikes. But why ask too many questions if you might not like the answers? By the way, this is a great policy in life I have been following ever since! You are sure to get in more trouble this way, but you will have a lot more fun on the way!

Now that we had approval to take the bikes we needed to somehow get the bikes to the farm. It is about sixty kilometres outside East London, so no way can we ride them out there. I made a few calls and managed to borrow another friend of mine's dad's motorcycle trailer to transport the bikes and my mum drove us out there with the Land Rover. The motorcycles were a 50cc Yamaha DT and the other one was a Suzuki 200cc of some kind. I can't really remember the model, but his dad was pretty holy about it as it was some sort of classic.

We spent the entire weekend riding all over the farm. We had a can full of extra fuel and the bikes only stopped when we had to fill the tanks, eat, drink, or pee. I really can't remember even sleeping at all that weekend. The riding was exhilarating. We chased through valleys and over hills to the savannah grassland at the far end of the farm splashing along the river banks.

With the wind blasting through my hair and wildlife scattering before us, we kept going and going. Soft, fluffy white clouds drifted across the blue skies and the warm sunshine was on our backs. I see trees of green, red roses too...I am getting a bit lyrical here, but it was the best experience of my young life. I had never felt so free and so, well, just being the right guy at the right place. From that time on, I always knew that I was a biker.

Getting home after that stunning weekend, we first went to drop Leslie and the bikes back at his house. It became clear how he managed to convince his dad to allow us to take the bikes out to the farm. He hadn't asked him! We just loaded the bikes and went off on our weekend. Later I found out that he did tell his dad that we were going to the farm, but he said nothing about the bikes. His dad didn't even know the bikes were gone until we stopped in front of the house to drop them off.

Needless to say, this was a once-off experience and his dad did not "agree" to let us take the bikes out again. In fact we were not allowed anywhere close to them again. Not that it would have done Leslie any good as the hiding he got ensured he wouldn't have been able to sit on a bike for a decent amount of time. He was busy mowing the lawn for the rest of his childhood anyway.

I didn't get off scot-free either. After this incident, I was banned from motorcycles for a long time. My father, a neurosurgeon has seen the aftermath of many motorcycle accidents and banned bikes outright anyway. This little incident did nothing to improve his viewpoint. The fact that my grades were awful didn't help my case convincing anyone that I deserved to get a motorcycle.

Bike-less time passed and after I left school I moved to Pretoria and ended up moving in with my cousin George. He is a strange character with a few quirks that can drive you insane, but he always came up with the best ideas for cool things to do as well as being well-connected. After a bottle of cheap whisky one night, I said I was keen to get a motorbike. I left it at that as it was just drunken, wishful thinking.

A few days later George said he had a surprise for me. He had called around and found a friend who was trying to sell his motorbike. He assured me it wasn't even that expensive and was in my price range.

It was an old 1980 Suzuki GN400. It had extended handlebars making it a cruiser style bike and a really cool scorpion paint job on the petrol tank. Apparently it was in decent enough nick so we went to look at it and the deal was done. We left so I could get the money and riding gear to be able to ride the bike home. It was love at first sight and with that I became the proud owner of my very first motorbike.

To protect my stunning good looks, I had my uncle's (who passed away the year before) old stuffed-up helmet, no visor, no chin strap, about three sizes too big and with almost none of the interior padding left. I rustled through the storeroom and grabbed this high-tech and crucial piece of biker's safety gear. To protect my super-athletic legs, a pair of jeans and a t-shirt made up the rest of my biker gear. Everything you need to ride safely and off we went to fetch the bike. I geared up, meaning I dropped the helmet onto my head and jumped onto the bike and I was ready to ride off on my new bike.

In defence of the events that happened on the trip home, it had been a good five years since my last ride on a bike. I had never actually been taught to ride but had picked it up along the way and only ever on 200cc and smaller bikes.

The few glasses of whisky before didn't help neither did the lack of a license. But hell, I was twenty years old and bullet proof. But hang on, let's back track a bit.

It started off well enough and I managed to get on the bike without incident. The guys standing around me must have thought I looked like a real Hell's Angel, or it might have been a Charlie's Angel? I elegantly flicked the side-stand up with a flick of my foot. The key slid effortlessly into the ignition and I smoothly turned it to the "On" position. The lights on the control panel went on and the headlight shone like fire. Confidence growing, I managed to kick-start the bike on the second try. The bike was even in neutral so I felt, if not looked quite the pro. I pulled away slowly enough to mask the few jumps and skips and then I was off. Having started off so easily of course only lulled me into the false believe that I knew what I was doing on the bike.

On the way home I managed to notch up my first motorcycle accident. Going into a tight corner, I hit a large patch of gravel. I wasn't lying over like the F1 racers or anything. In fact I barely lent over at all, but the bike's tail skidded out. Looking back, the bike might have only wobbled a bit or had a slight skid, but having almost no riding experience plus whisky and adrenaline pumping through my veins, it felt like sparks could start shooting as the tailpipe hit the ground.

In this instant of chilling fear, everything went into slow motion. I had to decide if I would try to save the situation and get the bike under control. It might sound like a dumb thing to have to decide, but there was some logic there. If I managed to bring the bike back under control I would spare myself a lot of pain and be the bull's balls! The price of failure would be a slide along the tar road, across the gravel and onto the side walk.

Alternatively I could steer the bike onto the grass in the kid's play park straight ahead, but this meant a certain wipe-out with no chance of getting the bike back under control. The grass was directly in front and the decisive factor for me, it was grass! I have no love for picking out tar from where my skin used to be neither am I too fond of grass burns, but if I was really lucky I might even survive this if I take a dive onto the grass. As time sped up again I decided to choose door number two, thank you Larry. Let's see what my prize was?

Wipe-out! After hitting the ground, a few seconds passed where I cannot be clear of the exact chain of events as it is now just a bunch of still pictures in my head. I jumped up from my tuck-dive-roll emergency brace position and surveyed the situation. I had a deep gash where the clutch handle had punctured my gloveless hand, a tailpipe burn on my leg courtesy of cheap jeans, blood in my mouth where I had bitten my tongue as my chin had hit the grass,unprotected by the useless bloody helmet and finally a good few bruises.

Taking stock of the damage and waiting a few seconds for my heart to slow down, I realised that the main damage was to my ego. Then I realised that I did not yet know just how bad my accident was. I quickly hobbled back to the bike expecting the worst. Oh, the relief! The scorpion paint job on the petrol tank was fine, so no serious damage done. The bike did have a bloodied, broken clutch handle and a few small scratches here and there but otherwise was none the worse for wear. I lifted the bike up and got on with shaky legs. I kick-started it and it jumped from under me, ran a few meters before falling over leaving me flat on my back.

With the clutch cable being broken the bike was in gear and this caused it to jump forward when I kick started it. I heard laughter and opened my eyes. There were school kids on their way home and a group of nannies in the park looking after rich peoples' kids who were enjoying the show. I felt my face go red and my ego smarted like hell. I got up, walked back for my useless bloody helmet and this time put the bike in neutral before I kick-started it. As I pulled away, the smart ass kids applauded and I flicked them the bird. A bottle of cheap whisky helped sooth my damaged ego when I got home. George had a good chuckle over the story and I managed to laugh with him....eventually.

It was during this period of my life that my then partner decided we were splitting up and I took some time out and went for a bike trip across the country. After a thousand kilometres passing through busy Gauteng, though the mined Southern Transvaal, across the barren Orange Free State, and into the bushy Eastern Cape, I thought I would do the responsible thing and register to do my motorcycle learner's licence. I duly did the thirty questions, scratch and sniff test and passed with only four wrong answers. Gaining the learners did little to get me legal on the road as that only allowed me to ride motorcycles up to fifty CCs.

But doing the learners did teach me those crucial basic skills and knowledge required to be a good motorcyclist. The test ensured I could recognise a stop sign and slow down when there is a school bus. Thus, I was now fully educated to ride a bike.

I was in my early twenties, single, bullet proof and not afraid of anything, so I wasn't too stressed about puny things like licences anyway. More important at this stage was to change my diet of flies, moths, grasshoppers and other bugs by investing in a helmet that had a visor plus a chin strap and padding, actually fitted me and had a cool design on the shell. After a quick shopping trip, this was accomplished. I now looked even cooler with a nice design on the helmet and of course started to lose weight with the reduced protein in my diet.

While on this trip I also visited my brother Hein who was in Port Alfred doing his Private Pilot's License at the flight school. I rode into the air base on my metal beast, flashing my fancy helmet and feeling like Tom Cruise in Top Gun. Planes were taking off while I rumbled down the runway towards the school. I stopped and puked trying to get the image of me being like Tom Cruise out of my head. Why did I have the sudden urge to change religion, donate all my money and then sit and wait for a spaceship? Pushing that out of my mind I continued down the road to the barracks.

If you had ever learned to fly in Port Alfred, you would understand how I could just ride in there and pick Hein up. They were grounded due to bad weather. They had been grounded for days by then, so it wasn't a tough job convincing my brother to come riding with me. Nothing grounded my bike... except me of course, but he didn't need to know that. We had loads of fun riding all over the place, even all the way out to Knysna, which was a hundred kilometres down the coast towards Cape Town. I will remember this as one of my favourite memories of Hein. It cemented a new friendship between us brothers, which saw us moving in together later on and having a great few years of partying!

After dropping him off and hitting the road again, I spent some alone time getting myself sorted out. I cruised where I wanted and camped anywhere I felt like. I even slept on the lawn of one of the large petrol stations just outside Bloemfontein one night. I learnt a lot about myself on this trip, including the fact that I loved long distance bike trips. I didn't only enjoy it, I loved it. I was addicted like an addict on crack cocaine. This trip probably saved my life and got me out from under the dark cloud of depression because of my breakup back into the light.

I learnt as many lessons as possible on my first bike including the importance of checking the oil regularly. Having covered almost four thousand kilometres since I got it without checking the oil once, the trip did not end well. As I passed a little hick town called Voggville my engine seized up. I don't know if you have ever been on a bike when this has happened or even seen it happen? It is quite a scary experience.

I was gently cruising along the deserted highway, taking it easy by keeping the revs just under the red line when my back wheel locked. I could smell tyres burning, hear the awful sound of screeching as the vehicle tried to stop quickly The bike fishtailed and gave a final "THUNK" from where the moving parts of the engine used to be. I managed to keep the bike up through this and then with a final flick of my foot, I lowered the bike's kickstand for the last time. I sat down next to the bike hyperventilating and cried softly. That was the end of the bike. It was written off. Goodbye Scorpion rider.

Many years passed till I finally decided it was time to get back onto the saddle. I was in my early thirties now and I no longer believed I was bulletproof. I had married by then, had a few more scars, more responsibilities and a couple of sports injuries. I understood the bulletproof feeling was in actuality just stupidity. Thinking I would do it properly this time, I started off by doing my learners licence again, this time in Wellington, New Zealand. I now had a little more money so I could buy a slightly better bike. Having said that, I went ahead and bought a really shit bike! It was a cool looking two hundred and fifty cc cruiser. It had loads of chrome and silver/grey fairings. I loved it, but it was a shit bike. It was a Jingeng 250JC. No, this is not a spelling mistake. It is a Chinese motorbike that looks very cool and is guaranteed to start falling apart within months. The quality of the bike was shocking.

I went on a long weekend trip across the north island of New Zealand on the Jingeng and fell in love again with cruising on the open road across the country. The bike nearly took my body apart, doing some damage to my ass, as it is not made to do long distances..... the bike not my ass but it was pure bliss. The scorpion rider was back in business. A couple of mates planned this trip and invited me along, starting my friendship with Tim, who I still often ride with. We covered about one and a half thousand kilometres in the weekend.

One morning, not too long after that trip, while on my way to work, I had my second bike accident. I was riding from home, along the bays towards the city. A woman driving in front of me pulled over onto the left-hand side of the road stopping in the cycle lane. I thought this was a bit stupid of her and slowed down and moved to the centre of the road to pass. Then without checking her mirrors she gracefully made a u-turn.

Time slowed down as in my first accident, giving me a moment to make a decision on what to do. In the first accident I made the safe, if rather pathetic decision to go for the fall rather than try to save the situation. In this incident, I made the second worse call I could. The worst would have been to speed up to try get around her, which would have gotten me killed for sure. Of all the possible options I had available to me, Deon the quick thinker, master of solving complex issues quickly and deftly chose to...

...blow the horn at her.

In retrospect this seems like a rather feeble response to the life-threatening situation of a car trying to kill me. One of the witnesses, a cyclist on the other side of the road was almost killed by my motorbike sliding across the tar towards him. Afterwards he told me his experience of the accident having just looked up hearing the crash. Seeing me flying over the bonnet while my bike was sliding straight towards him, all he could hear was the metal grinding across the road and the string of obscenities I let out in mid air and the hysterical screeching of the stupid female driver. Luckily my bike did not hit the cyclist, but slid past him onto the sidewalk and half way through the barrier and almost into the sea.

This was the second bike I owned and the second one I wrote off. I decided this was a bad habit that I would need to break. They say smoking is bad for you! At least this would be a habit I would be happy to break.

Talking about breaking stuff, I did need some time to recover from the accident. I was lucky that I was cruising slowly and I was dressed in full bike gear. I hyper-flexed my hip, my lower back was bruised and stiff and a piece of the skin on my foot was missing. Apart from that, I learnt some very valuable lessons from this accident. I improved my awareness of other vehicles and I had a better understanding of just how stupid some people are as drivers. Also never underestimate the value of proper riding gear and that not all cyclists are really assholes!

When I was ready to get back on a bike again, I got my full licence and upgraded to a BMW F650CS. This was now getting into more serious biking. The bike was amazing! Suddenly my love for motorcycles changed to a full blown obsession. The quality of the bike was more what I had in mind and the bike was still quite new with only 5000kms on the clock. I got the bike from a dealer in Nelson on the South Island and flew over to collect it.

From the second I got onto the bike until three hours later when I got on the ferry, the rain poured down. It wasn't just rain, it was as if the sea had lifted up and comedown right on top of me. There was not a dry piece of me to be found. This started me thinking of getting better organised for wet weather. I rode the 650 for a while and then made the mistake to test ride the BMW GS1150. The bike I tested wasn't in great shape and had way too many kilometres on the clock, but the difference in performance and power was mind boggling. Of course I had to upgrade and eventually I got myself the BMW R1150R.

The bike is the only mistress I would ever cheat with, and a wonderful love affair started....

Chapter 3 - Trippy idea

After the trip up the North Island's East coast, the idea of doing a proper trip kept nagging at me. The question was where to go? New Zealand is too small for a proper trip and could be done anytime. What I was looking for was something really special. Visions of cross country USA along route 66, or a trip along the Mediterranean Sea, or even Northern Europe and places like the Black forest flashed through my mind. I even considered somewhere like Russia, a place less travelled and mostly undiscovered. Then I had more realistic visions of my bank balance and my dreams evaporated. All these trips would just be way too expensive. The realities of money can be such a downer and the idea was shelved along with going into space, finding out who really killed Kennedy and telling Tom Cruise to his face I think he's an ass.

A short while later, Elizna and I were travelling to South Africa for a visit to the family and due to my lack of planning I forgot to pack a book for the 20 hour flight. Luckily the airports are prepared for travellers like me and have bookshops selling overpriced books. I bought "The Long Way Down", a story of Ewan McGregor and Charlie Boorman riding their bikes from Scotland through Africa to Cape Town. Even though I can't afford to do a trip like this, it did reignite my desire for one. I got really excited about their story and thoroughly enjoyed the adventures they had. I might have mentioned once or twice (ok probably a thousand times) how great it would be to do something like that and Elizna encouraged me to go for it and plan something. With her supporting this adventure I was fully into getting it going.

When we were back home after our holiday I had a look at a world map and the obvious solution for a trip was Australia. The country is large enough not to run out of road, easy and cheap to reach as it is close to us in New Zealand and has so much to see. Being an ex-South African, living in New Zealand the only real downside to this choice of Australia was that the country was full of Australians. The only time I really like the Aussies is when they lose in rugby or cricket! This dislike of the Aussies is mainly due to sport, but I can honestly say I have enjoyed the company of pretty much every Australian I have met, so there shouldn't be any problems once I was there.

With my mind made up on the country, the next step was to round up my riding posse. I needed some amigos to ride with me. I managed to get some of my friends excited about bikes with all my jabbering about them and hoped that a few would take the bait and join me for this trip. Darryl, who I am ashamed to say, was riding a scooter when we met, was into the idea from the first mention of it. Just to ease your mind, he became aware that a scooter just wasn't going to cut it and he also went through the process to get his licence. He bought a Suzuki Intruder 250, which was a pretty cool biker while he had his learners. Then when he was still months from his full licence he did the right thing and traded in his 250 cruiser for the Suzuki V-storm 1000. What a lovely machine! At around forty, Darryl still believes he is bullet proof so licence issues didn't stop him from taking the bike on a weekend trip when we went all the way up the west coast to New Plymouth.

I also had some other guys like Rudi, Otto and Tim interested, but it didn't work out for them for various reasons. Rudi ended up selling his bike and saving to buy a house, Otto started building a house so all funds were funnelled into that and Tim was keen until he heard we were planning to camp. This put him off as he just isn't into camping. He had also just finished a month long bike trip through India, so both funds and his leave allowance were all used up.

So we would be The Two Amigos. Sounds two thirds familiar.... mmm. Whatever. Dusty, play us that "Little Cowboy" song. There are some of you who will get this one. Back to the story though. Darryl and I spent some time discussing the concept of the trip to see if we could actually make it happen. Everything we discussed and researched looked promising and suddenly the trip changed from wishful thinking to pretty likely. How exciting!

This brings me back to the coffee issue I mentioned in the first chapter. One of the major challenges for a long distance motorbike trip is to plan what to pack. People don't really understand what you can and cannot fit onto a bike. There is very limited space and without proper planning you will end up filling that limited space with a lot of shit you don't need and nothing you do. Additionally we fly to Australia, so the standard 23 kilograms baggage weight limit applies. So now I needed to think of how to get all the crap I wanted to take with me packed properly. We would be camping so we needed camping gear, we might not have access to fresh water or food every day and we would need to be able to cope without anyone close by to help us out.

I needed to learn how to prepare a camping site in a hostile environment. I do know how to camp, but there are important precautions required for camping amongst potentially deadly wild life. I haven't grown up in a bubble, but honestly I haven't been the world's greatest camper lately. It has been many years of comfy lodges, B&Bs and so forth. Also, there are no snakes in New Zealand and nothing that is deadly that can bite you at night. There are snakes, spiders, centipedes, thingamajigs, convicts and road-trains. Australia has a long list of things that want to do you harm.

Not to sound like a broken down record or a radio station playing the same tune over and over, but back to the coffee. I have become a real coffee snob. I refuse to drink powder coffee and I am worth less than a month old slice of bread without my morning coffee. I either get up and have a coffee or I don't get up. It is as simple as that. Of course being on the bike in the middle of nowhere we will not have an ample supply of baristas to choose from.

So, how do I cope with the coffee problem? Well, I investigated many options, from "moer koffie" to ordering those lovely Dutch coffee filters, which allow you to have a small cup with a double filter at the bottom with the coffee in between the two filters and you just pour hot water in. Christine, my father's partner, introduced us to it and this would have been ideal. It is impossible to get these in New Zealand though, like so many other things. Luckily Elizna went for a visit to South Africa a few months prior to our trip and managed to bring back some of the filters. At the time of planning though, I did not have access to them, so back to square one. I have tried coffee bags, pretty much the same concept as tea bags just with coffee, but it tastes awful and I will not drink that crap. Things were going to be tough on the road and I could take that but there are some things you don't compromise on, coffee and sex being at the top of the list. It's either the best or none at all. Ok, so maybe I will even take substandard sex, but not coffee!

Elizna got involved in the mission to help me find, what has become known as "The coffee solution". She comes up with the best ideas. We found a number of solutions that could work. First up was the Espresso maker. It is made of tough, light metal so is small and robust. I could put any ground filter coffee into it, so quality was right up there and I could use a butane gas stove to boil the water. Elizna had found some of those elusive Dutch coffee filters, so I had two boxes of those and I had also found a coffee cup with a built in plunger in the cup. You chuck some coffee in, pour the hot water and then plunge in your cup. Amazing what you can find if you really start looking.

With the most important issue sorted, I went to the library to look at maps of Australia. You would think with a country as large as Australia, finding a good route to travel by would be easy. I got a large map of Australia and after an hour or so at the library I was nowhere closer to knowing what I wanted to do. I had nine different major routes I considered. Again, master mind Elizna stepped in. She got me a large map of Australia and had it laminated. So back home and armed with a whiteboard marker and the ever faithful Internet, I sat down and started looking at what is out there and what I would like to see.

It was time to call in my partner-in-crime so we could decide which way we wanted to go. At this stage I had narrowed it down to four basic routes. The general idea was to fly over to Adelaide or Melbourne and ride up the coast to Sydney, keeping to the coast through to the Gold coast and up to Cairns. I had a number of different versions of this route, but the general idea and direction was the same for all of them. Some took us inland through Victoria and New South Wales and others all the way along to the coast to Queensland. Again, luckily I was blessed to know people smarter than me as Darryl gave it one look and said... "No dude, it's a shit idea. This route takes us through all the busiest cities of Australia. Why would you want to do that?"

Couldn't argue with that! Just because we were going to Australia doesn't mean we have to run into every bloody Australian there. My thoughts were to keep to the coast most of the time, but he was right, it wasn't the best way to go. So we wiped the routes from the map and redid the planning. After an hour or so we had it all planned out and what an amazing route. We would fly over to Melbourne and ride along the coast eastwards to Adelaide. Once we got to Adelaide we would head up north into the Outback, also known as the Never-Never. The route would take us straight up the centre of the country past Ayers Rock (Uluru) up to Alice Springs, which is one of the most isolated towns in the world. Once there we would turn eastwards and ride to Rockhampton which is at the northern point of the Gold Coast. Then we would turn north again and follow the coast to Cairns. We would fly back out to New Zealand from Cairns

This route changed as we progressed our planning as we would have needed to travel about six hundred kilometres on very rough dirt road from Alice Springs if we wanted to follow this route. This dusty road is one of the least accessible roads in Australia if you get into any trouble. We decided we would pass through Alice Springs further north up to a nothing place called Three-ways. Here we would turn east and then head back east-south-east to Rockhampton. We also had the option of first heading up to Darwin if we were ahead of schedule before coming back down to Three-ways. This decision we would leave up to when we get there.

Our plan was to travel somewhere between seven thousand five hundred and ten thousand kilometres. To put this in perspective, if we were to pull out of Cape Town and travel north up Africa, straight up seven thousand kilometres will take you into the centre of Libya. Have a look at a map of Africa. That is the last country you get before hitting the Mediterranean Sea. Seven thousand five hundred kilometres takes us to the water's edge and eight thousand takes us a fair bit into the Mediterranean Sea. That is just about the whole length of Africa. Ten thousand kilometres will mean we can order a pizza in Italy. Or if you were to travel from Seattle in Washington State across the USA to New York city, then turn back west and go all the way to Dallas, Texas you would have travelled roughly 7000 kilometres. This should give you some perspective of the magnitude of what we were getting ourselves into and we had twenty three days to do this.

With the route all mapped out we felt we were making progress. Now we needed to move to the next stage of the planning, who wanted to go and would we have bikes to ride? It would be disappointing if we ended up arriving in Melbourne and having to walk all the way to Cairns.

We looked at a few options for finding motorbikes. Well, there were basically five options. First option was to get corporate sponsorship and have bikes given to us for the trip. As you can imagine, this idea, while very attractive from our point of view and certainly the most cost effective, sunk like a big old rock. Believe it or not we did not get many responses back. I know, how rude! So, option one went down the drain with last night's dinner.

Option two was to get to know someone in Australia who was willing to lend us their bikes. Trying to make the most out of my new Facebook account I sent out friend invites for Aussies who looked like bikers. I tell you what.... Facebook is not as amazing as it is made out to be. Again, this would have been a very cost effective way of doing it and could have saved so much of the negative press the Aussies are getting in this book, but alas, no one was interested in saving the Aussie culture from this terrible fate. Option two was off the list.

We needed to start looking at less cost effective options. Stealing bikes was briefly discussed, but after watching a show on Aussie prisons and not wanting to feel like an Aussie sheep for a few years (I'm sure you get it!) we decided that being Bruce's prison Sheila was not the way to do it. This idea didn't even make the cut as an official option.

I then looked at what it would take to ship our bikes across to Australia. This idea had a lot of advantages as these would be our own bikes that we were comfortable with. We could make sure the bikes were serviced before we sent them over and we would have spare parts for our bikes. Plus, we already owned the bikes so no need to spend extra cash. Additionally we could pack a lot of our stuff in the crates with our bikes, so we could travel light when we flew.

Well, that was the theory until I got a quote for sending the bikes to Melbourne and back from Cairns. Not only were we not guaranteed of the arrival date for the bikes, but also the crates are pretty expensive. To buy the crates, ship them over to Melbourne, have the crates transported to Cairns and ship it back to Wellington would cost a small fortune. It would be cheaper to gold plate the whole bike, tie a few bags of money to it and run it into the sea. Another idea gone bust.

So, to the last two options. We must either buy or rent bikes in Australia. Each idea had its pros and cons. Buying bikes meant we could sell them again afterwards and recover a large portion of our costs. Renting the bikes meant we needed to fork out the money and get none back, except of course for the rather stiff deposit. But it would be newer bikes in good nick.

I looked at the bikes in my price range in Melbourne and found reasonably decent motorbikes. We would need to start looking for bikes available to buy close to the time we plan to get there and then once in Melbourne go and test ride them. Once we found what we were looking for, we would need to service them and make sure they are ready for travelling the distances we are talking about and add on panniers and a top box. Once we got to Cairns, the motorbike capital of Australasia (wink, wink, nudge, nudge), we would need to sell them again in this thriving financial Mecca. It might take us a while to get rid of the bikes as some of the bikes for sale in this area had been there for a while. I believe there is a 1920 motorbike that has been for sale in Cairns ever since 1920. Plus, what do we do with the bikes until we sell them? We can't hang around Cairns until then and we can't just leave them on the corner of Queen and King Streets and tell prospective buyers the keys are taped to the back wheels!

The time we would waste getting rid of the bikes and the risk of having older, more run down bikes was worrying me. Additionally, the fact that we might not even be able to find a bike able to do what we are going to need it to do also made me nervous. Getting the money back would be great, but considering that we had to beg like spoiled little girls to get our leave approved, begged like spoilt little boys for permission from the wives (ok, that one is not true. Darryl's not married and Elizna supported me completely in this adventure). The point is if we were going to spend a fortune on the trip anyway, we thought it would be such a waste to have shitty bikes that broke down all the time. We might have to eat road kill to survive while watching some other cool dudes cruising by on their new, rented bikes flicking us the bird as they roar past our desolate camp site.

So, that meant we had to find a place willing to rent us, a couple of guys who never really grew up and with visions of grandeur, motorbikes. I would have politely said, "Sorry, I have to wash my hair and the bikes that week." if it were my bikes, but luckily there were no Skype interviews and as long as your money is green they'll take it. I think the fact that we were willing to pay our deposit eight months in advance, right in the middle of a recession also helped. Anyhow, there we had it.

For the most part, I was the person organising this. Darryl was just as involved and did his part, but at the end of the day I took on the main responsibility of planning and arranging the trip in detail. Although this did add some pressure to getting everything sorted, what it did also give was more control of what and when things happened. I wanted a BMW 1200 GS or GS Adventure bike and would not budge. Why the hard assed attitude you might ask?

Good question! Well, it was my dream. I had dreamt of this, day and night . I wants this! My precious.... Ok well I live in New Zealand a.k.a. Middle Earth, so excuse the LOTR reference. It had to be done and now that it is out of the way, we can round up some hobbits and continue on the journey to Mordor. We now had two BMW GS1200 motorcycles booked with panniers, top box, freshly serviced before we got them, washed, waxed (Brazilian I believe) and ready for a couple of adventurers.

Chapter 4 – Preparation H

There is a difference between planning and preparing. Planning was now done and we were continuing to fine tune the plan, but we needed to get prepared. With it all mapped out on paper we managed to get ourselves to the part where we needed to start the prep. First thing was to book a meeting with the boss. No, not with Elizna, she was already on our side. I have another boss as well.

Our mission here was to get half an hour of our boss, Cobus' time, without alarming him, and then to get him to agree to both Darryl and I being on three weeks leave at the same time. The thing is we usually stand in for each other and believe me, since I started working at Deloitte, I have not had a quiet moment. So getting approval to get leave at the same time where we will both be out of contact for three weeks was always going to be a bit tricky.

We booked a meeting in the boss's diary to discuss this and then the two of us sat down to look at our options of when we would go. We originally planned to go in August of 2011. This falls right in the middle of the best time of the year to do this weather wise. It is right at the start of the spring, which means we will not need to hit the 50 degrees Celsius of the summer heat in the Outback and it is not the freezing cold of the Southern winter down at the coast in South Australia. There were only two problems with this. First, it was still sooo far away. We couldn't wait that long for it. Secondly we were due to be on a pretty big project at that time and it would be an awful time to do it. So, we looked at the other option of going in April. April had the benefits of being quite a bit closer and not falling during any crucial project times. It also fell over the Easter weekend, which is also when Elizna and my wedding anniversary is. We can incorporate this celebration into the trip and Elizna could fly over to join us at the Great Barrier Reef to spend a few days in the sun, surf and warm waters.

As it turned out, after lots of planning and payments and looking at flights and schedules it wasn't going to be possible for Elizna to come over for this. We would like to do some dives, but we only have a few days available for this. Elizna cannot dive and fly the next day due to bubbles in the blood. Also, she used up all her leave to go and visit the family in South African in November. Sadly she would not be able to join me there. It turned out to be a good turn of events as diving would not have been possible for her anyway.

Armed with the dates, we went to the boss's office. I have to give the man credit. He handles situations well. We started the conversation with a "We have to talk". He didn't flinch, although I am sure there was a "What the fuck did you guys do?" moment inside his head. Laying it out for him the reaction was not what we expected. No tears, no threats on our lives and nuts, no screaming or tantrums. He simply said:

"I hope you didn't think you would go without inviting me."

This was a little bit different from how I envisioned the conversation going and the brilliant "you can't handle the truth" Hollywood arguments I had prepared so well were rendered useless. What this did do however was to add the tick that our leave was approved and another obstacle overcome.

Right, so now we had the dates, the leave, the bikes were lined up and the route planned. Things were starting to take shape nicely. The next step was to plan our kit. We had to carefully consider what would be absolutely essential to have with us. We had to focus on things that could save our lives or provide us some comfort.

The first thing I needed to look at was the riding gear I own. I had cold weather riding gear as New Zealand is not known for its long hot summer days. Also, the gear had been through a crash and was quite worn. It was in bad shape and absolutely not the type of gear for a hot environment! I would need to find more appropriate gear or I would be in big trouble. I also freely admit that I am far behind in technology. My cell phone can't even connect to the internet... yes, I know. Spare me the rolling eyes. Shopping had to be done.

The other lack in my gear related to the plan to get out in the Outback and camp a few nights. At this stage I didn't have a tent, sleeping bag or for that matter, any camping gear. I sleep in motels, B&Bs and fancy hotels. I am a travel snob. Oh and Elizna doesn't camp... ever.

Nothing to it, I went shopping. Walking into Kathmandu, the sales people fired away with their standard Kiwi sales pitch. Which, for you non-New Zealanders, means they ignore you until you come begging for help. I walked up to one of the sales people and asked for help and he rolled his eyes and managed to break away from sitting behind the counter, and staring into the middle distance. I did manage to make the salesman's day by saying;

"I know nothing about camping and need gear." This is like saying "Just watch my medium-rare steak there, I'll be right back" to a hungry dog. The other sales people hissed like trapped cats at the lucky salesman for being the chosen one, while giving me a few sour looks for not coming over to them. He ushered me away from the circling vultures who were still hoping I might turn around and ask for a second opinion.

And so the shopping started and soon I had a four-season tent, which means it can handle both relatively high temperatures to pretty cold ones. I must admit, I wasn't too worried about how the tent was going to cope; I was more worried about me. I mentioned that all I wanted was something small and light. This made his eyes light up even more and I felt like a deer frozen in the headlights of an approaching truck. I heard another hiss from one of the closer sales people still circling hoping for some scraps. This was not a good sign.

"Then you will need the Tentmaster 2000. Made from ultra light, polyphysitrical chemically stabilized, blah blah technical mumbo jumbo materials. They used this material on the mission to Mars you know." I just nodded in agreement to his analyses of how durable the material felt. I wondered what they used the stuff for in space. Just saying it was used on a mission into space doesn't qualify it as the best thing since sliced bread. They could have used it to wipe their arses in space and how would that qualify it as being a good material for a tent?

I randomly wondered if sliced bread was also such a big deal in space?

"What else do you have?" I foolishly asked, not being impressed with the price tag. The salesman froze and it looked like he had just chewed on a lemon. I decided to put the Tentmaster 2000 in the trolley and move on to the sleeping bag section. Agreeing to everything else the salesman said, his face did a slow relax and he even managed a smile as we strolled up to the till with a tent that can be used on other planets, a sleeping bag that can be used on Everest, a self-inflating mattress that is used by the US military on missions in Iraq and a 50% discount voucher for a camping trip to Sudan if I booked in the next three weeks, I was wondering how he managed to completely miss the fact that I was actually going to Australia.

After signing the credit card receipt, the transformation was incredible. The salesman sat down on his chair behind the counter and ignored me as if I hadn't just spent a fortune. I played with the idea of seeing if I could get a reaction by asking for more stuff, but thought the humour would be wasted on him and his nose might actually just managed to swallow his face if he realized I was kidding so I just left.

Brushing off the strangeness of the encounter, I suited up in my space suite and went for a space walk. Actually I got home and pitched a tent. No, I mean I really just set up the tent in the backyard, much to the amusement of our two cats. Their nails playfully ruining the waterproof guarantee within a few seconds of its being out of the bag. But, I needed to make sure everything was there and it was all in good working order. If I was going to have to go back there to exchange damaged goods or get missing pieces I needed to do it while the taste of my blood was still fresh in the salesman's mouth.

Fifteen minutes later I had the tent up. Everything was there and working fine. Now I needed to check the self-inflating mattress. The salesman had one exactly like the one I bought on display and all he did was open the valve on the side and a few seconds later it was fully inflated. Opening the valve on the side of mine, nothing happened. Cold chills ran up my spine, knowing that I had gotten a dud and I would need to get him to exchange it for me. That would of course never happen. It would be sent to the manufacturers, who were probably based in Mexico for repairs and I will get a voucher. Then when it had been fixed six months later it will be returned with a few "stains" as it was "field tested" by the amigo fixing it when he took it to the drive-in with his best friend's girlfriend. It will never work properly and I would have wasted a good deal of money on crap.

Fear was edged away by anger. Pure furry took over my senses and I started to feel my blood boil. Why did this have to happen to me? What did I do in a previous life? Did I kill a nun? Did I bully Adolf as a kid in nursery school? I grabbed the bag and saw a white sheet fall from the bag.

"Instructions for use. Important information, please read before using".

This looked promising. But I cannot admit to have read the instructions. I am a man and I can figure things out myself. I don't need some ten year old sitting in a sweat shop in Bangladesh writing the instructions to tell me how to inflate a self inflating mattress. Or maybe I did...... it was all so confusing. Well, I had to either read the instructions or take it back to the salesman. Rationalization took place at rapid pace. He was probably betting on me not reading the instructions and would be very condescending when he showed me where my major flaw in reasoning was.
I would show him! I will read the instructions myself and show him how I operate! Just as well I did as it clearly said that you would need to inflate it by blowing into the valve. This would only be required when the mattress was brand new or had been deflated for a long time. Ah the relief! Tears of joy. Dancing in the streets! To help celebrate, the cats added a few small punctures to the mattress which would help the mattress deflate slowly overnight leaving me on the hard ground just after 2:00 a.m. next to Uluru. I really love those cats.

I needed a few days to get over the experience of shopping for the camping gear, but couldn't put off finding better riding gear. I went to Wellington Motorcycles to see what type of boots they had and ended up buying a pretty damn expensive jacket and pants. They were made by Revitt, a good brand and perfect for desert riding. It had three layers, the outer being the normal protective layer, but a cream/white colour instead of the standard black. This would help to reflect the sun's rays and I would bake a little bit less under the harsh Australian sun. It had a few well designed vents that would cool me down while riding and was 100% waterproof. The inner thermal layer would help me stay warm in the winter here in New Zealand. So I had some new riding gear. Riding home I realised I still did not have riding boots! Darryl ended up buying me some boots for my birthday, so one more tick in the box.

The shopping wasn't over though. This trip wasn't a case of just getting on bikes and riding. It was about survival in the Outback, men being men... with toys. Free from commitments, rules and must-does. Men with useless gadgets and toys hanging off the back of bikes. State of the art GPS, new iPod classic with a million and twelve songs on it, edible underwear, a voice recorder, a pocket knife, waterproof matches, camelbacks, water bladders, oh it is a man-boy's dream to prepare for such a trip. Gadgets and manly stuff need to be bought and tested.

I bought a high power, miniature flash light that uses LEDs and can light up a cricket stadium for a Day/Night match, all on two AAA batteries. I found a tyre inflator pump that runs on a specially ordered convertor plug which plugs into the bike's auxiliary power outlet. I ordered a waterproof helmet camera that records video in high definition onto SD cards. Add to that two, eight gigabyte SD cards to record the whole experience. The recorder runs on two AA batteries at about the rate of a battery per fifteen seconds of recording. I decided that four sets of rechargeable batteries would need to do, so got a battery car charger and 8 rechargeable batteries.

Most of this is totally useless in the real world but not for this! As you can see the shopping started in quite a subdued fashion and quickly spiralled out of control.

My friends are really important to me. Elizna most of all as she took the brunt of this insanity, but guys like Otto, Rudi and Lisa were very patient with my total obsession with this trip and gave me all manner of crap that was perfect for my needs. Stacked camping pots, various options for kettles, a spork (I will get back to that) and a lot of advice. I love my friends, especially for having indulged my one track life.

Spork! This is a typical example of the Kiwi ingenuity the Kiwis are so proud of. It is a plastic spoon on one side and a, you guessed it, a fork on the other side. Mind bending stuff really.... No wonder the Kiwis were the first to travel to space...

Man in his element.

Chapter 5 – Dry runs

Reading the chapter title you might be wondering if perhaps I had some Indian or Mexican food and now had the runs and was feeling dehydrated. Not so, this time when I refer to dry runs, I am talking about practice runs. Just like anything else, the more you do it, the better you get at it. I think it was Gary Player who said,

"The more I practice the luckier I get".

That is relevant to my situation somehow. Maybe I should go play some golf and figure it out. Anyhow, I think I am getting off track here, so back to the dry runs.

I'm not sure if you have tried motorcycle riding and more importantly long distance riding? Riding a bike is a lot of fun. You can smell the earth when you ride past a field that had just been ploughed. You can feel the temperature changes as you go through a dip in the road. You are fully engaged every moment as you are not sitting there and turning the steering wheel as you do in a car. You have to watch the quality of the road, you have to look for objects like gravel or ice on the road surface and you have to look at the trees next to the road to gauge the strength and variances in the wind. You have to watch every car anywhere close to you as you are at risk if they do something stupid. You have to fight fatigue after riding for hundreds of kilometres and being exposed to the elements for so many hours.

Let me take you through a moment's riding experience. You cruise down the road to KFC to get their new Rounder burger. You have to keep the bike upright and with your left hand pull the clutch, indicate for turns, honk the horn and dim/bright your lights. With your right hand you control the petrol and the front (main) brakes, with your left foot you change gears and your right foot controls the back brakes. They are all busy all the time. When you stop, you have to reduce petrol, while pulling or stepping on the break, gear down with your left foot while your left hand pulls the clutch, indicate if you are going to turn and then if you come to a complete stop, you will need to keep the bike upright, so you have to compromise one or both of your feet by putting them on the ground. Now you have to use your right hand for the front brake as your back brake is not being used by your right foot. You should already be in the correct gear by now as well, as your left foot's also on the ground. After all of this there's a cute girl walking past so you feel compelled to wave. Your iPod is stuck on ABBA and you desperately need to change it, the sun shines in your eyes, so you have to lower your sun visor. It's a very busy moment and the curry of last night is threatening to cause the runs.

You get the point that when you're riding...you're a busy chap! Go driving in your car up to 120 kilometres an hour and stick your head out the window. It's cool how hard the air pushes you back. Well, keep it out there for about 10 hours. This is the force on your body while you ride. Even if you have a screen on your bike, the wind hits your helmet and pushes your head back. Never mind that you have a heavy helmet on your head as well.

What does all this have to do with Indian curry? Not much really, but I am quite hungry at the moment and think that will be dinner for tonight.
No, where I am going with this is Fiji. Or to be more specific a photo of Fiji. This brings me to the issue of a photo of me in Fiji recently for Elizna's birthday. Elizna took the photo of me from behind, where I am standing looking out over the sparkling blue waters of Fiji. The fat rolls around my hips obscure the view of the ocean for anyone looking at the photo. Working long hours and travelling for work means you eat rubbish and gain weight. I haven't really gotten fat, I just have a comfortable tyre I carry around with me. I also no longer do any kind of exercise. Again I use the excuse of just working too hard.

If we put the physical strain bike riding puts on your body and the physical condition of my out of shape body together, we do not get a happy scenario! I needed to get some type of fitness routine going to increase my stamina and I needed to get riding fit as well.

But wait, that's not all. If you play a sport, let's say cricket or rugby you practice the skills required to do the sport well and you have to work on your fitness to make sure you can keep up. I needed to apply that logic to my situation. I get to ride to work at least twice a week and most weekends we do manage to get out and take a ride for a few hours. What we don't do is get out and ride for days. We were planning three weeks of solid riding. We did plan to spend a few days off the bikes once we got to the Great Barrier Reef, but that was two weeks of riding before we got there. We had spoken about some potential off days, but what exactly do you think we will do on an off day in the middle of the Outback? Disneyland has not yet opened an Outback theme park with croc-o-hunter rides and sitting in a camp site for a day is not what I rate as a classy day. I had a feeling we are going to keep riding until we got to the Reef where we would go for a few dives.

To get the feeling of spending a few days in a row on the bikes, plus give us the opportunity to test out all our gadgets, we would go for a four day ride across the South Island in the first week of January. It was still a few months before we planned to get to Australia, but it would have to do. It would be a small glimpse of what was waiting for us there on the other side of the Tasman Sea. As this fell inside most companies' shutdown period, we would hopefully have a few extra amigos that could join us. We also planned to do a stop and meet up with someone really special. Twisting Throttle. The man is a legend in our world and one of the people who inspired this trip. I mentioned earlier that the story of Obi wan Kenobi and Mr Boorman was an inspiration with their trip down Africa, but they were not the only ones.

We have a man living in Christchurch who calls himself Twisting Throttle. He did a trip around the rim of Australia. He kicked off in Sydney and rode anti-clockwise around Australia along the coast and he did this in thirty odd days. He rode many miles a day and wrote the story of the trip. Darryl found the book and we both loved the story and his great sense of humour. He also did fifty states in fifty days. That is pretty much the whole of the USA in less than two months. Wow, that is impressive.

So Darryl had contacted the man and he was keen to meet up with us and maybe go for a ride with us. What had been a dream many months ago was turning into the opportunity to meet up with celebrities who wanted to go riding with us. I can now see how going after a dream starts a ripple effect that ends up changing the way the world sees you. Amazing how the universe works.

As for the fitness, well at the time I am writing this, I am a ball of muscles. I have less than five grams of fat on my whole body and can run ten miles in twenty minutes without breaking a sweat. Considering that no one will believe this and the fact that it's complete bullshit, I will not include a photo to prove it. Actually I am still just as unfit and have not yet started my exercise routine. I am getting to that. I am thirty five years old and know myself pretty well. I knew for a fact that I could get to the fitness level that will take me through the trip, but I also knew that it was no use getting ready too early. I would need to start a month or two before we go. Starting too early gives you too much time to fall back into old habits. So, come February, I would be running every day. I knew that the excitement of the short waiting time would keep me going

As to the "being game fit" idea, as I write this it is end of December 2010 a few hours away from being on holiday. We are planning to do our prep run over the first week of January. We will be out of the house on the morning of the 4th January, across to the South Island for four lovely days of riding.

Part 2 – Aotearoa, Land of the long white cloud.

So what do you know about New Zealand? It is probably best known for its rugby team, the All Blacks. In a country with a population of around 4.6 million people, it is amazing how they keep producing such high quality rugby players and consistently seem to be the best rugby team in the world. Rugby in New Zealand is pretty close to being the national religion.

But what else is there to know about New Zealand? It is a small country in the bottom right hand corner of the world, hiding in the shade of Australia, seeming to drift closer and closer to the South Pole. If you have ever been in New Zealand for a winter you would agree.

New Zealand is basically two main islands, with a bunch of smaller islands making up the whole. The North Island houses the largest city in New Zealand called Auckland. It is in the Hauraki Gulf where the fishing is good and the weather is ok. If you are a keen fisherman, you can catch a lot of large snapper, Kingfish and the occasional baby whale here. I would be careful to skin and eat the whale before getting back to the land, as the Green movement is very strong in New Zealand.

The North Island has a total of forty volcanoes, of which three has erupted since my birth in the mid seventies. There are also places like Rotorua, which you can smell from miles away with all geothermal activities. New Zealand has some serious vault lines running up and down the country, causing a large number of earthquakes on a daily basis. Some of these earthquakes are really strong. Just have a look at what happened in Christchurch recently.

Talking about Christchurch, that brings us to the South Island. The South Island, or Mainland as it is called by the Mainlanders, is absolutely beautiful. The Southern Alps runs down the West coast providing a few pretty decent ski fields in the winter. There are also a few glaciers down on the South Island that you can fly to by helicopter and walk on top of these immense blocks of ice.

A bit of interesting history, New Zealand was the first country to allow women to vote back in 1893. So now you know who to blame for letting the women out of the kitchen. Ha ha ha ha. Ok, I am just kidding! Give me a break. I warned you about my sense of humour.

The other thing that a lot of people know about New Zealand is that the Lord of the Rings trilogy movies were shot here. It is what every movie goer thinks Middle Earth looks like. As you can expect, everywhere you go there is some old movie site close by where you can go for a guided tour to experience the movie. Nerds, step in from the left please.

I spent seven years in New Zealand and my experience of the country is that it is a friendly, far behind the rest of the rushing world type of place. They are not backwards or technologically challenged, far from it in fact. I am referring to the life style and the pace of life. People trust each other and you do not need lock up your house, car or anything else in fear of being burgled. It is still one of those places where if you go to the shop and you will only be a minute or two, you really do not need to switch your car off. You can just let it idle while you run inside the "dairy" for your Pineapple Lumps and L&P and jump right back in and drive away. No one will even look at your car funny. Even if you were blocking their way, they will not really get mad, as long as you wave to them when you jump back in your car. The people are very patient in general.

It is ridiculously safe in New Zealand. Kids still play in the parks long after dark, without parents being worried about paedophiles and murderers. It is a country where people respect each other and crime, even little crimes makes the headlines in the news.

Politically it is a very stable place, with the two main parties not being extreme in any way. They differ in the way they want to look after the workforce, but otherwise pretty similar. They do lean over to the socialist type of ideology, but yet again nothing extreme. I know it is a bit more complicated than that, but in general life, it feels simple enough. I think the politicians here, like everywhere else just makes it look more complex.

Economically it is a pretty small place, but the country has enough industry to support the population and even to allow the New Zealand dollar to be a pretty strong currency. Unemployment is really low at 6.5%, which is the twelfth lowest in the world. The middle class rules the country.

Back before the 1900's New Zealand was governed as part of the New South Wales territory in Australia. In 1901 New Zealand was given a choice to become one of Australia's states, but chose to become an independent country.

But that is like reading the specs of a car from a website and claiming to know what the car feels like to drive. How about more interesting facts about the place to really get to know New Zealand?

New Zealand is a fairly liberal nation with homosexual marriage (Civil Union), prostitution, soliciting, and brothel keeping all being legal. The driving age is 15, the consensual sex age is 16, and the drinking age is 18 (though minors accompanied by adults are allowed alcohol in some restaurants). The funniest about these facts is actually quite an obvious oversight. Kids aged 16 may legally have sex, but they may not watch a movie with sex scenes, which will be rated R18. DHUUU! You can screw, but you can't watch someone screw.... what the hell?

Let's get to one of the more popular Kiwi activities, which are claiming to be the first.

The best known case of a Kiwi being the first is Sir Edmund Hillary. He was the first man to conquer Mount Everest. He became an icon and was knighted by the Queen later on and by all accounts was a great man.

A little less well know person, Richard Pearce got a heavier-than-air machine into the air fourteen months and another machine nine months before Wilbur and Orville did. This means that a Kiwi was the first to have built an airplane. In the true Kiwi fashion, being friendly and polite he allowed the Wright Brothers to take the fame because, he said that they were capable of controlling their plane, and he could not control his in the air. He crashed every time. So he could fly, but not land. He also invented those silly emergency cards in the seat pocket in front of you showing the brace positions the air stewards always yap on about. The interesting thing about this is that the flaps on the wings that he invented are still the basic design for what is used today. His mistake was that he fitted them to the leading edge, rather than the trailing edge of the wing.

Bring up the Pavlova and who originally came up with it at your own risk. The Kiwis and the Aussies both claim it is theirs and neither is willing to budge. I have tasted a pavlova once and honestly do not know what the fuss is about. Now if it was the Sticky Date pudding, or caramel slices I could still understand, but the mountain of cream that is a pavlova? Well, to each his own I guess.

New Zealand also lay claim to have invented the hair pin with the kinks in, which ensures it does not fall out of your hair. Other inventions they are so proud of? How about the tear-back Velcro strip, the pop-lid on a self-sealing paint tin and the child-proof pill bottle?

And then one final fact before we go riding. New Zealand has the longest place name still in use in the world. A free Tui beer for anyone who can pronounce it correctly. Here you go:

Taumatawhakatangihangakoauauotamateaturipikimaungahoronukupokaiwenuakitanatahu.

It is a hill in Porangahau in the Hawkes Bay area. The Maori name translates to:

"The place where Tamatea, the man with the big knees, who slid, climbed and swallowed mountains, known as Landeater, played his flute to his loved one."

With that let us get going on a lovely trip through the south Island.

Chapter 6 – Heading South

4January 2011
As a rule I hate getting up early in the mornings. Normally it's the worst moment of my day. As you can probably tell I am not much of a morning person. However, today is not one of those mornings. Today I am forcing myself to lay in as I have been awake on and off for a while and I will be getting up earlier than I do for work! I am like a school boy the night before Christmas. I am awake often and when I do sleep, it is light with disturbed dreams.

Finally the alarm goes off and I get up so quickly I have to sit down for a moment to stop me from passing out. The cat that had been sleeping between my legs jumps up and hisses at me. Shame, not the start either of us wanted. Maybe tune back to excitement levels a little bit. I stand up again and now I feel a bit better and this time the cat only glares at me. Can't please everyone. I hop into the shower and am dressed in my new bike gear in no time. I make coffee for Elizna and me and we sit together on the bed and have a chat. Even though it will only be a few days I will miss her. We are close and don't spend a lot of time apart. Especially not over holidays.

After the official bathroom duties have been taken care of, namely "shit, shave and shampoo", I carry the kit down to the bike and load it up. It all fits exactly as I tested it earlier the week, so it is all good so far. That done, I quickly head back upstairs for the goodbyes and then walk down the stairs mumbling excitedly to myself. I have to stop myself from running down the sixty two stairs leading down from our house to the street. It would be a bloody shame if I fall down the stairs now and break a leg. This thought manages to slow me down enough to ensure I get to the bottom of the stairs in one piece.

Standing next to my fully loaded bike I get the feeling this is going to be a great trip. Anticipation and exhilaration rushes through my body. I jump on the bike and take off down the road leading along the Wellington bays. It is still quite early morning and Wellington is deserted on this public holiday. The sun is cresting from being the Wairarapa hills to the east, casting deep orange light on the flat surface of the water.

My first stop is a whopping twelve kilometres away. I know you must be thinking how tired I must be after this long ride. Well, the first stop is the Inter-Islander ferry terminal. The ferry, Aratere will take us across the Cook Straits from Wellington to Picton, which is our landing place on the South Island. The ferry is large, with six decks and is over hundred and fifty meters long. It is officially also a part of the State Highway 1, which runs the full length of New Zealand. It can even fit sixty train carriages into the lower level.

Darryl is already on the South Island so Otto and I will sail over together and meet up with him there. Otto is just as crazy about bikes as Darryl and I, so I am very glad that he managed to also make the trip. We had known each other all of ten minutes when the first discussion about bikes came up and we haven't stopped since. My arrangement with Otto is to meet up at the ferry check in area, but he is never on time, so I imagine I will get there before him. As expected there is no sight of him as I ride in, but there are a number of cars in the queue already to get onto the ferry. I send him a quick text to tell him I will board and meet him on the ferry and then I get into the queue and get myself booked in. As I ride onto the ship I see Otto pulling into the queue in my rear-view mirror. I have my first giggle about his hi-viz vest.

I make my way to the area where the bikes must be parked and start strapping it down. I have just finished tying down my bike when Otto rides up and parks next to me. I am happy to see he is just as excited about the trip as I am. Boys will be boys, no matter how old we are. We strap down his bike and go upstairs for a pretty uneventful sailing across the Cook Strait.

The cook Straits is a pretty mean piece of water where quite a few boats had been sunk over the years. At its narrowest point, the strait divides the North and South Islands by a mere twenty two kilometres, but the trip on the ferry takes a full three hours. If you visit New Zealand, make sure you put this trip on your list of activities to do. You get an amazing view of Wellington as you leave the harbour and cruise past some of the suburbs and then when you get to the South Island, you enter the Marlborough Sounds, pass through the Tory channel into the Queen Charlotte Sounds where you will eventually get to the Picton township. I assure you that this is some of the most beautiful scenery you will see in your life. The colour of the water is enough to boggle your mind. On the way you will also be able to see the salmon farms. I recommend the salmon in New Zealand. Very, very yummy!

While the fish are being farmed, we sit and drink coffee while chatting about a book he is reading about the Hells Angels. After the three hour sailing we ride off to meet Darryl. He has been on the trip for a few days already as he decided to go straight after Christmas. He definitely has the look of someone who has been on the road for a while! He has a grey beard which elicits a few remarks about his age. With the first age joke done, we are ready to get going. We ride out of Picton as quickly as possible as it is filled to the brim with tourists. Darryl has had time to plan the route for us to take to the west coast, so he takes the lead and we shoot out towards Blenheim. This area is well known in New Zealand for the wine it produces, especially Sauvignon Blanc and Pinot Noir. I am a fan of neither of these two wines and we are not here to taste wine anyway so work our way past the vineyards towards Blenheim. The road is very busy and slow, but luckily when we reach Blenheim we get off State Highway 1 and head west on the West Coast road. Immediately I feel more relaxed and think, "This is more like it". The road is quite, there is some cloud cover and it is warm but not hot. Great riding conditions!

Shooting ahead, the rhythm of the road starts humming away and I feel a song bubbling up. Anyone that has heard me sing will know this is not a pretty thing, so to stop me from singing I switch the I-pod on and select the lounge playlist I had setup the night before. Nice tunes drumming away and the tar skimming past I feel the call of the road ahead. I feel the need to just open up the throttle and fly into the future. At this exact time, Darryl pulls over and I can almost see myself riding ahead in that trance like state while I pull over. The rhythm is gone for the moment, but that's ok. I am sure I will catch up with it somewhere up ahead.

We have just covered the first hundred kilometres. Wow, I must have been in the trance for a while as it feels as if we had just pulled away. We chat a few minutes, water the garden of the picnic area and then get going again. Otto uses this opportunity to lose his sunglasses and he only realizes this a few miles down the road. I realise something is happening as he is swerving all over the road, scratching around in the bags on the back of his bike. The groan chokes the giggles chokes the moan.

When we get to the road that splits with one road going south along the West coast and the other North to Westport, Darryl pulls over again. He did not fuel up when Otto and I did in the previous town and the sign next to the road warns that there is no fuel for the next hundred and fifty kilometres, so we turn back and go to Westport. This is also then lunch time so I quickly scoff down a toasted sandwich with roast beef and processed cheese while the others eat a hot dog each. I quickly pop in to the bottle store and buy a small bottle of Jack Daniels. It will come in handy sometime soon I am sure.

With the bikes and riders fed we retrace our steps back to the fuel warning sign and fly past it to come up to the West coast a few minutes later. Fog drifts over the road as we cross over the hill and get to see the sea. The fog gets heavier and the scene becomes more and more surreal. Darryl sees a sign for a campsite and lodge area when we get close to Punakaiki where we planned to spend the night. It is a stunning place deep in the forest along a long and dodgy gravel road. It is completely quite and breathe taking beautiful.

Unfortunately they are full and we ride back through the green forest disappearing into the mist.

Just around the next corner we see a sign for the Punakaiki Beach Hostel & Backpackers. We pull over and the owner says they have no rooms available but we are welcome to camp on his lawn for $20. We can then use the bathrooms and kitchen. I am very keen to get our first camp going so with a whoop-whoop, I show my approval. Even before the others have finished talking I am scoping out where to camp.
I pitch my tent right next to the small road that is the only thing between me and the sea. It is exactly the spot I wanted when I said I wanted to camp. A spot where you are out on the edge of life, where nature speaks loudly and man is quite. Sitting there lighting up a cigarette the sea calls out to me. Funny enough, the moment for the Jack Daniels arrives right on schedule and we chuck back a quick one before Darryl and I go down and take a swim in the freezing water. Refreshing and exhilarating.

As I have mentioned before, Otto is not the most rushed person I know. While we are taking a swim he is still busy setting up his double storey, four bedroom, 2 bathrooms, with a lounge, indoor swimming pool and a kennel tent.

"Fuck Otto, how many people are you planning to house in there?" I ask, but he doesn't go for the bait and only laughs. Once his tent has been pitched, he goes about getting the rest of his camp setup.

Otto has brought his inflatable mattress along. It is a BIG mattress and the idea is that he will use my motorised tyre pump to inflate the mattress. We never tested the fittings before we came on the trip and as you can expect, none of the fittings I have fits the mattress. So Otto will need to sleep on the ground. Not ideal after 360 kilometres on the bike and a 500 kilometre trip planned for the next day.

We go for a pie and beer at the pub down the road and then sit down and have a couple of Jack Daniel's looking out over the sea. Life feels pretty good at this moment. The exhaustion sets in and we all disappear into the tents for a well earned sleep. It doesn't take me long to be fast asleep.

I wake up in the middle of night and hear the crashing of the waves almost touching distance away. It fills the whole tent and rolls over me as if I am right there in the waves. The absolute darkness and the rolling hypnotic waves cause my senses to warp and I can feel myself becoming one with the sound. I drift away on this sound into a deep, happy sleep.

Chapter 7 – The West Coast, rain and John Cleese

05 January 2011
I wake up at 6:00 a.m. and get up. I can't remember the last time I have felt so rested out so early in the morning. The mist is heavy and I can barely see the sea. Everyone else is still asleep and there is no movement in the early morning mist. I sit outside the tent for a few minutes just taking it in. Finally I get up and go to make some coffee. Easy, I have achieved success. I have quality coffee in this remote camp site. Pride boils over at my wonderful achievement. I sit and drink my coffee and smoke a cigarette and appreciate the fact that I am the only living creature awake right here right now. I feel like I am in my own world.

There is a long beach in front of me with pretty large waves. Behind me are steep cliffs running as far as I can see in the mist hugging the coastline. The mist dampens all sound except for the rolling waves and slight chill in the air makes me hug the cup of hot coffee a bit tighter. This alone moment is pretty special and part of the reason why I like bike trips. After about half an hour there is movement from the other two tents. We finally get going at about 8:00 a.m. and shoot off down the West Coast into the mist.

Within seconds from being on the road, the rain starts coming down. In less than a kilometre after starting off Darryl pulls over and we both don our rain gear. It feels like I am kitting up to go scuba diving and there is a moment's panic as the rain suit chokes me. I loosen the neck a little bit, but still do not feel that comfortable with this condom over my riding gear. Once back on the bike it feels a bit better and within a few kilometres I have gotten used to the extra layer. With the rain suit and waterproof over-gloves, I am staying completely dry in the down pour and again, I feel that all the months of planning are paying off. The road is quite this time of the morning and although it is raining hard, the bikes are handling well and we are feeling the groove close by. More about the groove later when I finally slot into it.

Small towns and settlements flies past us as we ride through the down pour. This early in the morning these little villages and towns are not worth trying to stop in. Nothing will be open and in this weather I am sure most people gave the rain one look, pulled up the blankets and snoozed a bit longer.

We eventually pull over in Greymouth where we fill up the fuel tanks and grab some hot coffee at a small coffee shop on the esplanade. Greymouth is pretty much the capital of the West coast. It is by far the largest town on the west coast, with about 45% of the west coast population living here. Greymouth was a stronghold of the Maori in the early years and only when coal and gold was found here did the Europeans move in. Recently the biggest mining disaster in New Zealand history happened here at the Pike River mine where twenty nine miners died in an explosion and collapse of the mine.

Where we are standing on the esplanade, Otto is freezing as the temperature has dropped and he does not have waterproof gear. His boots is also leaking so his feet are freezing. I keep my mouth shut about how dry I am. I remind him of his heated grips, which he then switches on and this helps a bit.

I had been riding behind Otto for the last while and warn him that his gear that he has stacked onto the back is hanging over his indicators. When we have a look at it, we find that it is his blow up mattress and it was not only covering the indicators, but also it was pushing up against the exhaust pipe. It now has a hole the size of my hand burnt into it.

"Well, it didn't do you much good last night anyway, but now it's properly fucked. Chuck it." I offer some wise advice. Otto is a good tempered man, so he does not attack me, but I think it was touch and go there for a moment. Darryl helps him to pull the mattress from under the rest of his stuff and they inspect the hole. It is too big to even think of fixing. He asks the shop owner if they can get rid of it for him.

"Don't worry Otto. I have had my camping experience last night so know now what I still need. We can stay in rooms for the rest of the trip so you will not need the mattress anyway." This helps make Otto feel a bit better about the sleeping arrangements. Little did I know about the revenge that will be his for my wise ass comments. After finishing the coffees, we mount up and ride out further south along the west coast. The rain has not let up for a second.

Riding along the west coast we can feel that this is a sparsely populated area. There are very few signs of civilization and then it is mostly very small settlements or villages and the occasional farm house. Not the greatest place to live if you want to go to the 3D cinemas, but a very enjoyable area to do motorbike riding.

Otto had mentioned on our ferry ride over that he is not comfortable with riding in the rain. He had an accident years ago while riding in wet conditions and he was really hoping that the trip will be dry. The amount of water that has been dumped on him has not fulfilled that wish, but it has done something else which is much better. As he leads us down the road southwards I can see he is getting more and more comfortable with the wet conditions. His speed is increasing and the way he is starting to trust his bike through the corners is great.

We finally get to the town of Fox Glacier, where the glacier tourist traps lay about like mouse traps. Lots of busses full of Germans, Japs and Poms crammed into the tiny town. They pile out of the busses like toothpaste being pushed out of the tube and then walk about in their matching tour organizers labelled rain coats on their way to or from the glaciers. We fuel up again and then also decide it is a good time for brunch. Our eating routine will quickly settled into a noonish brunch and a dinner when we get to our stop for the evening. I think we will do the same when we get to Australia, but then again, who cares at this stage.

The lunch stop also gives me a chance to call home and chat to Elizna. It is the only part of these types of trips that I do not like. We are such great friends that time away from each other always miss that final ingredient to make it perfect.

We leave the town after lunch and after a few kilometres Darryl turns off at the highway onto a mud trail that takes us into the rain forest and up to the glacier viewing point. We slowly make our way through the thick forest and thicker mud and finally get to the lookout point from where we can see the Fox Glacier. It is a strange concept standing in a rain forest looking at a Glacier less than five kilometres away from you. Only in New Zealand. We decide it is not worth trying to hike there. We have our bike gear and rain gear on and a challenging hike up the mountain will be very difficult. So, we decide to rather take a few pictures and then carry on doing what we came here to do.

We slowly work our way down the slippery mud trail back to the highway and then head further south. Going along at a comfortable pace around hundred and twenty kilometres and hour I notice my petrol light has come on. Dammit. How long has it been on? My bike does not tell me exactly how much fuel is left in the tank, only that it is almost empty. I try to remember how far it is to Haast, which is the next town. It can't be that far, can it? Well nothing to it, we will just have to push on to Haast, where we plan to spend the night and hope for the best. Every corner I take has a long strait road following. Every hill I crest has a bigger hill hidden behind it. I hate riding on fumes, it stresses me out. I also don't really look around, so all I do for the remainder of the ride to Haast is watch the road ahead for signs of fuel. We finally get to the thriving metropolis of Haast. There are a few caravans on bricks and a small shop. Fuck. No fuel. Darryl goes into the shop to ask about fuel.

"Good news, a couple of kilometres back there is a fuel station." He says and gets back on his bike.

I could have danced of joy, but was conscious that my bike is on its last fumes and while I foxtrot down the street, it will cut out. We turn back and head back towards the promise of fuel. Hallelujah! We found it.

The fuel is priced about twenty cents per litre dearer than we would have paid in Wellington, but I fill the tank to the brim and I am smiling while doing it. Having sorted out the stress point of fuel we have a look around at exactly where we are. I must admit, after the beauty of the coastline, this dump is not on top of my list of places where I want to stay. We have a quite chat and decide we will not spend the night in this crappy little settlement.

"Let's cross the Haast Pass and see if we can make it to Wanaka. If we can make it to Wanaka tonight, then it will probably allow us the time to cross over both Arthur's Pass and Doubtful Range Pass later on. It is an extra zig-zag across the country, so if we stay in Haast, we will not have enough time to do this." Darryl explains his thinking and shows us on the map on his I-phone what he suggests.

"Anyway, it is too early to stop. I really feel like riding a bit more." Otto adds.

I agree with both of them plus I can feel the groove is just ahead of me somewhere and I want to get there. So, we are all in agreement and thus set out to cross the Haast Pass that will lead us inland to the Wanaka and Hawea lakes.

Crossing the Haast pass the scenery is stunning. This is one of the most beautiful areas of New Zealand! We ride past Mount Aspiring which is truly spectacular. Getting to the other side of the pass, the groove is finally waiting for me and I thankfully slide into its warm glow.

So finally I can get back to the groove. To explain the concept, think about a quality sportsman. I am a cricket fanatic, so let's say Jacques Kallis. No one can debate that he is one of the most skilled batsmen in the world. Still, some days he would walk out onto the pitch and swing and miss ball after ball. He will nick a couple of balls he should have put away. Then he would top edge the ball, it flies out to the outfield and is dropped by the dumbass Australian fielder. Ha ha ha. Nice drop there Pointing! The next ball hits the middle of the bat. And then the next one as well. Suddenly he cannot miss hit a ball and ends up with a huge score.

How did this happen? He was tensed up and just not feeling it. Then something snapped and he moved into the groove. The groove is that mental and physical place where your mind and body suddenly gel and you do the thing you do effortlessly and brilliantly.

This is also true of motorbike riding. As Lake Wanaka comes up on my right, the groove was there and I settled into it. Darryl is riding in front of me, but I easily pass him in a tight corner without slowing down. I feel my legs shoot their nerve endings into the side of the bike and it connects to the electrical system of the bike. I can feel every bolt, the oil flowing through the engine, the gears mashing easily with the clutch. I can feel the tyres gripping the tar tighter now that I have a direct connection between my brain and the bike. I feel the metal and rubber become part of my body. Being one with the bike, I fly through corners at pretty high speed. Darryl loves it when I get the groove on and he tucks in behind me to just ride my lines.

Too quickly we crest a hill, which leaves the lake behind us for now as we will now ride along Lake Hawea until we turn back east later to get to the Lake Wanaka township. I quickly look back and can see we have lost Otto. Not surprising as we were doing low flying and Otto is a bit slower than us. He needs to wait for a bit more of a gap to overtake and there were a few slow cars on the road back there. I pull over and lovingly pat the bike as we tear apart.

Taking off my helmet my smile disappears immediately. Something is wrong with my bike. A fast ticking noise is coming from the bike and does not stop. Darryl also worriedly looks on as we try to find the source of the ticking. It is coming from the control panel. It must be some electrical issue. I can see no loose wires and nothing feels over heated. But we were riding real fast so maybe it is just cooling down. We light up a cigarette and when Otto pulls up it is still ticking away. Now I am really getting worried. Something as serious an electrical issues might stop me from being able to continue on the trip.

I switch the bike off completely, but the ticking carries on. Maybe if I remove the key it will work? I take the key out and listen closely to the bike. Removing the key had done nothing except leaving the key hole empty, the ticking is still going on. I walk away to relieve unnecessary pressure on my bladder and Darryl excitingly calls out that the ticking has stopped. How bizarre, I still hear it. The ticking is carrying on just like when I was standing right next to the bike.

Relieve floods through me as I figure out that it is me ticking and not the bike. However, this raises the question, if it is me ticking, what could it be? I take out my mobile phone and listen to it. I hand it over to Darryl and stand back. The ticking does not follow the phone, but stays with me. Now I have to have a look at what else I have on me. The next thing that comes to mind is my I-pod. I open my bike jacket and remove the I-pod from the deep inner waterproof pocket. I really hope it is not my I-pod. I hand it over to Darryl as well and stand back, but I am still ticking. Again I am relieved, the I-pod was a present from Elizna for my birthday, so I am a bit precious about it.

The plot thickens and I have to keep looking at what else I have on me. Then it strikes me, "Of course! The supposedly waterproof bullet video camera is in one of my other pockets."
I mutter to myself

I had used it to film some of our riding across the Haast Pass in some pretty hard rain and it must not be as waterproof as the seller claimed. I take it out and hold it next to my ear. Yes, the ticking is coming from it. I am a bit disappointed that the camera has some electrical fault, but generally I feel pretty happy that it is just the camera. I take out the batteries to try minimizing the damage and hopefully saving the footage on the SD card, but then am unpleasantly surprised when it keeps ticking. That is really strange as there is no alternative power source for the camera and no moving parts. I put the batteries back in the camera and decide I will look at it later and put it away in my top box. As I stand back I realize something is wrong. The ticking is not coming from the top box, but still originating from me. It is not the camera after all.

What the hell? Going through my pockets all I still have on my body is my wallet, but there is nothing electrical in there.... is there? Surely coins cannot tick? Maybe I have a bug planted on me and I am being followed by the CIA. What could I have done to have drawn their attention? Did they check out my Facebook page and found out what I think of Tom Cruise? I go through my wallet and hold it next to my ear. It sounds like the ticking is definitely coming from the wallet. I open the coin pocket and there at the bottom is the E-tag that Air New Zealand has given me to tag in when I fly. It must have a malfunction of some kind. Wow, what a relief! Laughing talking about the CIA moment I put the wallet on the bike and walk over to Darryl.

I am stopped in my tracks within two steps. The ticking does not stay with the bike and my wallet. As far as I can now determine, it is me ticking. Can it be my pacemaker?

"But I don't have one." I say out loud which is causing a few frowns in my audience.

I have never been operated on, so have no mechanical parts able to make such a noise. Now the CIA is back on the map. I am now not only thoroughly puzzled and slightly concerned about this, but have now also become the other two's entertainment. They laugh, but I can hear the tension in their strained laughs. They are possibly now also thinking about the CIA or what if Al-Qaeda has planted some type of bomb in me while I was busy scoffing down a pie at the petrol station?

I go through every pocket I have, to see if I have anything else on me. There is a lighter in my pocket and worrying about what they put into lighters now days I hand this last item over to Darryl, yet I am still ticking. Now I will need to resort to more drastic measures. I take off my jacket and put in on my bike and stand back. I am still ticking. Visions flash into my mind of me standing naked next to the road seconds before I blow up and become the next 6 o'clock news headline story about a terrorist target.

I scratch my head wondering what exactly the protocol is in such a situation. To quote the movies, should I, "Freeze and put your hands on your head"? Should the others stay back or call the National Guard or something? Is this one of the weave-duck-roll-tuck situations? As my hand comes closer to my head the ticking gets louder and I prepare for the worst. I wish I could have said goodbye to Elizna and tell her how much I loved before I blow up into bite size chunks. Tears boil up as I wait for the blinding, flashing blast that will rip me into low fat (yes low fat!) mince meat. Maybe I will end up in a good spaghetti bolognaise. It will be a fitting end to me as I have a reputation as a bolognaise killer.

A couple of seconds pass and then a few more and I do not blow up. I cautiously lower my hand and as my hand lowers, the ticking is softer again. I raise my hand back to my head and the ticking becomes louder. Down, softer, up louder. All I have in my hand is my bike keys. I don't even wear a watch. Do I have a built in nail clipper?

And then the moment of truth. It was John Cleese. The sick, Pommy bastard just had to have a laugh on my expense. The fear and anger is washed away by an outburst of laughter. The others don't know what I am laughing about, but join in anyway, as I have either cracked and it is better to laugh with someone who had just cracked so they don't go postal on your ass, or I have found the source of the ticking.

While I was on a project in Auckland, I stayed on my own in a hotel room every night. To break the boredom, I one day bought a Monty Python movie and included in the DVD was a key chain. The little black box on the end of the chain has a button, which if you press it, chirps away: "He is not the Messiah; he's a very naughty boy!" For anyone who doesn't know Monty Python, this is a quote from the Life of Bryan.

This little box was obviously not waterproof and had shorted out with all the rain and started ticking. Bloody hell.

With the major mystery solved, we mounted up and rode past Lake Hawea and then finally turn back to Lake Wanaka. There is no accommodation available in the Lake Hawea settlement, but Otto did have a bit of fun with me though. As we ride into the town, we passed three pretty girls walked on the side walk on their way somewhere. As I passed them, Otto blew his hooter. I did not hear it, but I did see the girls give me a couple of sour looks and one interested look.

"What the hell?" I thought and when we stopped while Darryl asked the B&B if they have place Otto laughed at me as he told me what happened. I was tempted to do the same on the way out of town when we passed them again, but felt I have had enough humour with my John Cleese moment so just rode on past. I did wave at them this time though.

Aside from the waving and hooting, Lake Hawea is a stunning place. The lake is surrounded by huge mountains and the colour of the water is mind boggling. It is a pure turquoise and if you look down, it seems like you would be able to see miles underneath the clean water. This must be some of the cleanest water in the world!

The lake is about 140 square kilometres in size and three hundred and fifty meters deep, yet in 1958 the lake was raised artificially by twenty meters to increase the capacity. Here's my question, how to you raise a Lake?

Wanaka is twenty kilometres further on from the lake and we quickly covered this last stretch for the day.

Wanaka is home to a pretty interesting attraction. I would recommend you go there and take the time out to visit it if you are in the area. The place is called Puzzle world. It has a number of interesting illusions, but the most amazing one is a tilted room. The whole room is tilted at an angle of fifteen degrees. You cannot believe how this messes with your mind. I have pretty good balance, but there is just something about being in this space and having to stand at an unnatural angle where water runs uphill, a snooker ball will run to the higher end of the table, but not to the lower end and a chair slides up on a banister when released. You know why it is, but there is no way for you mind the process this.

We ride into Wanaka, which is a little bigger than the Lake Hawea settlement and stop at the first motel as you enter the town. My ass is hurting so bad! I am done for the day. Thinking I might be due a bit of luck after the John Cleese moment, I really hope they have rooms available.

Darryl comes back and informs us that they have one room left with four single beds.

"Yes please!" Otto and I reply at the same time. We cannot sit on the bikes any longer. Darryl books us in and we pull the bikes to the back of the motel. Just walking around while unloading the bikes already makes me feel a bit better, but I think it will be a while before my ass recovers. I grab a shower to wash away the day and this revives me. I call Elizna and we have a quick chat about what she had been up to and how the ride was.

Later we walk down to the town centre to get some food and drinks. We go into the steak house just down the road as we just can't be bothered walking any further. We order some locally brewed beers and I order a burger.

OUCH!

Funny how every restaurant we have entered only has hard wooden seats. Surely there must be at least one that has soft seats in the South Island? My ass needed a soft padded cushion, not a hard wooden seat. What has happened to cushions? Is it outlawed in the South Island? Darryl grabs one of the couch's cushions and uses that and Otto and I follow suit. That's much better. I can now actually concentrate on the food rather than just thinking of the pain in my ass.

After dinner we trudge our way back to the room through the pouring rain and hit the beds. I am asleep within minutes, ending a day of great riding and amusing moments.

6 January 2011

It is about 1:00 a.m. and the world is coming to an end. Loud rumbling vibrates of the walls and I can feel my bed vibrate. No, it is neither an earthquake nor a nuclear explosion, it is Otto snoring. Good lord! How does his wife manage to sleep next to that? A few little giggle initially turns into a wide awake, grumpy Deon after ten minutes. We have to cover a lot of miles in the morning and I cannot fall back to sleep with the V12 engine gunning away in the bed next to me.

"FOR FUCK SAKES OTTO! TURN THE FUCK AROUND! FUCK!" I finally scream. To my surprise he does exactly that and the snoring stops. I could have cried as it has been about half an hour since the snoring woke me up. Soft breathing is all I can hear and I feel myself relax. Then, as if Otto has passed the baton over to Darryl, he rolls onto his back and pulls a nice deep snore. Not as loud as Otto, but not a shabby second place. I feel the tears boil up. For the next hour the tag team that is Darryl and Otto first passed the baton between each other and then upgrade to the new improved "stereo" version. Somewhere in all of this I did finally fall asleep again, but when Darryl wakes me up I felt tired and not ready for the long ride ahead of me.

As a disclaimer, as I know both these lads will read this one day, I am well aware of the fact that I also snore and I at no point claim otherwise. All I am saying is that my snoring never bothers me!

Luckily I can make a decent cup of coffee, which does make help waking me up a bit, but does little to improve my mood. I go through the process that is to take place every morning on the bike trip, I load the gear back onto the bike. Heavy clouds seem to count down the seconds before opening the taps and as we pull out of the motel's parking area, the rain starts falling heavily and my grey mood is not improved. Within a couple of kilometres with Enya humming away in my helmet I start feeling better. The cool, wet air wakes me up and soon I am riding along happily again. There is nothing like a nice early morning ride to clear the cob webs.

We briefly head further south west till we get to Tarras, where we turn north on the 8 highway. We go over the Lindis Pass while buckets of water keeps being poured over us and then get to Omarama where we stop to fuel up again and do the normal morning coffee and call home. We grab some coffees at the Oasis cafe, but due to the grim looks we get from the waiter for dripping all over the cafe, we stand outside under the roof and drink our coffees. When I call home Elizna is still asleep as she had a good night with the girls and needed the extra sleep. It is still pretty early anyway.

As soon as the coffees are done, we saddle up and head on up the highway. Small settlements like Twizel, Pukaki and Tekapo go past me in a blur as we slow down while in town and use the lower speed to stand up on the pegs to give my ass some blood circulation. By the time we stop for lunch in Fairly we have covered a good three hundred kilometres for the day and I can see Otto's bike swerving across the road as he is shaking of the cold. It had not stopped pouring down a moment since we left Wanaka and he was drenched to the bone. We sit down for brunch and Otto orders the hot soup and I can see him relax as he defrosts. Shame, I really feel for the guy. It makes riding tough if you are cold as it tenses you up.

When we leave Fairly we cover a whole bunch of miles that has nothing exceptional. After a few hours on the bikes we all point up at the same moment. There, ahead is something we haven't seen for a while. Something that could grab our attention simultaneously. Blue sky and sunshine.

As we come around the corner an abandoned motorboat sits next to the road with no trailer or anything. It looks like it was riding down the road and then just pulled over to the side. How bizarre. Good looking boat though. I have a giggle.

When you are on the bike you are on your own. There is no one to talk to, no one talking to you. This carries on hour after hour, day after day. It is quite therapeutical. I believe it is because I ride motorbike that I do not need a physiatrist. It is like a meditation at high speed. Anyway, while you are on such a long ride, your mind is free to wander where it wills. And sometimes it is really amusing to see where your mind goes when unleashed.

Seeing the boat standing next to the road my mind started to do the afore mentioned wandering and I could see the family driving up from Christchurch to Lake Wanaka for the holidays. Dad had packed the car late last night while mum packed meat balls, sandwiches and the last leftover KFC form lunch and then make sure the kids have all their favourite toys packed. Dad had spent the week before making sure everything on the boat works and the fishing rods have enough line on. The dogs have been dropped at the kennel and the hamster and the gold fish are all but forgotten to die of hunger during the week the family is on holiday.

They get away at 3:00 a.m. with the kids sleeping on the back seat. The wife falls asleep after twenty minutes while the husband drinks cup after cup of coffee from the flask to stay awake. Finally after hours of driving the tired husband and father wakes everyone in the car saying loudly, "Wake up my dear family, we are here. Let's head straight out to the lake to get the boat in the water!" Happy cheers from the back seat as little Willy, or Bill as his teacher calls him, excitedly think of all the fish he is going to catch while little Martha can only think of getting some sun on her white body. Mary, his wife, turns and smiles at him while thinking of all the hours he will be out on the boat giving her some time to lie on the couch and finally finish reading Oprah's biography or continue with her affair that started last year with the neighbour. As soon as the wheels stop turning they all excitedly jump out the car, brushing the sleep from their eyes, everyone talking excitedly. The happy husband turns around, stretching his tired back and then, "Fuck, where's the boat!?!"

Hehehehe. Well, maybe you had to be there to get it. I thought it was quite funny.

The giggle is strangled quite quickly when the sun hits me and immediately I feel the heat cooking me in the rain condom. We pull over and shed the rain layer. It feels so good to ride without the extra layer.

At 2:00 p.m. we arrive at Springfield. Not only is this the famous town where the Simpsons family lives, it is also at the base of Arthur's Pass and our intended overnight stop.

Not feeling tired and after yesterday's last stretch having been such a good ride, regardless of the poor humour shown by John Cleese, we check the current weather reports for the Pass and also for tomorrow. What we see is not good news. The Pass has a current weather warning for severe wind gusts. Further bad news is there is heavy rain falling up there and that the weather is due to only get worse tomorrow morning. Wind gusts are around hundred and twenty kilometres per hour at the moment and it is expected to go up to about hundred and fifty kilometres per hour tomorrow morning.

Chatting to the shop owner, he warns us that the Pass is not good to go over right now. He would advise we wait till tomorrow afternoon when the wind is due to drop down a bit. He says it is pretty bad up there at the moment and no place for motorbikes.

We stand there wondering what to do, feeling it is too early to stop and we cannot spend the whole day till tomorrow afternoon in Springfield, regardless of whether we could find Homer Simpson and he invites us for a beer.

In these situations, you have to do one of two things. You either listen to your gut feeling, or you look for a sign. The gut feeling was that we should not cross this mountain in severe weather conditions, but then the sign came. A Harley rode past, with his wife riding pillion and they had just crossed the Pass.

"Fuck, that. If a Harley can do it, it can't be that bad!" I say and get confirmation from the others. We decide that we will push on and sleep somewhere on the other side of the hill. We fuel up first, as we do not know where on the other side we will be able to get fuel again and then hit the road. Darryl asks me to lead and I happily ride up the hill. I think he thought I was going to slot into the groove as there are lots of tight corners and I did such a great job the day before.

I have on occasions felt unsafe on my bike before. I had once ridden in pretty gusty winds with Elizna on the back and had felt unsafe. I have once skidded on ice when crossing the Wairarapa hills. I had once hit a pothole on a very wet road and almost lost control at about hundred and ten kilometres per hour. But until going over the crest onto the top of Arthur's Pass, I have never felt certain that I was going to get killed on the bike. The wind is like nothing I have ever felt before.

My bike is quite heavy as far as bikes goes. It has a dry weight of two hundred and eighteen kilograms, I weight a good seventy five kilos, it has twenty litres of petrol in the tank, it is fully loaded with two side panniers, a top box and camping gear on the back seat all adding up to probably thirty more kilograms and even with all this weight, I am being thrown around as if I weigh nothing. Wave after wave of the most horrible wind I have ever felt comes crashing over me, throwing me all over the road. Coming down to a dip in the road, the wind swirls around and where it was hitting me hard from the left a second ago, it is now hitting me from the other side. I correct for the change quickly and throw myself and the bike's weight to the right to counter the wind. Just as I do this the wind changes again and pushes hard from the left again. It is too much force pushing me to the left and I am laying far to the left already. I jerk it back as hard as I can and shift my weight as quickly as possible to try to pull the bike upright again, but the quick alternation of weight movement causes the bike to start wobbling and I lose control of it.

To make it worse, a second ago when I looked in my mirror, the car behind me was right on my ass and if I fall now he will drive right over me. The wobble gets worse quickly and instinct and experience both kick in at the same time and in a split second do battle for my life.

Riding bike you have the constant battle between your natural human instinct and your experience and it is magnified in extreme conditions. To demonstrate my point take the scenario where you approach a tight corner and at the last second before going into it, you realize you are going way too fast. This can be in a car, motorbike or even on a bicycle. Your body tenses up to allow your muscles to respond to the physical danger. Muscles tense up to help the adrenaline surge through your body. Your heart start racing, your eyes expand, your breath is a deep quick gasp to provide your brain and body with the maximum amount of oxygen to respond rapidly.

All this is exactly the opposite of what you would want to have your body do on a motorbike. The bike is like an animal, feeling your tension and also tenses up. It becomes sluggish to respond and difficult to control, seemingly with a mind of its own. What you need to do it relax your shoulders and arms, lay into the corner a bit more, trust your tyres and bike and lay over some more. You should be calm and relaxed and just go into it and your bike will feel your confidence and do exactly what you ask it to do. It will grip the tar road tightly and you can throw the bike around as you like as long as you seem relaxed and in control. Your bike does not know if it is in trouble, it trusts your leadership.

In this moment where I lose control the battle for my life is quickly fought and won with experience coming up trumps. I relax my shoulders, pin the bike with my thighs and do the most unnatural thing you can think of: I open the throttle and accelerate hard. This is what the bike was waiting for. It needed to know what I wanted to do. Being told that I am in control and that I want it to pull out of the wobble and jump forward, the 1150cc beast responds to my command and jumps ahead, the wobble disappear and I pull the bike upright. The car behind me brakes hard as the driver would have thought I am going to crash, but I speed up and then lay deep into the corner.

The next few miles this battle keeps being fought over and over. The tension builds up, but every time the experience comes up winning the fight. Sweat pours down my body and my eyes sting. A bug is blown into my helmet and of course ends up in my eye, just as another serious gust throws me and the bike in front of an oncoming campervan. I swerve hard back into my lane, but the wind keeps pushing me into the oncoming lane. The driver of the van sees this and makes space for me to get past. I throw all my energy into pulling the bike back into my lane and with little room to spare I manage to get back far enough to miss the van. Thank goodness he was watching and also responded.

The bug in my eye starts to settle in and I think he was busy pouring the concrete for his new house's foundations. I open the visor, which compromises my control with only one hand on the steering, but I have to stop the bug from settling down or I am not going to make this. I rub the bug out and as I close the visor, I start wondering if the tension has gotten too much and I am going postal.

Up ahead in the road is a naked man.

Surely not. As I get closer, swerving all over the place, I see that indeed there is a naked man walking next to the road. His friends are sitting in their camper van just a hundred metres ahead and he must have lost a bet, or maybe it is his bachelors. I hoot as I go past and wave at him. Having seen that he is less well endowed than I am, I did not feel threatened at all and thus the happy wave.

With the comic relief moment over, I carry on riding through the insane winds and then round the next corner the dark clouds loomed up ahead. Heavy rain is coming our way. I pull over and we take a few minutes to smoke a cigarette and pull the waterproof suits back on. Darryl leads as we ride on towards the half way point of the pass.

Coming up to the half way point the rain comes down in buckets. The wind drives the rain into me so hard it feels like hail. Visibility drops to a few meters and rivers flow over the road. It gets more complicated as we have to cross many long, exposed, single lane bridges. We stop at the half way point and take a moment to recover, but we have to carry on. We cannot stay here and the longer we stay, the worse it is going to get.

We push ahead and then mercifully ride into a valley. The wind picks up more speed as it is funnelled through the valley, but at least it is coming straight from the front. Now it is not trying to throw me from the bike anymore, but is directly challenging my bike's power. The wind still had a chance when it took on my riding skills, but my bike does not take kindly to challenges to its power. It calls on all the horses built into its lovely engine and it thrashes into the wind. After showing the bike I am in control, it is now responding and showing me it has all the power I could ask for. Together we fly through the wind and rain and that connection between us deepens.

Then the wind is left behind as we start the decent. We have pushed through it. The rain intensifies though, but the steep drop to the left and the rise of the sheer cliffs to the right causes the world to turn into millions of waterfalls. It is so beautiful! Up ahead a huge aqueduct has been built over the road as a large waterfall crashes onto it and then off on the other side of the road down the cliffs to some pool far below. My I-pod is suddenly giving me issues, as the one speaker is not working. I fiddle with the connection that hangs in my neck. I usually keep this connection under the waterproof layer, but in my rush to get the rain gear on in the howling wind I had left it outside. As I fiddle with it, it shocks me. Dammit. Now it doesn't work at all. I switch it off completely and can only hope I haven't just killed my I-pod.

We continue down the road and then get to the settlement of Jacksons. The total settlement consists of one bar/restaurant and just down the road, a couple of cabins. The guy at the pub recommends the cabins as the best place to stay around here and the when we get there, they quickly recommend the bar up the road for dinner. I believe the same people own the two places, but that suits me fine. The cabins are cheap, dry and warm. It also has the extra crucial ingredient of separate rooms. I cannot afford to lie awake again listing to snoring. Otto and I am in the same cabin and I close the door between our rooms and ask Otto to do a snore test. I can't hear much more than a soft growl, so it is ok. With that we go down to the pub to get some well deserved drinks and hot food.

We first settle down on the couches and drink a couple of beers and talk through the riding of the day. That was hectic, but we are getting our money's worth as far as riding experience goes.

I have a look at the menu and decide the steak will do. The menu has the steak with a sauce and two sides. The sides are fries, mash, veggies and salad. I decide on the fries and veggies. I go to the bar to order while the other two still sit and sip on their beers. As I do not so much sip as gulp beer, mine is finished long before theirs.
The barman walks over to take my order and I notice his prison tattoos. He also has a funny (and not in the ha-ha sense) twitch where he squeezes his eyes shut and give a rapid shake of the head.

"Heya mate. Can I have the steak with the pepper sauce and for the sides I want the fries and veggies. Also can you give me a Heineken?" I place my order.

Not that easy. He seems a bit upset.

"You-you-you-you can have fries an-an-an-and the salad, or ma-ma-ma-mash and veggies." He says and twitches.

Man. Does he have to also stutter? Just how long can I keep a straight face and not laugh at the comic of errors that is our barman? I think it was mostly the prison tattoos that helped me keep a straight face.

"Um, ok. I will then have the fries and salad." I mange to solve his issue easily without getting him upset.

"Ok. He writes it down carefully while the twitch causes him to need to stop writing every so often.

"And how d-d-d-d-do you want your steak d-d-d-d-done?" he asks and looking at him I can see he is squint as well. What the fuck did they feed his mum? Well, I have heard of the sheep related issues in these parts where some of the farmers get real lonely and those sheep start looking mighty fine. I wonder if they also have other types of issues where brothers and sisters get too friendly with each other? Or maybe someone dumped toxic waste in his drink water. It is also possible that he was fine until he went to jail....

"Just make it medium rare." I ask now starting to feel sorry for the guy.

"NO!!! We can only do m-m-m-medium, or rare. D-d-d-do you like blood or not?" he asks looking me partly in the eye.

Not sure if we are still talking about the steak here and I start thinking "Deliverance".

"Um, Ok, just make it rare then." I say and watch him write it down. I swear to you this is what he wrote:

Steak. Pepper sauce. Fries and Salad. Steak rare to the medium side.

What the hell? Isn't that just another way of say medium-rare? WTF? Never mind. I pay and then Otto walks up to order. I take my beer and start heading back to the couch.

"Can I get the steak, medium rare with veggies and salad?" he asks and as the barman twitches and goes over his rules on how you can order I start giggling and go and sit down with my beer.

After all that I can tell you that the stake was very good. It was cooked medium rare and was a very good piece of meat.

After dinner we walk back to the cabin and then crash and burn.
As we don't have any reception on the cell phones I cannot call Elizna to say good night, but at least we did agree that no news is good news, so if she hears nothing it would be because of reception.

I fall asleep immediately and do not dream or wake up with snoring at all.

7 January 2011

I am woken up by a loud knock on the door.

"Come, come. Let's get going." It is Darryl outside getting us up. I am still a bit groggy, but get up immediately and brew some of my lovely coffee. Sleeping went much better last night without the snore machine next to me and Otto is also well rested. Obviously my snoring also did not bother him.

I walk outside with the coffee and light a cigarette, watching the rain pour down. Today will be just as wet as yesterday. We load up the bikes, put the waterproofs back on and hit the road. There is no wind today, just loads and loads of rain. We come up to Inchbonnie, but it is still too early for anyone to be open to be able to give us some coffee, so we just ride on through. When we get to Moana we find a place where we can get ok coffee. I am a bit loath to drink the coffee as it comes from one of those coffee machines that pretend to make real coffee, but this does give me the opportunity to call Elizna. She sounds relieved to hear from me. She knows we have agreed to the no news is good news, but there will always be that nagging doubt somewhere in her mind while we are on the bikes in bad weather and she can't get hold of us.

Anyway, after a coffee, we are on our way again. Today we have to cross the Doubtful Range Pass back over to the East Coast. After our crossing yesterday on the Arthurs Pass I am a bit apprehensive, but on the way to the pass we ride into a forest, which is picture perfect. I pull over to switch my camera on and Darryl takes the lead. We stop again just before the start of the pass for a stretch of our legs and then we kick off what ends up being the best riding for all three of us for the whole trip. Doubtful Range Pass flies at high speed below us, as Darryl sets the pace and slots deep into the groove. Having been on the bike now for three solid days and one and a half thousand kilometres, I am right in the groove as well. Otto is also right there and we pick up the pace even more. Darryl leads at about an average speed of hundred and thirty kilometres an hour and we stick to him like shit to a wool blanket.

A bright orange Ford of some kind crawls up to me from behind and tucks in behind me. It falls back a little bit and then joins our race across this stunning mountain pass. I actually start enjoying the relationships with the Ford driver as he drive a respectful distance behind me, but is flying through the corners at the same speed we are. I can see him enjoying himself. Too soon we come to the turn off to Kaikora and stop on the turn. We are all bubbling with the overflow of emotion of the riding we had just done. It was amazing.

On the next stretch there is no traffic at all along the ribbon road through farmlands. Darryl suddenly accelerates hard and drops down behind his screen on his petrol tank. I see what he is doing, he is going to set the speed record. Not to be left out, I open the accelerator and fly after him. The BMW's large engine screams in pleasure as I hit hundred and seventy kilometres an hour and then pull back as we approach a corner.

Otto takes the lead from here and then we hit some pretty tight corners. There are no signs warning of just how tight the corners are. It is pretty intense riding and we know Otto doesn't like these tight, technical corners. That doesn't stop him however and I can see he is still deep in the groove as he leads us quickly through this piece of tricky road. We show no respect for the one way bridges and do not even slow down, but rather speed up as it is strait road.

Finally we go over the last hill between us and the east coast and ahead of us is Kaikoura. Kaikoura is a picture perfect town on the coast with turquoise water and white sand. Also half the world's population as tourists are milling around here. It is now hot and we have passed out from under the rain at some stage while crossing over the pass into a clear blue sky.

Kaikoura is best known for whale watching and providing people the opportunity to swim with dolphins. The other great thing about Kaikoura lies in the meaning of its name. Kaikoura translates from Maori to English as "Kai-", which means "Meal" and "-koura" which means "crayfish". I love crayfish and have on a previous occasion when I passed through here on a motorbike, bought a couple and carried it all they way back home.

Once we entered the town, we stop next to a restaurant that doesn't look too busy and kit off. It feels good to get the kit off for a bit, as it is pretty hot here after the few cold days. We grab a table and like all bikers do, we all look up as a bike rides in and parks next to our bikes. It is a Suzuki M40 and it is packed like ours for a long ride. The guy does not have any proper riding gear on though and this is one of my dislikes. I prefer to think that bike riders are responsible and will wear the correct gear. The guy takes his helmet off and immediately I lose interest. He has short cropped hair on the sides and longer Mohawk style hair on top. He looks a bit dodgy, but Darryl is not put off. He walks over and starts chatting to him. I think this was mostly because Darryl is interested in buying the same bike.

I get up and also go and chat. It turns out the guy is from Russia and this is day seventeen of his trip. He has cruised the South Island for the whole of his holiday. He is quite interested in our bikes and especially mine. While reading the piece about what he says, read it out loud in your best Russian accent.

Trust me, the heavier you lay it on the closer you will get to how he sounded. Trust me you cannot overdo the accent!

"My name Roman. Like warrior of long time back."

"Hi Roman, I am Deon.... like .... dumbasses of today." He smiles and shakes my hand. He missed that one, but I am never keen to be outsmarted with come backs and really I do not have a "Deon like..." It is usually just "Deon the Great", or "Deon the Amazing" or something plain like that.

"What is size of your bike? Roman asked.

"It is an eleven fifty." I reply proudly and lovingly pat my bike on the petrol tank.

"Yes. I like big bike. I ride two litres in Russia. I like bike that goes very fast" he says and frowns at his eight hundred cc bike. There are obviously some love issues there. "This bike too slow and I like two litres." He confirms and walks closer to my bike.

I allow him to get closer, but then he pushes the newly formed friendship boundaries.

"I can get on bike?" Roman asks and to give him credit he did wait for me to think this over.

"Sure. Go for it." I allow reluctantly. It was the right thing to do as he is in the biker's community and he smiled happily and respectfully climbed on.

"Yes, I like heavy weight. It is right bike." He says and I have strange mixed feelings of jealousy and pride at the same time.

"Yeah, she's a beaut." I casually confirm and then he gets off and I can relax my jealous streak.

We chat a little bit longer and then our food is brought to the table so we say goodbye and go and sit down for a well deserved lunch. While we sit in the shade under a sun umbrella overlooking the clean blue ocean, scoffing the food down our throats, in walks Roman. He stands there with his plate and a ginger beer in his hands looking for a place to sit down, but all the tables are full.

I wave him over and ask him to join us. He is quite chuffed and accepts the offer and sits down. As he sits down, he starts talking. I swear he must have a "talk-on" button on his ass. He just keeps talking and talking.

"So, Roman, what do you do for a job?" I ask.

"I am cutting people open." He says and demonstrates with his bread knife how he would be cutting people.

Ok, so here we have a Russian who has the financial means to ride around for weeks on end and he cuts people for a living. Maybe it is because of too many movies or books, but the first thing that I can think of is Russian mafia hit man.

Cool.

"Um, how do you say? I am surgeon. I cut people to fix." He tries to explain further.

"Ah." Interesting. I don't know if I am impressed, confused or disappointed.

"What type of surgeon?" I ask.

"I work on nervous." And then he goes into a lot of detail I will not be able to repeat in very broken English on how he works on the nerve system and connecting prosthetics to the nerve systems so that people can actually feel heat or cold and can use prosthetic hands pretty close to a normal hand. He explains how the electrical impulses are negatives and all you need to do is understand how to replicate the impulses to make the stuff work. I probably have this all wrong, but it was pretty interesting.

Talk about judging a book by his cover and getting it all wrong. After a while Darryl gets up. He is not a fan of people who talks a lot and Otto also gives up, but I am really enjoying the conversation. We change the conversation to the riding. He has ridden in so many countries. He is trying to improve his English to be able to qualify to go to MIT in the USA. Wow. He asks about riding through Africa and we talk a while about what it would take to do a trip there and also what route he should take.

After lunch we decide we should head off to Blenheim, as we need to be in Picton the next morning at 7:30 a.m. for sailing back to Wellington and we cannot sleep in Picton as there are a million tourists there already. Darryl has met someone earlier on the trip that said they will have place for us in Blenheim if we come past there, so we head out that way. Just before we gear up I ask them that I want to stop for fuel before we leave Kaikoura, but before we know it we are out of town. I flash them to pull over and Darryl checks his I-phone and the next fuel stop is about fifty kilometres away. We are sure we can make that, so we head on out along the coast. We are now on the busy State Highway 1, so the riding is tough. Lots of large trucks and fancy sports cars make it quite dangerous and I have a moment that I miss the safety of the wind on Arthur's Pass.

Looking down I see my fuel light is on again. Fuck. I hate riding on fumes and here we go again. As we get to Darryl's fuel stop, we realise that there is no fuel stop in the little settlement. Now I need to slow down to hundred kilometres and hour to conserve fuel. I creep on and eventually we get to the fuel stop. Again their prices are high enough that Oprah would have had a light heart attack, but we fuel up with a smile.

Standing there with our last hundred kilometres of the trip laying ahead the mood is a bit moot. We have been waiting so long for this ride and it is almost over. The heat is stifling, so we decide to push on to Blenheim. As we turn away from the coast the wind hits us again. It is strong gusty winds and again I am thrown around a bit. It is nothing like the winds we had on the Pass and after spending so much time on the bikes, the wind is a minor bother. It is actually enjoyable to have the wind add some extra dimension to the ride. Funny how much things can change in such a short time.

When we get to the accommodation it is a pleasant and unpleasant surprise. The pleasant part is that there is a swimming pool. With the heat as it is now, the swim will be very nice. The not so pleasant surprise is the trailer park itself. It looks exactly like the scene of every cop show on TV. Dodgy trailer trash. To be fair though, it wasn't that bad. I am sure the people in Baghdad sleep in worse. After unpacking we go for a swim and then head out for a few beers at a pub across the street. We play a few games pool and then end up having dinner early afternoon.

At this stage the heat of the afternoon is worrying me. Darryl and I are going to ride in heat quite a bit worse than this for days on end when we head over to Australia. We will need to think of some way to be able to keep cool.

After a few beers I am totally drunk and I will blame the beer for the poor pool I was playing. I call it the night and we head back to the trailer park. I go for another swim and then get in bed. It takes me less than five minutes to fall asleep.

8 January 2011

Darryl knocks me awake again and I get up pretty groggily. The room was very hot and I couldn't open the window as there are millions of flies due to the horses kept next to my room. I dress and pack up and neither of us have much to say. Otto is still sleeping, as he is on a later ferry.

He gets up just before we leave and we say our goodbyes. Darryl and I ride out and he takes the lead. Suddenly he stands up on his pegs, hand high in the air. He had just crossed the five thousand kilometres mark for the trip. Great stuff! I ride up next to him and hold my fist out to him. He taps my first with his in recognition of the milestone. Just before we enter Picton I cross my 2000 km line, but make no big deal of it. I am just happy that we are pulling up to the ferry after such a long ride with no issues what so ever and a wonderful experience.

As we stop at the ferry, they wave us on. We had not read the ticket properly and we are just in time for the ferry. The time we had as final boarding time was actually our sailing time, so just as well we got up early and rode a brisk hundred and thirty kilometres per hour through to Picton.

On the ferry Roman pulls up next to me. Great. I help him tie down his bike, as he does not have his own tie downs he has to use the shitty tie downs provided by the ferry guys. It is horrible and I can see him freaking out at just how dirty his hands are. Must be a surgeon thing.

We go upstairs to the lounge and then when I want to go get a coffee Darryl says they do not accept EFTPOS or credit card. Just cash. Fuck. We only have fifty cents between the two of us.

"You want coffee. Here, take money." Roman says as he hands over his wallet to Darryl.

Darryl agrees to take twenty dollars and he will give it back to him once we get to Wellington. I love experiences like this and I am now a Facebook friend of Roman, the crazy Russian.

The ferry trip is pretty much listing to Roman telling me how their progress is going in the study to try keeping a sheep brain alive outside the body. Basically they just feed it water and sugar and something else and that is all the brain needs to be able to live. Interesting. They do have some moral issues on trying it on a human brain, but I can see that if it was up to him, he might just try to do that.

Eventually Darryl has enough of the talking and lay down next to the table on the floor for a nap. Roman thinks this is a good idea and this gives me a bit of quite time to reflect on the ride.

I am now so ready for the trip to Australia I am wondering how I am going to get through the ninety odd days still to go.

Chapter 8 – Best made plans

Stress...

Fear...

Uncertainty...

Words filled to the brim with feelings. How long can one second last?

"All and all, it looks good. The heart beat is strong and as expected, the spine is well defined, the liver and tummy is there and the expected size. Let's see.... there we go, two arms and two legs."

And then the dreaded moment arrives. Time slows down even more.

"Let's measure the neck." The scene on the black and white monitor changes as she swirls the scanner around and I feel my heartbeat increasing. My lungs are screaming for fresh air but I simply cannot take a breath.

She clicks on the fist measurement point and then the next.

"Good, that looks normal" she says and I slowly manage to let go of the breath that has been caught in my lungs. I try not to make too much noise as I gasp for fresh air.

"Mmm. Wait, let me have another look at that." She says and grabs a different scanner.
The breath that had just been expelled hangs in front of me as I am caught without air in my lungs and now cannot get myself to breathe in again.

"No, no, no, no" is all my brain can manage.

"The umbilical cord is lying against its neck so we would just need to do an additional measure. There we go. The babe looks all good and now if you wipe your tummy and go to the girls up at the reception they will print your pictures for you and give you a CD."

As softly as I can I gasp for air feeling a bit faint to be honest.

I rush back to the office and quickly look for our previous picture dated 23 March 2009.

0.879 millimetres.

I open the pictures we just got. Scanning through the pictures until I get the one where she took the measurements.

Again my heart picks up the pace again as the picture opens.

Wrong one. This one shows the nose.

Fuck.

Next picture. There we go. 0.232 millimetres.

That's a lot less. Google. Normal range.... anything less than 0.300 is considered normal.

Relief

Joy

Breathe

I am going to be a dad.

PART 3 – The Myth of 'Roo

Australia is a land mass of 7,617,930 square kilometers. It is the world's smallest continent and the sixth largest country in the world. It is the only continent with only one country covering the whole continent. It is one of the few places in the world where they measure population in square kilometres per person, instead of the standard people per square kilometres. Once outside the big smoke (Australian slang for big cities), you will see very few people.

The Australian east coast is where the main centres of civilization are (if you can call it that!), with Sydney being the main commercial centre of Australia. Other cities like Melbourne and Brisbane are also really big, but from there it becomes smaller cities, like Perth, Adelaide, Cairns, Darwin and the capital, Canberra.

The majority of the Australian landmass is known as the Outback. The Outback itself does not have a specific defined area, but is pretty much anywhere in Australia that if you look around you and see no one and wait an hour and there is still no one, then you can be sure you are either blind, or in the Outback.

Most people know the old story of the British exporting their criminals to Australia, but what most people don't know is that even though that is true and this was done, it was never serious criminals like murderers, rapists and the likes. These criminals were executed in England. No, crimes that would get you shipped off to Australia were things like recommending that politicians get paid, starting an union, stealing fish from a river or pond, embezzlement, receiving or buying stolen goods, setting fire to under wood, petty theft, being suspected of supporting Irish terrorism or disgraced politicians found with hookers in their cars behind the shed by a reporter from The Sun news paper. Once they arrived in Australia, they had to serve out a sentence as criminals, and then they were let free and could go and settle on any piece of land in the Never-Never (Australian slang for the Outback). This practice was mostly stopped by the end of the nineteenth century. It was the practice for about eighty odd years and in this eighty year period a total of about 165,000 prisoners were exported to Australia.
At the same time and often on the same boats, were people flogging to Australia for the gold rush. During the same eighty years, the number of people going to Australia for the gold rush was more than twice that of the criminals. So the old myth that the majority of people in Australia being descendants of criminals is not quite true. It is believed that the current population descendant form these globe travelling convicts are about 22%. It is just because they all act so dodgy that people tend to believe they must all be descendant of some criminals!

So, what else make Australia an interesting place? Well, here are some interesting facts about Australia.

How about the Anna Creek cattle station? It is the largest working cattle station (or ranch as they are known in the United States) in the world. The area taken up by this station alone is more than the whole of Belgium. It is a total of 34,000 square kilometres. The largest range in the States is a measly 6,000 square kilometres. Now who said the USA was always bigger?

Each country has its own special "country day". The USA has Independence Day; Azerbaijan has a National Day and Brazil a Proclamation of the Republic Day. These all seem to be the country's celebration of becoming an independent country. A day to celebrate being freed from being held prisoner by another country. Well, Australia took a similar, yet different view of this concept. They have Australian day. Australian day is to celebrate the arrival of the first convicts in Australia. Well Whoopi-doo. Break out the champagne!

But a country is not all just about the history and land mass. It is also about the people. So how about some of the classic people of Australia. We all know Crocodile Dundee and Russell Crow (although no one really likes either of them), but who else is from this spectacular country that is worth mentioning?

Meet Bob Hawke. Mr Hawke managed to get himself written into the Guinness Book of world records in 1954 for drinking 2 ½ pints of beer in 11 seconds. Bob then later became Prime Minister of Australia. I imagine it wasn't later on the same day, but this is the type of leader a country needs. I am sure I would be happy to sit and listen to his political views.

How about someone more interesting? Well ok. How about a certain Mister Francis de Groot? Francis was a retired cavalry officer who in 1932 managed to get himself selected as part of the honour guard at the opening of the world famous Sydney Harbour Bridge. So there he is on the wonderful, sunny opening day sitting on his horse when inspiration strikes. He swings his horse around and gallops towards the celebrities preparing to cut the ribbon to officially open the bridge. He races up, draws his sword and slashes the ribbon. As he cut the ribbon he loudly declares the bridge open in the name of the decent citizens of New South Wales.
That of course went down poorly with the celebrities and the rest of the honour guard and he was immediately forcefully removed and taken away while the ribbon was tied back together and the ceremony continued as if nothing happened.
He was then taken to a mental hospital and declared insane. I think he was mostly declared insane for thinking there are decent citizens in New South Wales. He was later fined for the replacement cost of one ribbon.

So, with all this wonderful knowledge of what is waiting for us in Australia, the journey continues....

Chapter 9 – Going down under to the big smoke

Day 1
Friday 8 April 2011
From: Wellington
To: Auckland

It is the last day of work and the day drags on and on. How long can is still be until this day ends? I see my skin start to wrinkle, my hair start going grey, my eye sight deteriorate and I feel the need to have my prostate checked as I age waiting for the work day to end. A number of people come around to wish us well on the trip, which is nice.

The last meeting just seems to go on forever and both Darryl and I keep watching the clock, not really listening to the presentation.

Finally it is time to go and Darryl and I rush out of the place like the kids rushing out of school for holidays in the movies. I need to go home now and get the last things sorted out for the trip. I will need to pack my toothbrush and other last minute items and then get the last few hours to pass without going insane before we go to the airport. Nervous tension sets in and I am struggling to keep calm. I finally tell Elizna it is time to go to the airport, even though we are probably an hour too early. I just can't stand around waiting any longer. I carry the heavy bag down the stairs and load it into the car. It barely fits in the boot of the Peugeot 206 and I briefly wonder how this will fit onto the bike. I push that thought from m y mind as I cannot start doubting what I packed now. If it doesn't fit, I will through it away.

At the airport we go and check my bag in and it is just under the allotted twenty three kilograms. There is one final thing to be done before I can go through to the lounge. I go to the bookshop to get the notebook for me to use to record the trip in. It is the same shop from which I got the "Long Way Down" so many months ago. Talk about going full circle.

And now for probably the toughest part of the trip. I have to say goodbye to Elizna. We kiss and says goodbye and she immediately turns around and walks away. It is better that way so neither of us can get to teary. I watch her walk away and when she is out of sight I go to the Koru lounge and get myself a beer and the first of many bad dinners. This dinner is made up of cheese, biscuits and some Cookie Monster cookies. Darryl turns up a short while later and we excitedly talk about the fact that the day has finally arrived and that we are now officially on the trip.

"From here of on, whatever happens is the trip." I confidently state. I had barely finished saying this when an announcement is made that our flight will be delayed by thirty minutes. That's a good start! I grab another beer and sit back and try to relax while reading my book. Finally the call is made for us to board. I have pre-booked my seats for the whole trip long ago, so I have the very front row seat. I sit down and the man sitting down next to me gives the bike jacket a look. I immediately put my I-pod on and start reading my book again as I am just not really in the mood to chat with strangers now. There will be enough of that later in the trip I am sure. I am a little emotional after saying goodbye to Elizna and Chloe, our cat wasn't home when I left and I didn't get to say goodbye to her. Yeah, I know boo-hoo. That together with the excitement of finally being on the trip is not putting me in a mood where I am mister chatty.

The flight is uneventful and when we get to Auckland our bags are out quickly. When I put my phone on there is a missed call from an Auckland phone number. I had made a booking for tonight's accommodation and part of the deal is shuttle transport from and to the airport. It is the only pre-booked accommodation for the whole trip. I call them back and they say that their shuttle is on its way and will be there in two minutes. We hurry outside and look for the shuttle, but it is nowhere to be seen. Darryl spots the shuttle driving away so I call them again and they say that they waited and we did not turn up. They had to go drop off some other passengers so we will have to wait, they will be back in ten minutes to come and get us. We smoke a cigarette while we wait and finally after about twenty minutes the shuttle returns and we load our stuff into the back. He then heads to the international terminal and pick up a couple who had just arrived from abroad.

As the guy sits down he gives us one look and asks about our bike jackets. We tell him about the planned trip and he tells us about his seven bikes he has back home in a strong Yankee accent. His girlfriend leans over and whispers something in his ear. He looks a bit deflated and then falls silent. I must admit I thought it would be a bit later in our trip when people were going to start ignoring or avoiding us. Never mind, we have arrived at the hotel. We book in and go to our rooms. How can I best describe the place? It is a roach motel. It is very, very dodgy.

I packed my bathroom bag in my big bag and it is sealed with a cable tie and I have no way of getting it open. I try using my key to open it, but it doesn't work. Just as I decide I will go and ask for a pair of scissors at reception, I get a call from them.

"Good evening mister le Roux. I am sorry to tell you, but you have only paid the day rate, so you must come to the reception and pay the rest." The lad says in a strong Indian accent.

"Oh, well that's correct then, we will only be staying here one night." I reply.

"No sir. You paid the day rate and it is different from the night rate." He clarifies. "You still owe us sixteen dollars for the two rooms."

I go to the front and think about who would be paying the day rate? Cheap hookers or maybe pilots and the air stewards having a little cock-pit party? I pay the extra money and ask if I could use their scissors. I have to promise twice that I will return the scissors. Armed with the scissors I manage to get my bag open and can brush my teeth before finally I get into bed. As I settle down I hear that a very rowdy bunch is making a lot of noise outside and it doesn't sound like they are wrapping the party up either. Groan. It is not the best start to the trip.

After what feels like hours I finally fall asleep. Sleep is not restful though. I dream I have been captured by an African dictator who is determined to break me. He tortures me to get me to talk and tell him my secrets. I can't remember what I was supposed to tell him and the burning knife he uses to cut my face still stings when I wake up. I am relieved that it was only a dream, but our friends outside are still going strong. I manage to fall asleep again and now dream that I am in Russia and they want to arrest me for being an American spy. I keep telling them that I am not American. I am a Canadian spy. Not sure which dream was worse.

Day 2
Saturday 9 April 2011
From: Auckland to Melbourne (flight)
To: Wye River
Distance travelled on bike: 191 kilometres

I wake up at 5:00 a.m. when my alarm goes off and quickly get up and get in the shower. Having not slept well and not being an early riser I am potentially in a foul mood. However, the mood is easily and thoroughly overridden by the excitement of being on our way to Australia. I also get the opportunity to make the first of many coffees using my coffee solution.

When I get to the reception the shuttle is ready to take us to the airport and without any further delays we are on our way to the international departure lounge. This time of the morning there is not much traffic so we get to the airport quickly. After grabbing our stuff from the shuttle and working our way inside we go to the Air New Zealand booking counters, but then Darryl says: "Fuck this, where's the premium book in area?" We have both travelled a lot over the last year or so, so both have Koru lounge access and also have gold status as far as frequent flyer goes.
We get to the premium counter and I tell Darryl I had used one of my complimentary upgrades for this flight to be upgraded to business class. He

also asks for the upgrade and now we are both going to travel in style in business class. The lady booking us in says we are lucky. We will be flying in Air New Zealand's brand new Boeing 777. Way cool.

After checking in we head through customs without incident and then go up to the Koru lounge. There we have a breakfast and I use the opportunity to charge my cell phone. After all the planning and testing I had forgotten to pack the cell phone charger. I do have a car charger, but will only be able to use that once we are on the bikes. A very attractive woman comes and sits right across from us and she is wearing a very, very short skirt that rides up enough for us to be able to see that she is wearing blue underwear. Luckily we get our call to board, so we leave the sightseeing behind and head out to our gate.

As we have gold status we can board immediately and the amazing surprise of business class is waiting for us. This is the first time I travel in business class in my life, so I am pretty excited about it. The chairs are very cool, each in its own cubicle with an automan for your feet. As soon as we sit down they serve champagne and I do not say no!
After takeoff we are served fruit smoothies and muffins. Again I do not refuse the treats and it is very tasty. I start to watch the movie "Tron", but quickly lose interest as it is very predictable and basically terrible movie. Man, why do they waste so much money making crap like this?
I decide to rather have a snooze. There is a button next to the chair that says you should press it to turn the chair into a bed. I press it and the chair automatically converts into a bed. This bed is much softer than the one I slept on last night and I am asleep within seconds.

After a snooze that lasts about an hour I wake up. I immediately know that I will not be able to sleep any further right now, so decide to get back to watching some TV or movies. I press the button to revert the bed back into a chair and about half way up with a grunting noise and a small jerk, it stops moving. Mmmm. This is not good.

Ok, so now I am sitting on a half folded bed/chair. It is a brand new plane and I go and break the chair. I try to casually manoeuvre it back into the bed, but with a bit louder cracking noise it now sounds like it is properly broken. The thing about business class is there are a lot of air stewards so within seconds one of them is there and smiles while looking at me half folded and blushing bright red.

"Don't worry sir, I will fix this. If you don't mind getting up for a second?" She says and when I am up she tries pressing a bunch of the buttons which I had also tried, but figured she can sort this out. Eventually she is down on all fours under the chair switching it to manual. Then with some effort she manages to get it back up to the chair. For a second I consider telling her I actually wanted to put it down into the bed, but her red face and sweat running down her temples makes me reconsider my wonderful sense of humour. Of course by this time everyone in business class is also looking over to see what the commotion is about, so I just smile and settle down back into the chair. It gives one final crack and then settles down. We seem to have reached a point where the chair will no longer move and I will just need to sit really still. If you are flying on the new 777 and the chair is busted, sorry about that!

I have a look at the rest of the entertainment options and find an episode of the Big Bang Theory. Half way through I catch a glimpse of what Darryl is watching. There are two totally naked chicks making out and doing a dam good job of it. What the hell? I feel like such a nerd! He laughs when I say this and admits that this is actually a romantic comedy and he did not really know that the movie becomes this racy. So he is also feeling a bit like a nerd watching the romantic comedy. Good start for a couple of tough guys roughing it out for three weeks!

Not to long after this they announce that we are now approaching Melbourne. The usual story of having to switch off all electronics and fold away to the tray tables and television screens is blared out over the scratchy intercom.

Chapter 10 – Debbie Does Victoria

As states go Victoria is pretty compact. It is the second most populous state in Australia with about five million people and the smallest main land state. It is 228,000 square kilometres in size with Melbourne as its capital. Melbourne used to be the biggest city in Australia back in the 1800's when the Australian gold rush was on and it kept that status until Sydney eventually became the biggest city. When the two cities were roughly the same size, the argument started about which city should become the country's capital city. This was apparently a very ugly war between the two cities, with rude comments on talk shows and the big tobacco companies playing both sides. While all this mayhem was going on, Canberra snuck in and took the title of "The capital" from under their noses. Melbourne then promptly decided to become the cultural capital of Australia.

Victoria is the proud record holder for the world largest gold rush after gold was found in 1851 and the population increased sevenfold in ten years.

Victoria is also home to the barbaric sport known as Aussie Rules Football. In our time in Australia we would watch a few games and even though I started to enjoy it somewhat I cannot claim to actually have understood a single moment of it. Some tough blokes playing this game though!

More importantly on the most famous island off the coast of Victoria, Phillip Island, the Australian MotoGP is held. This is the world's premier motorcycling class racing.

I look out at the mainland below us and the green grassy hills. We are approaching from the east so the scenery is not anything we will see on our way out once we have landed. They must have had a bit of rain as it is very green out there. Finally I see the first suburbs and then for the next fifteen minutes the city unfolds underneath us as the plane speeds towards the airport. Seeing the stretched out expanse of building and suburbs, I realise just how big Melbourne is.

After we touchdown the pilot informs us we have been asked to park next to the runway as we are ten minutes early and the gate is not ready for us. Sitting there on the runway looking at the small clouds and blue sky through my little window I put my I-pod on and let it pick a song randomly. Michael Buble starts singing and I seriously try to remember when and why I would have loaded that? Maybe the I-pod comes out with it pre loaded... I guess that's the only way he gets to sell any music.

I skip the track and then Louise Armstrong starts singing "What a wonderful world". Now that's better, as it suits both my mood and the scenery much better. After what feels more like half an hour than ten minutes, we finally seem to have received to all clear as we are heading over to the gate. The stewards hands us a leaflet that will give us rapid processing privileges to get through customs. All we have to do is flash this card and they will let us go through a quick, short line. Again the rich and privileged are treated as such and it is almost depressing knowing that next time I travel someone else will be getting this luxurious treatment. Next time you see people just flying through a short line in customs, you are welcome to feel grumpy. I know I will. Yet, this time I am one of them, so smugly walk out of the plane towards to one place in the world no one likes. Customs.

I get to walk up to a counter where there is no queue and they stamp my passport within seconds of getting there. The rest of the people get to stand in a long queue which will take at least twenty minutes to get through. Shame, so that's how poor people travel. As I stand there waiting for my passport to be handed back to me, I see Darryl is in the long queue. He had misplaced his card, so cannot use the rapid processing lane. He does not look too happy about that I can assure you.

Once processed, we get to the baggage carrousel and wait for our bags. It takes forever for it to arrive. Twenty minutes later the bags starts coming out and by now we are feeling as if we will never get to the bikes. We grab our bags and in shuffle away with the ugly plastic bags that is our luggage towards the duty free area, Here Darryl buys a bottle of the good stuff, Jack Daniels and we each get a carton of cigarettes. The end of this trip also signals the end of my smoking, so this carton will be smoked up and if there is anything left on the last day, I will give it to Darryl.

The final step for getting out of the airport will be to get through quarantine. We should have no problems here, but it is funny how an apple or half a kilo of coke just by accident sneak into your bag when you are not watching, so there is always the odd chance of something holding us up here. When I get to the quarantine area there is another long queue, which I recon will take at least half an hour to get through. Luckily my "I am important" pass is valid here as well and thank goodness they allow Darryl to come through this side as well.

A very bored looking quarantine officer asks me if I have anything to declare. I promptly declaring that I have nothing to declare and he waves me through.

Stepping out into the arrivals hall I wonder if I should have declared the coffee. I really do not know, but it matters not. I am in Australia and now feel that magnetic pull of the bikes. They are so close I can almost smell them.

Outside, Darryl has found a dodgy Middle Eastern guy that will take us to Sunshine where we are to pick up the bikes. I saw a sign inside the terminal saying it is a better idea to use certified taxis as there are people ripping off visitors. I leave it though, as Darryl had already negotiated that it will be $60 to get us there and that sounds like a reasonable rate.

We get into the car and as we drive out of the airport, he asks for the address again. I give him the address and now he claims that this is in Sunshine West. This is much further than Sunshine, so we will need to pay extra. It is even further than going all the way into Melbourne city, he says.

I had checked on Google maps before we came to Australia where this address was and it looked to be quite close to the airport. This asshole was trying to take us for a ride. Then inspiration strikes and I grab my back ripping out my GPS and switch it on. He sees this and asks what I am doing.

"I am looking where this address is." I say and for a moment we lock eyes and I am reminded of our poker games. One or both of us are bluffing and we both know it. The whistling tune from the spaghetti western, The Good, The Bad and the Ugly would have been quite appropriate at this point as my eyes narrow to a small sliver.

Darryl sees what is happening and catches on immediately. With him sitting in front he takes his GPS out as well and puts it up against the window so we can all clearly see. Oh, it is twenty kilometres away. It is hardly as far as he claims it is. I had called his bluff and he had lost out. As we get closer he seems to know the area pretty well. He doesn't even need the GPS. I put my GPS away as it had served its purpose for now. We get to the depot where we are to pick up the bikes in good time and now the excitement of getting to the bikes makes my bladder feel weak. It looks like we are at a truck depot and while Darryl sorts out the taxi I go and look for the guy who has our rides.

Ray, the guy we are to meet to get the paperwork sorted out is really friendly and we have a good chat about the ride and where we are heading today. While we talk about riding and his adventures in his younger days, I sign my contract and then go and look for Darryl.

"I have dibs on the blue one" he says when I find him. He has obviously managed to find the bikes while I was inside doing my paper work. I lead him back to where he needs to also do his paper work. When we get back inside is seems the blue one had already chosen me. The contract specifically matches me to the blue one and Darryl to the silver one. After Darryl signed his contract we head out to the back of the store room and I can now see why he didn't want the silver one. Instead of an engine it has paddles, the back tyre is flat and it has an old tractor steering wheel! Actually the only difference is that it has silver fearing and the other has blue fearing.

We do the check on the bike to make sure it is in the condition stated and then I try to find the power point. This is a small, but crucial piece of the bike as all the gadgets, and the are a lot of them, depends on us having these power points. I did confirm it with them many weeks ago, but now cannot find it. Normally the power point is on the bike's control panel, but I'll be dammed if I can find it. I ask Ray about it and he also searches all over the bike. I am getting a bit worried, as we are royally fucked if we do not have power. Ray eventually calls the BikeAroundOZ guys and they have to look it up on their system. Eventually we find it on the side of the bike almost under the seat. I am too relieved to have found it to be upset about the dumbass who decided to fit it there.

At this point the guy from the Satellite telephone rental company turns up. I had arranged that he meet us here and bring the phone to us. Shahid explains to me how the phone works and gives me the pre-paid bag I should put the phone in and mail once we get to Cairns. Honestly I am too excited at this stage to really listen to what he is saying about the codes and I think he realised it. He gives me the phone and tell me to enjoy the ride.

The bikes are in good condition with brand new tyres and basically save for a few small scratches, no worries what so ever. The bikes have over hundred thousand kilometres on the clock, but that is why we went for the BMWs. They are able to do quite a few hundred thousand kilometres before they start giving problems. I get on my new best friend and start it up. The height is ok, but I will turn the preloaded suspension a bit softer to allow for me to get closer to the ground. Also, once the bike is fully loaded, it should sink down even more. I ride outside where we had left our bags

Now we need to pack all the stuff we have in the large bags onto the bike. The panniers are quite a bit smaller than the ones I have on my bike back home so I struggle to get everything in, but eventually it is all in or on the bike. Darryl is done long before me and I am sure his is bigger than mine. Later I would find out that they are expandable and my panniers were collapsed.

As we get ready to leave Ray says we should stop in Geelong and go to the golf course. They have good meals and there are kangaroos on the golf course.
Before getting on I take a moment to have a look at the bikes standing there fully loaded. We have made it! We are on the verge of starting off on the ride that has been planned for more than a year. Moments like these are few and far in between in your life and knowing that I do relish the moment.

We mount up, start the bikes and here we go, we ride the first metre of our journey. We ride out onto the four lane highway heading out east, away from Melbourne city. The road is pretty busy and there is a strong, gusty, hot wind blowing. I am also not used to the higher riding position and the tyres are brand new on/off road tyres, where I am used to pure road tyres. It takes some getting used to and so we are taking it easy. We have also been warned that there are a lot of speeding cameras on this highway, so we are happy to keep to the hundred and ten speed limit.

I still need to get a cell phone card so we pull off the highway at Geelong and look for a shopping mall. Darryl also wants to get a tyre repair kit and luckily on the way into Geelong we spot a motorcycle shop and pull over. While Darryl goes in to get the repair kit, I have a chat to the one salesman who had come out when we stopped in front of the shop. I ask him where I can find a Vodafone store, as I need to get a prepaid sim card. He says I should buy a Telstraclear mobile card rather than Vodafone. He says Vodafone is good in the major cities, but has almost no coverage once outside the big cities. Telstra has pretty good coverage most of the time in the smaller towns as well. Great, I was going to get the Vodafone so am glad for the good advice. When Darryl comes out we head down the road to the shopping mall in the city centre. I will also need to take out my thermals and rain layer as it is really hot and I have all of it on.

At the shopping mall we park right in front of the mall doors and while Daryl fidgets with his GPS I head onto the mall to look for the Telstra shop. I get the Telstra shop on the second level of the mall and after a bit of a wait I am finally helped. It is kind of strange as I am greeted immediately, but then added to the waiting list. I almost expected them to ask me if I want to wait at the bar while they prepare my table. Regardless, I am now the person on the list to be helped, so no time for drinks at the bar. The sales lady listens to what I want and rips open a starter pack. She needs to make sure that my phone will work on the network, as I had been on the Vodafone network. Unfortunately my mobile's battery is completely flat, so she has to take it to the back where she can plug it in to charge. After checking that my cell phone will work on the

Telstra network the sales woman gets all the paper work ready and asks me for my address in Australia.

"I don't have an address in Australia. I am visiting from New Zealand" I reply.

"Ok, so where will you be staying most of the time?" she asks.

"Nowhere. We will sleep in a different place every night. We are doing a motorbike ride through the country and will not sleep in one place for more than a night. We haven't; booked any accommodation either as we will see where we sleep when we get there." I tell her about our plan, always keen to tell anybody who would listen about our trip.

This does not work for her and she whispers something to the other sales lady. It looks like she just cannot sell me the phone card without completing the form. And without an address there is just nothing she can figure out. Panic starts to show in her eyes, as she had already opened the card and put it in my phone. She will not be able to sell it to someone else and she doesn't have the home address for me. Of course the fact that I have just told her in detail what we are doing leaves me with no room to make up an address just to get the paper work done.

"How about my address in New Zealand?" I offer, wondering if I made up a relative who lives in Australia if she would call my bluff or just accept it.

"No, it has to be an Australian address." She says after consulting the form and now looking close to tears.

At that point the more senior sales woman comes over and after being filled in on the dreadful situation I feebly offer the motorbike rental company's address.

"Yeah, now worries. That will do." She says and the relief was felt by everyone. Even the guy standing behind me in the queue sighed with relief. Now I had a phone card, but my cell phone battery is still flat. Back at the bike I hook it up on the car charger and we decide to go to the golf course and get lunch there and see if we can see the kangaroos.

We ride out to the area where we believe the golf course is and after a few wrong turns find it. We see a few kangaroos on the golf course but I feel a bit cheated. They all have tags in their ears and are fenced in. That's no different from seeing a 'roo in the Wellington zoo. Only animals seen in the wild counts, so my animal count stays on zero. They are big animals though! We will need to keep an eye open for them. Hitting that large mouse with the bike will be the end of the trip. I doubt I would survive a crash with one of those!

We have a look at the restaurant and I suggest we move on. I really just don't want my first meal in Australia on the road trip to be in a fancy golf course restaurant with a bunch of old men in funny clothes. I had visions of pies and milkshakes bought at the petrol station.

We ride out and now the cloud cover is getting seriously dark and heavy. It starts getting darker and darker, even though it is only 3:00 p.m. As we go over the hill to get to Torquay the temperature drops by ten degrees instantly. I can't remember if I have ever felt such a dramatic change in temperature before. I do know that when nature has dramatic changes like this, something big is happening. Having grown up at the coast, it is one of the things I was taught to respect the sea and if something dramatic changes, make sure you are extra alert. I believe we are going to get wet up front and I am pretty tense waiting for some extreme wind or hail to start falling. We pull over as we get to the beach and go into a shop selling fish and chips. It is not the pie I mentioned earlier, but not bad. I like this. The order is for $10.30. In New Zealand we live in an almost completely cashless system. Everything is done via EFTPOS, which is pretty much a debit card. In Australia most transactions are still cash based. I still have an Australian $10 someone in New Zealand accidently gave me for change instead of a New Zealand $10, but that is all the cash we have between us. The lady looks us up and down and then says not to worry. The ten dollars will be ok. So far the Aussies had not been the monsters I had imagined them to be. Everyone had been friendly and smiling and I am feeling really happy right about now.

Sitting outside chomping away at the deep fried fish and the super hot fries, we see a whole flock of parakeets flying over. It is so strange seeing them in the wild and not caged up. While we sit there on the bench looking out over the ocean the first few rain drops splashes down on us. They are large, heavy drops and I think my prediction of earlier is about to become true.

I had considered bringing my waterproof gear that worked so well on the New Zealand South Island trip, but in the end decided against it as the weather had been really good for the last few weeks in this area and this is the only area I thought we would have any possibility of rain.
In any case, my bike gear has a waterproof layer, so should be able to keep me relatively dry. I put my rain layer back it and then we ride out onto the Princes highway and then the Great Ocean Road. This is one of the best rides in the world, but for the moment I am all focussed on keeping the bike going through this down pour. I was correct earlier when I thought something

extreme is coming, as the heavens have opened above us. Heavy rain welcomes us to the Great Australian Bight and after riding through this for an hour or so we stop at Lorne and grab a coffee.

Lorne is a very popular beach tourist resort town with lots of cafes and boutiques creating a Mediterranean feel to the area. Sitting on the Mountjoy parade under an umbrella I start shivering. It has been pissing down now for the last sixty or so kilometres and it has gotten cold quickly. Not exactly what I had imagined the first day's riding would be like. The other thing that is tapping my energy is the slow riding. The road is pretty slippery and there are surfers all over the place cruising around in their old cars, making the riding very sporadic and slow.

The coffee helps warm me up and while sitting there Darryl tells me he and his girlfriend are getting pretty serious. They are even discussing moving in together. This is a big change for him as he has been the eternal bachelor. While we are sharing, I then tell him that Elizna is pregnant again and I will always love Darryl for the genuine happy response from him. He had been such a good friend and support to us through our previous failed pregnancies.

With the touchy feely conversation over, we turn back to the business at hand. We decide that we will not push too hard the rest of the day. We don't know the bikes yet ad the new tyres are a bit slippery. We have a look at the map and decide we will stop at whichever place looks to have dry rooms and somewhere to eat close by.

Riding along the coast I see a camping area in Separation Creek, but they do not have any cabins, only tent camping. With the rain coming down like it is, I am not keen on camping tonight. We rather push on and when we get to Kennett River we stop at the camping area there. They have cabins but are fully booked. So yet again we have no joy. We continue down the coast and when we get to Wye River we finally find a place to sleep. Wye River is a small holiday town with only about two hundred permanent residents. The place we found is a camping ground, but at least they do have cabins. We take the budget room, which means we will have to share the ablution block with the campers, but that's ok. We will share the room tonight, so I am glad that I remember to pack my ear plugs.

We unload the bikes and then head on up the hill to the pub. It is a nice pub, where we get to test out our first Australian beers sitting overlooking the grey and moody ocean. There we sit and talk and have a few more beers and end up with dinner. After dinner we both feel the exhaustion after our early morning, the airport and the excitement of finally being out here, so we head back to the cabin. I fall asleep easily, but it is pretty cold and I wake up a number of times in the night shivering. I fold the blankets double over me and still feel cold. Sitting on the bed shivering, I considered getting dressed in my riding gear again to heat up, but when I pick it up it is still damp, so just give up on it. Honestly I had been worrying about how we will be coping with the heat in Australia, not the cold!

Day 3
Sunday 10 April 2011
From: Wye River
To: Kingston SE
Distance travelled: 541 kilometres

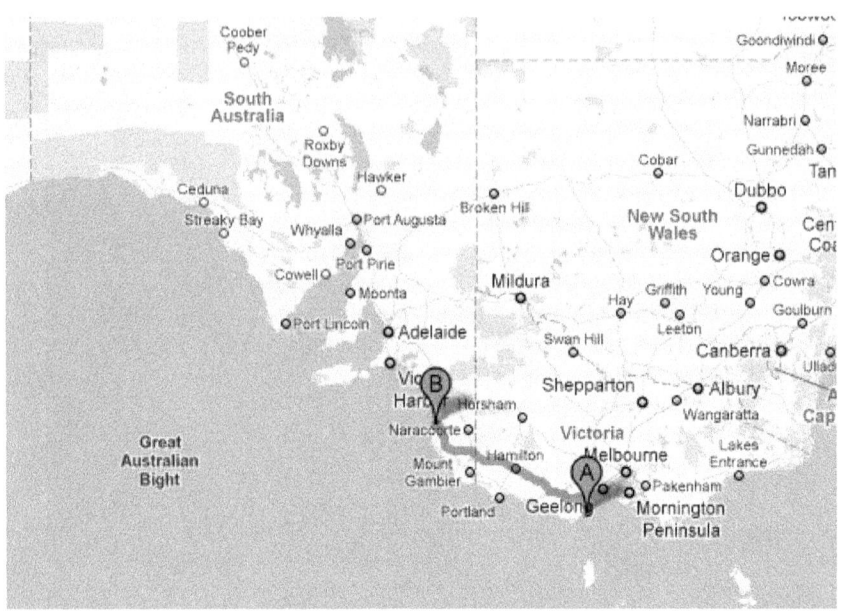

We get up quite early while it is still dark outside. I go for a shower in the ablution block to wake me up properly and also to warm me up. As I walk back to the room I look up into the lighting sky and am happy to see that there are no clouds. That is great news, but then I feel drops of rain. It seems to be raining from clear skies. How strange, but maybe I am not fully awake yet and I am only imagining it. We load up the bikes and head out of the camping grounds as people starts to move around.

As we get onto the Great Ocean Road the rain starts coming down again. It is raining pretty heavily, but the sun had just crested over the ocean turning the sky into a blood red canvas. There is a perfect ten rainbow ahead which is stunning, but then also that means it will be raining upfront as well. I was right thinking it is going to be wet as I can see the grey sheets of rain coming down up front. When we reach it, the rain pours down and soon I can feel my boots filling up with water and the rain seeping through my gear. Unfortunately the heated grips on my bike don't work so soon I am shivering again. We work our way towards the point where the road turns away from the coast just after

Apollo Bay. The road now twists through a forest of eucalyptus trees. The smell of the forest is stunning and with the low laying clouds the whole area is covered in mist. It is beautiful and I take every opportunity to look around as we ride through this magical forest. Then my attention is jerked back to the moment as my bike's back tyre has a slip in a corner. It turns into a little bit of a wobble but I easily correct the bike adding a bit of gas to straighten the bike out.

"What just happened?" I think out loudly as the bike slides again and this time I am on a straight piece of road.

"What the hell?" I ask again, now completely focused on the road.

The road has a layer of eucalyptus leaves and bark covering it, which with the rain has become as slippery as Godzilla snot. After a few more slips and slides, I have a front wheel slip. A back wheel slip is scary enough, but if you keep your wits about you, not really that dangerous. A front wheel slip is very dangerous however. Powering through a front wheel slip will not work, as you will just fall quicker. I do manage to get the bike under control quickly and now slow down to a crawl. I miss most of the rest of the scenery through the forest and am purely focussed on the road, trying to miss the large patches of leaves and bark.

As we come out of the forest we are on a hill and I feel myself relax a bit. I look back in my mirror to see if Darryl is still there, I had not looked back once through the whole forest. He is riding a little behind and just as I think everything is ok, Darryl's bike slips from under him. We had just started speeding up again and I have no idea of how this happened as it is a straight piece of road and no there is no bark on the road here. It must have been something on the road, but basically the whole bike slides out from beneath him at hundred kilometres an hour. He kicks hard onto the road with his left foot, which pushes the bike back up and over and he has to kick on the road with his right foot now. This kicking and change in momentum starts a serious wobble and I can see how he is looking for a place to fall where he will get suffer the least amount of damage. I have a look at the side of the road and am worried about the fence running along the side of the road. If he hits that he will cut himself into pieces. Miraculously he gets the bike back under control. We pull over and smoke a cigarette to calm the nerves. First full day's riding almost didn't happen. If he fell there, it was over. He would have been taken to hospital, if he was lucky and then the trip was as good as over.

When we finally feel ready to go again we mount up and ride on. We are taking it really easy after that scare. We come down the hill, ride through some farm land and after a few small settlements we get back to the coast. This is also where the Twelve Apostles are. The Twelve Apostles are giant rock stacks that rise majestically from the Southern Ocean and are the central feature of the rugged Port Campbell National Park. The Twelve Apostles have been created by constant erosion of the limestone cliffs of the mainland that began ten to twenty million years ago. The stormy Southern Ocean and blasting winds gradually eroded the softer limestone, forming caves in the cliffs. The caves eventually became arches and when they collapsed rock stacks up to forty five meters high were left isolated from the shore.

I have a moment where I have a look out at the scenery but am pretty nervous at this stage so to be honest, miss most of it. All eyes on the road, we just keep going until we get to Warranabool. Here we decide to get some coffees and use the opportunity to break the tension. There is a guy pretty interested in our bikes, but he quickly puts himself out of favour when he starts talking about how the "Abos" had a fight with the good white kids of the neighbourhood last night and we need to be careful. Enough said. We were warned that racism is quite alive and well in Australia and here we have our first encounter. This is our queue to exit so we get back on the bikes and move along.

From here we now leave the Great Ocean Road behind us. I must admit I had quite high expectations of this part of the trip and am feeling a bit disappointed. I had really not seen as much as I had hoped and the cold rain has not made it the most pleasant riding.

Now we are still pretty close to the coast but not close enough to see it. We are back amongst the farms and although beautiful, the rain keeps our nerves on edge. Darryl laughs and says that this is supposed to be "Some showers" according to the weatherman. That's crap if I had ever heard it! "Showers" means the rain must stop from time to time. The rain has been solid since we mounted up this morning so don't come and talk to me about showers!

After another hour's riding I finally see a break in the clouds up ahead and we manage to ride in between two large patches of rain. It tries to outflank us on the left, but we are only just quick enough to out run the wet tentacle of the clouds. I scream joyously at our victorious sprint to outrun the rain when Darryl pulls over. His old man bladder has turned traitor and the rain catches up to us. We get going pretty quickly again trying to outrun the rain as we pass over the border into South Australia.

Chapter 11 – Waltzing South Australia

Fact: South Australia is the driest state on the world driest continent. This simple, yet extreme fact carries my hope, as I am now very tired of being cold and wet.

To prove the extreme lack of rain, South Australia is home to Lake Eyre, which is the world's largest salt water lake at eight thousand four hundred and thirty square kilometres. It is dry as a bone most of the time, so calling it a lake is somewhat pushing the concept of a lake. But let's not be pedantic about that. The fact that it is almost always dry produces an immense saltpan, which is actually quite famous.

It is the site of a number of attempts to break the world land speed record. Sir Donald Campbell broke the record here in his Bluebird in 1964. Going at a speed of six hundred and forty eight point seven three kilometres and hour, he managed to log the new record. Even though it became the new world record officially recognized by the FIA, an American actually reached a speed of six hundred and fifty seven point one one four kilometers an hour the previous year. It was not officially recognized as his car had only three wheels and was not wheel driven as the jet engine did not power the wheels. Can you actually imagine driving at that speed? It must be scary as hell!

A bit more on the civilized side of life, South Australia also produces some of the finest wines in the world. The Barossa Valley produces excellent wines, including the 1998 vintage of the Penfolds Grange, of which a single imperial sized bottle was sold at an auction for US$35,000.00. Good lord. Would you actually drink that?

So, back to the story...

We get to Mount Gambier, which is the biggest regional city in South Australia. It currently has a population of around thirty thousand people and is one of the fastest growing cities in South Australia. As we have been swimming up to Mount Gambier and I am sure we would have made better time if we rented jet skis rather than motorbikes, we decide a bit of food would do us well and lift our spirits. We stop at a shopping centre next to the highway and get some food and hot coffee.

I had been ordering long blacks, as this is how I like coffee. It should be about half a cup and basically just have nice hot, strong coffee in. This is one of the things the Kiwis do exceptionally well. You cannot live in a city like Wellington and not get to appreciate good coffee. Soon you will cut out milk from your coffee and most certainly stop polluting the pure taste of coffee by adding sugar.

The Aussies have a slightly different method of serving coffee. They make sure it is so hot that it would heat up the surface of the sun. Then the next characteristic of a good Aussies coffee would be to fill it to the absolute rim. If you can fit a single extra drop in the cup, you have failed. This accomplishes two things. First it will ensure the coffee is weak. The half a litre of water ensures it as strong a glass of slightly dodgy milk. Secondly it makes it impossible to drink the coffee. It needs roughly seventeen years to go from scolding hot to boiling hot. From there, it takes another month or two to get to drinking temperature. The problem is that from the moment it has cooled enough to only burn blisters in your mount instead of burning your bone to ash, it now turns cold with 11.3 seconds.

This time I am determined to get a strong coffee I can actually drink instead of shying away from the heat. I order a short black, which is also known as an Espresso coffee. This is now two pounds of ground coffee for every drop of water. As you can imagine this is now a little bit stronger. The spoon is discoloured when I take it out and the paper cup sounds like crystal when I put it down on the table. It takes a strong coffee to get to me, but my response after swallowing the two sips of coffee in the cup was a meek; "eeeeeeek". Once it hit my stomach it is as if the world slows down and I speed up. I rambled off on more than one conversation at a time and one or more of the conversations with people that may or may not have been there. Now that is much better coffee.

After lunch we ride out in the rain and head to Milliscent. Contrary to its name, it smelled quite a bit like a paper mill. Large chimneys pump out smoke smelling of wet wood. I wonder what the carbon footprint of this place is.

We just ride past this ugly town and head further north. After a long stretch of uninspiring scenery we arrive in Kingston SE. The SE is short for South East. Maybe there is another Kingston further North West, but I figured that is a silly name for a town. I later found out that it was to distinguish it from the other Kingston in South Australia. This other Kingston was later renamed to Kingston-on-Murray. This naming issue does not inspire me to believe these South Australians are very creative people. Why didn't they call it Peterston, or

Flagpoleville. Surely you can come up with something a little better than the same name as the town just down the road and start a feud?

We ride into the town centre and find the Information centre. This would become our standard operating procedure for the rest of the trip. When we arrive in the town we will stay, we would look for the Information centre and find out about accommodation. They usually know where to find the cheapest and best suited for the range of travellers they get. I am sure some of these towns are not really swamped with tourists, but I found them to be very useful and normally staffed with very friendly people.

Kingston S.E. is no different and the lady at the centre is friendly enough and suggests we stay at the Royal Post Hotel. They have nice rooms, which are also pretty cheap, plus they have a pub downstairs which serves pretty decent food. This sounds like our kind of joint and I just want to warm up and get my riding gear dried out. We have a look on the map where the hotel is and after saying our fond farewell we head out to our rides.

We ride to the hotel and walk into the pub where they give us each a room. Prices are reasonable and there are a number of draft taps, so I am confident we will enjoy our brief stay here in Kingston S.E. With our rooms secured we head back to the bikes to unload and carry all the gear up the two sets of stairs and into the rooms. On one of my trips while carrying the bags and panniers up the stairs a young, very drunk guy, with very few teeth and dreadlocks looks at me carrying all my shit up the stairs and slurs,

"Ye don haf ti wurri bout teefs he." I smile and nod. A few hours later when I woke up in the middle of the night I finally got what he was saying. I believe he was trying to communicate. My take on it is that he tried to say:

"You don't have to worry about thieves here." I must admit I do not think he is the best candidate to put out there to pass on that message, as I was thinking I hope he doesn't steal my tent which was still on the bike when he spoke to me. I know it is my issue, not his. I don't always trust people. But I also could not afford for the stuff to be stolen overnight and I am stuck with no gear. It has taken a lot of time and planning to get all this shit together.

Anyway, Darryl decides he is going for a nap and I decide I will go for a hot shower. I feel much better after the shower and now I am inspired to take those beer taps for a test drive. As I walk down the stairs I can see out the window that the rain had stopped. I have to consciously decide not to get grumpy and think pure thoughts. Maybe we are lucky and this is the end of the rain. Little did I know at this stage, but that's for later.

I take this time to quickly jolt down my notes on what has happened over the last two days, with more than one mention of the stupid rain. About an hour later Darryl sits down and I as I am getting slightly tipsy after testing three of their drafts I go up to the lady at the bar and ask if we can get some dinner. The woman frowns at me and say that they only serve dinner in the evenings.

There is a moment where neither of us really knows what to say. The moment stretches into the next moment and I realise I will have to say something quickly before it gets to weird.

"Ok, so from what time is it evening here in Kingston....SE" I quickly add the "SE". I had almost asked her about the time of the evening in another town. I will have to watch myself here. You never know if it is a sensitive issue.

"Enni time fro seeks." She says and when I look at the clock behind the counter I understand why she was frowning at my dinner request. It is 3:48 p.m. It seems she was quite reasonable to feel I was out of place to be asking about dinner.

"Is that clock right?" I ask her.

"Eyup." She replies easily, knowing that she had me in the bag. She does relent and say we are welcome to go to the shop across the street and get some fries there in a mean time and come and eat it here.

I am still a bit baffled at how I could have it so wrong. Then it comes to me. We had crossed the time line and are now another half an hour earlier. I had not yet have my stomach change to Victoria time and now we are in the next time zone already. You see, Australia decided to be a little bit different in how they manage time zones. They have an half hour time difference between Victoria and South Australia. The same applies for when we cross from the Northern Territories to Queensland in a week or so. Why half an hour? Well, they claim it to be standard time, but I have never heard of half hour time zones before.

Darryl goes across the street and gets a bag of fries, which we eat while sucking down a beer and talking about tomorrow's ride. As we will find out in our time here, the only show on the television is Aussie Rules football. I have to admit, it looks like there are no rules what so ever. If that is what the Aussies call rules, we will be ok, as it will be tough to break any rules.

Two minutes to six I get up and go stand at the bar. I feel a bit beaten after my time issue with the bar lady. She asks me what I want, but I ignore her and look at the clock. I stand there and count the last minute down under my breath, but loud enough for her to hear and finally it is 6:00 p.m. I ask her if I can order dinner and she laughs. I had hoped she would find this funny and I seemed to have lucked out. We both order pepperoni pizzas, which is surprisingly good. I wolf it down and then with a full stomach and a slightly tipsy brain I head up to the room and the only reason I know I actually made it to the bed is I woke up in it later at night with a very full bladder.

Day 4
Monday 11 April 2011
From: Kingston SE
To: Port Pirie
Distance travelled: 515 kilometres

I wake up a few times during the night and from time to time I can hear a pretty rough storm raging outside. How is this possible? We specifically came to Australia as we knew the weather is warm and dry here. For crying out loud, most of the country is a dessert! A few days later I would be watching the news in one of the road houses up on Steward Highway and will see the devastating floods that had hit Melbourne just after we had left there. Trains were locked down as the tracks and stations were flooded, cars were washed off roads and scuba gear sales picked up 400%. We had just made it out of Melbourne in time. If we landed one day later we might have been stuck in Melbourne for a few days. We have been hit by the fringe of that storm so I would later understand why all the rain, but laying there in the bed all nice and warm and dry I cannot understand how we manage to get so much rain.

I fall asleep and in my dreams, if I had any, I was not too worried about the rain. A bit later when my alarm goes off I get up and open the curtains. To my utmost relief it is a good looking day out there. There are some clouds I can see, but they do not look too heavy and I can see lots of blue sky as well. Not that blue skies did us any good yesterday, the rain was falling from the blue skies.

Breakfast is included in the room rate, so after packing the bikes we get some breakfast. It is still very early and we are the only people awake. I eat some Weetbix, to make sure I get my roughage in and the plumbing keeps working and I have an orange juice as the coffee is instant coffee. I have already packed my own coffee away and we are keen to get going, so I decide I will get coffee at our first stop. After munching down the cereal we head outside and although cool, it is not raining. Great stuff, I struggle to really convey just how good news this is for me.

The plan is to head on out to Adelaide today where we will get whatever we will need for the Outback as it will be our last city for awhile. From Adelaide it will be small towns only for a week or so. From Adelaide we will carry on further north now to Port Pirie and sleep there tonight. Hopefully the rain is over and we can see more of the surroundings today and not be freezing cold. Also, it will be nice to do some dry riding and actually feel some warmth. I have had enough cold riding to last me a life time. Three quarters of the year is cold riding in Wellington. I have been looking forward to the dry heat of Australia for months now.

It is still early morning and this time of the morning there is no one else on the road. We ride north on the B1 highway and cover the last part of the Princes Highway. I feel a bit cheated with the ride up the Princes highway. It has been one of the pieces of the trip I had been looking forward to some stunning riding with lots of tight corners and exciting riding with stunning scenery to keep me in awe. It turned out to be difficult riding on slow roads with terrible weather not allowing me to see much of the scenery.

Getting to Meningie we now leave the coast and head inland. Lake Alexandrina is stretched out in front of us. According to Aboriginal dreamtime legend the lake is inhabited by a monster known as the Muldjewangk.
The Muldjewangk is a water-creature that inhabited the Murray River, particularly Lake Alexandrina. It was used as a deterrent for Aboriginal children who wished to play near the riverside after dark. Sometimes they are portrayed as evil merfolk (half man half fish), or times as a gargantuan monster. It is also inconsistent whether there are many of the creatures, or a single monster. Large clumps of floating seaweed are said to hide Muldjewangks and are to be avoided. Large footprints have also been seen. Some elders now say the Muldjewangks no longer inhabit the river system.

Knowing that these vicious monsters lurk somewhere upfront worried me a bit less than you might think. It must be the fact that being a biker, the monsters would have no power over us. Bikers are just too cool to be bothered by such things. Well, as long as they stay in the lake that is. Once we avoided the monsters of mythology we turned back towards the coast on the M1 highway, which will take us all the way to Adelaide.

Coming closer to Adelaide the traffic increases and I can see that there will be a city up front. Well, would have if I could see more than a few meters. The rain has increased into a torrential rain and I am soaked right through to the bone. We get to the start of a very long, steep downhill that takes us all the way down into Adelaide. As we ride out from a tunnel and into Adelaide, the rain stops and the heat picks up. Jippee!

We have done a bit of stock taking and have a few errands to run. I need to get a new car charger to USB converter as mine is now completely busted. When I unplugged it and turned it over last night, about four litres of muddy sludge poured out of it. For some reason the electronics inside did not seem to coexist peacefully with the mud. It refused to work, which means my I-pod, GPS and Cell phone are all without power. I also somehow managed to forget to pack my I-pod USB cable and now need to get one to be able to recharge it.
Also, as this is the last city we will go through before going into the Outback, I also want to get some cash and the petrol situation is nagging at me. I have a five litre can for spare fuel but that is not a hell of a lot for the two of us. I want Darryl to also get a can so we can feel confident to take on any of the long stretches in the outback.
Darryl's GPS has stopped working so he needs to get to a Dick Smiths to see if they can help him sort it out. So the road is claiming its toll on our gadgets, but that is to be expected.

Darryl takes the lead as we ride into Adelaide and we are now looking for the right shops. We ride up and down and this way and that way. At first I think it is to get to see Adelaide, but when we pull over Darryl say he is looking for an outdoor or electronics shop and just can't find any. We ride a little further and Darryl pulls over. Across the street is a big sign saying "Market". He reckons we might get what we are looking for there. I look up and down the street and notice that every other sign is in Chinese. He has taken us into Adelaide's Chinatown.

We walk up and down the street and then go into the market. There are some strange shops in there, but nothing strange enough to warrant investigation and nothing normal enough to actually have what we are looking for. We head on out into the street again and while Darryl is looking for an outdoor shop on his I-phone and only finding on-line outdoor shops, I see a cute chick and her mother walking up towards us.

Having had only Darryl to talk to the last few days, I am keen to talk to a cute blond, even if her mother is also there.

While I talk to them Darryl keeps finding on-line shops with the language getting fouler by the second, but no shops that we can actually just go to and get ourselves sorted out.
Just my luck the people I pick to talk to has just moved to Adelaide and they are walking around looking for a shopping mall. At least they have an idea of where to go so they show us on Darryl I-phone map and after thanking them we are off to go look for it.

After a few twists and turns we find the boulevard where all the shops and shopping centres are. Finding parking is a completely different story though. Being used to the smaller towns we have gotten used to parking where ever we want. So Darryl rides right onto the boulevard and we park there between the crowds of people glaring at us.

A young man walking past us warns us that we will get a ticket if we park there, so we decide to play it safe and go look for some other parking spot. At least we know where to go now. We ride back to the main street and I find a parking garage. Great, so we park in the garage and go down to the boulevard. First up, we decide to get to the technical shop. I manage to get the parts I need, but the techie does not seem to be able to help Darryl with his GPS issue. There is just no power coming through.

Next up we walk down the boulevard looking for an outdoor shop. One of the other things I am looking for is a butane canister for the Outback. I want to be able to boil water to make coffee and for that I need a butane canister. Hopefully we will be able to get a petrol can for Darryl at the same time. After what like a few lifetimes of walking around looking for the outdoor shop without success, we ask the people at the Information kiosk where we can find it. The man directs us four blocks down the road, where there are three different options, right next door to each to other. I have never understood why you would open your shop right next to your competition. Why not open it on the other side of town? Surely you would get all the business from that side of town and the competition all the business form the other side. Maybe I am just being way too simple and do not understand how this type of business works.

Be that as it may, we walk the few blocks and finally get to the outdoor shops. We go to the one that looks least like a big branded one, hoping things will be cheaper there, but I am sure that if you are right next door to your competition your prices will be pretty close to being exactly the same.

We find the butane canisters, but they do not have petrol cans. Walking back out we turn back the way we came and across the street is an army depot store. It is one of those dodgy shops where the guy behind the counter tries to look like an old war veteran, but just looks like a dumbass. I suggest Darryl go in there as they might have petrol cans. After about ten minutes he emerges with a ten litre can. Great, now we have fifteen litres of fuel between us, or as Darryl smugly said, he has ten litres and I have five. To which I of course told him to go and be intimate with a goat.

That out of the way we found a coffee shop and Darryl is pretty keen on getting a nice beacon and eggs breakfast. He has had a few strange looks by some of the smaller town folk when he asked for his eggs poached. It seems eggs can be fried or fried in the smaller places. We sit down and when Darryl asks if they do poached eggs for breakfast she says,

"Yes, but it is afternoon and we do not serve breakfasts during lunchtime."

This might sound pretty logical to you, but in New Zealand any cafe that does not serve all-day breakfast will be shut down within weeks. It should make the news headlines for at least three days and the papers for another week.

She says that there is one place about three or four blocks away that might still be serving breakfasts, but she's not sure.
There's not a chance in hell that we are going to walk another three blocks just for eggs. Across the street is a Hungry Jacks, which is the Australian version on Burger King, which is a burger fast food joint, pretty much the same as Mac Donald's. So Hungry Jacks will be lunch, simply because it is closer.

We eat our lunch and again rain pours down outside. I am getting pretty fed up with all this rain right about now. Is that really necessary? Feeling a foul mood approaching due to the combination of the rain and the fact that we are walking around instead of riding, we head back to the bikes. I even give up on the bank and decide to get money later on. Finally we are back at the bikes and will now work our way out of the last city we will see for a while. I simply can't wait to get out into the outback.

I don't think I saw the best of what Adelaide has to offer. By all accounts it is a very beautiful city and there are heaps of nice things to do. To me it was warm, then wet, then warm again, with no parking and no poached egg breakfasts. Mostly I think I am just over keen to get out into the Outback, so even if it was paradise, I would still be keen to get the hell out of there.

Well, getting out of the city onto the A1 highway is not as easy as it sounds. We ride around for a while and when we stop at a traffic light, Darryl squeezes between two cars and asks the driver how we can get to the A1 highway. Sitting behind him in the traffic I can see that his left pannier is missing the car's door by mere millimetres. It looks like the guy is pretty confident with his directions and is telling Darryl we should turn left at this traffic light. Which is great news for me as right next to me on the left hand side is a bus. I inch forward and when the light turns green I shoot in front of the bus. He blows the horn but luckily the bike is quick enough for the bus to not be too much of a bother. We still don't seem to have the way out of the labyrinth which is Adelaide right though as we are lost within a few minutes again.

Finally at a traffic light Darryl grabs his I-phone and manages work out how to get out of here and not too long after that we are back on the road. We head up north to get to Port Wakefield and the road is now starting to look like the roads I had been expecting to see once we get to the Outback. The vegetation is changing to become spares and drier. The rain has also stopped and now it is starting to get warmer quickly. It is now starting to feel more like the Australia I expected. We ride past a town called Baklava. This is the only town in Australia where no Greeks are allowed to purchase property. Ok, not really, but that would be quite funny. No reason to stop here though as it is just another small town, so we ride past. The next town is Port Wakefield. On the side of the round is a huge statue of a crayfish. I remember that when Mike from the Twisting Throttle book came past here he also commented on this. That's pretty cool knowing that we are passing through places I read about a while ago when another adventurer passed through with his motorbike.

We finally get to the turn-off from the main road that will take us out to Port Pirie where we intend to stay the night. I must say, I am a bit used up today, feeling that sore body I had been expecting after a few days on the bike. It is interesting that I thought the worst would be my bum and my lower back, but due to the sitting position of the bike, which is pretty much straight back, my back is not too bad. My butt is quite tender, but something I did not get on my bike back home is my left arm is going pins and needles from the high position of the handle bars.

We ride into town and just cruise straight down the main road until we get to the Central hotel. It looks like the only decent place in town, so we go in and ask about vacancies. The lady behind the counter is friendly and when she hears we are from New Zealand she tells us that she is from Thymes in the Corremandle, which is close to Auckland on the North Island. I wonder how you end up in this little dusty town, coming from such a pretty town like Thymes.

The rooms are pretty expensive, but we take a couple of rooms and unload the bikes. As is our custom, I go for a beer and end up drinking six drafts and Darryl goes for a nap and joins me later on. We sit and chat and then get hungry. I decide after a hard day's riding a man need a steak. I look at the menu and sure enough there is a steak on the menu. So, I order the T-bone steak with a pepper sauce. Darryl decides that sounds pretty good, so orders the same. We keep chatting, but I am so tired I am giving the steak even odds on turning up just in time for my first snore. I just can't keep my eyes open and am basically asleep, just waiting to fall over.

Then the steak turns up and I burst out laughing. On the plate is a steak that pretty much covers the whole plate, covered with a thick, gravy like sauce and a small twig of parsley on top.

Now this is a man's meal. No space wasted on goat food on this plate. It is so funny we take pictures of it and Darryl uploads it to Facebook. I do feel like at least some greens though. I check out the menu and at the bottom it says we are welcome to help ourselves to the buffet of the veggies. I get up and work my way over to the buffet and go fill my side plate with veggies. My wife would be so proud. I even loaded some salad on the plate and end up cleaning the plate. It is amazing how much of an appetite I build up riding all day.

After dinner I wobble to the room and fall over on the bed. I am quite excited about tomorrow, as we will next head up to Post Augusta, where we will finally leave the coast behind and head up north into the Outback. Then all thoughts about riding, eating or anything else are gone and sleep comes easy and quickly.

Day 5
Tuesday 12 April 2011
From: Port Pirie
To: Coober Pedy
Distance travelled: 642 kilometres

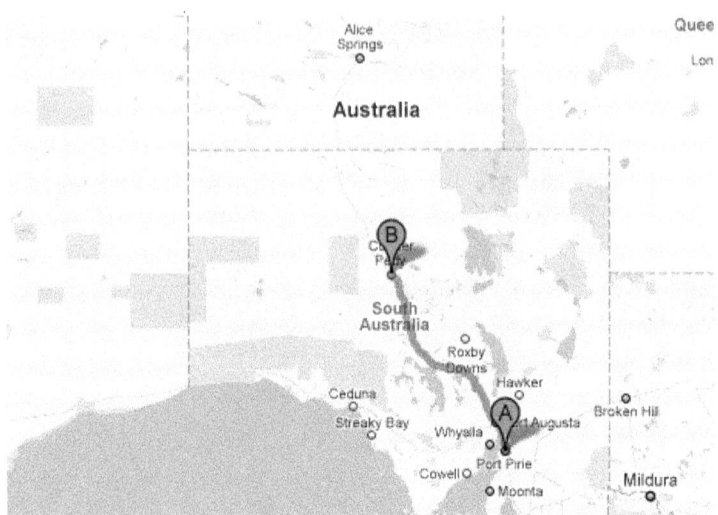

I wake up not feeling as rested as I felt yesterday, but after a big steak like the one I destroyed last night I could not expect the most restful sleep. I always have hectic dreams after lots of red meat, but I cannot remember any dreams. I do remember the fact that we are going into the Outback today. Any tiredness disappears as quickly as mist in the rising sun. Again breakfast is included in the price of the room, so we go to the breakfast room. We are up pretty early and need to feel around the room to find the light switch. Darryl grabs a few tea bags and sugars for the road ahead when we will not have access to these types of luxury and I have a couple of bricks of Weetbix. The way we are wolfing down the food you would not say we each had half a cow last night.

Then we head outside and get back on the bikes. As we ride out of town, the sun crests from behind the mountain range. The scene is stunningly beautiful. I can see some rain clouds around, but none close to us and none in the direction we turn when we get back on the highway. It is still pretty chilly, but it is still very early and I am hopeful that the fact that we will be moving inland will increase the temperature.

We ride into Port Germaine and as typical this time of the morning in these little towns, nothing is open. I am not too bothered that it is still so quite, it is quite magical to have the road all to ourselves so we just keep going further north. I have still quite few kilometres left before I need to get my second cup of coffee. Yes, again I had managed to drink a proper cup of coffee due to my planning and no, I am not yet tired of bringing that up. I am pretty chuffed with this.

We ride on and the flora is unexpectedly very green while the landscape is expectantly flat land on the left, stretching away to the horizon and to the right it is the low laying Flinders Mountain range. Further along, the mountain range becomes the largest range in South Australia, but where we are now, it looks like a long hill. As there is very little traffic and the road in pretty good condition progress is pretty fast and easy. The riding is so quick and easy that in almost no time we arrive at our last stop before we head into the Outback and the last decent sized town until we reach Alice Springs in the Red centre! We ride into Post Augusta and get to the shopping centre. I do not need to explain which shopping centre, there is only one in town. Now that we are about to head into the Outback I want to fill up my water bladders. This will give me six litres of spare water in my water bladders plus the three litres I have in my CamelBak. I have read up enough about the Outback to have a strong conviction that we absolutely must have sufficient water with us. We don't have much in the line of first aid, just one of those cheap first aid kits you get at the pharmacy which has a few things in I don't know how to use. To be honest, the only things in there I will be able to use are the three band-aids. I imagine that if one of us needs first aid, band aids will either have to do or we are in real trouble. At least we will not die thirsty. But to be able to do something for someone who had come off a motorbike, you will need a pretty extensive first aid kit and really good first aid knowledge. I figured that what we will need is water and a way we can call for help. This is the one reason for the extra water. The other reason is that after our trip on the New Zealand South Island where we hit the warm weather, I had decided that the best way to keep cool will be to keep my shirt and hair damp.

I walk inside the shopping centre and to start off buy some coffees for us. I firmly believe that special occasions need to be accompanied by either coffee or beer. It really just depends on the time of the day. Being mid morning and having miles to go for the day it is coffee. I ask the lady behind the counter if she would mind filling up my water bladders from the tap. She fills them both and also Darryl's so now we have plenty of fresh water.
So here we stand next to our bikes, a coffee in the one hand and a cigarette in the other, standing on the brink of the Outback. I am gooseflesh all over. And for a change it has nothing to do about the weather. In fact, it is getting quite warm. The warmest if has been so far on this trip. While we are standing there

I use the opportunity to take out the rain proof layer from my gear. From here of on I hope to not need water proof gear and will need the air vents in my gear to do their job.

After a pee and finishing the smoke and coffee we mount up and start off on the Stuart highway, which will be our home for the next week and a bit. As we pass out of the Port Augusta area the heat starts climbing rapidly. The heat is really welcome and I am now really enjoying myself. I realise something else. My mind is slowing down. No, I am not becoming a vegetable, I am starting to feel the effect of spending hour after hour in my helmet on my own. The meditation that is long distance riding is starting to take effect on my being and the frantic thoughts of how I need to enjoy every second, regardless of the weather or bad conditions is fading away and it is now becoming easier to just relax and let the trip happen as it will.

Then the first road train passes me and I am jerked back into the here and now. Good lord, it is like a wave of water hitting me, trying to jerk me from my bike. I have just met my first road train and just before I make up my mind that these are going to be a problem, the next one comes past and as he passes the driver waves. Wow, I had expected them to pretty rude bastards who attack small animals and scare children before going to bed.

Just to make sure we understand that although these road trains might have drivers that wave at us, to prove that they are not our friends we pass a dead kangaroo and then to make it worse a dead cow. Not only will these trucks drive over us without probably feeling a bump, but the other thing worrying me is the dead animals themselves. Don't get me wrong, I am not too worried about animal zombies attacking us, night of the living dead road kill type of thing, but I am worried hitting these large hunks of rotting meat. Hitting a cow or a kangaroo will not only destroy the bike, but also the rider. So again, even though we have discussed it before, I remind myself that we will not ride before sunrise or after sunset.

As we progress north into the Outback the scenery doesn't really change much. In fact, mile after mile looks almost identical as the previous mile after mile. I am starting to get a grasp of the sheer size of the country. After a few hours of pretty much straight flat road, we finally get to a Roadhouse called Gosses. The name sparks so many romantic and exotic images. Well, whatever you see in your mind when you hear "Gosses Roadhouse" is pretty close to what we got. It is a dusty little building with flies all over the place. The temperature has climbed into the thirties now so when we stop I take off my jacket. I get a cold Coke Zero and pour it down my throat to help cooling me down a bit.

We sit outside on the veranda just enjoying the shade a bit when a car pulls up. Two youngish girls in very skimpy outfits get out and go into the shop. Darryl has a comment or two and when they come out they get into their car and sit and eat some food they had just bought. Now this might not seem odd, but are they sit there for ten minutes with the car switched off, so no aircon or fan and the windows all shut. When we finally get back on the bikes to leave they are still sitting there. It must be stifling hot in there. The place feels pretty dirty to and run down. I hope that this is not the trend and that all the Roadhouses will be so dirty and full of flies. Regardless, what will be will be, I think to myself quite Zen-like as we ride away. We had covered about ten kilometres when Darryl pulls over. He had forgotten his I-phone at the Roadhouse and now needs to race back to hopefully retrieve it.

"Go ahead. I am going to wait here." I yell at him through the helmet. He nods and turns back and races away. I am happy to get this moment to get off the bike and step out into the wild Outback on my own and get to know the lay of the land. Visions of doing documentary style footage of me meeting the Outback and telling the spell bound viewers how the wild man from Africa is getting to know the wild Outback bush.

I pull over to the side of the road and get off. The heat is now stifling so I take off my helmet. Within seconds I am attacked by Australian wildlife. I am fighting to get away from it wondering if I will survive. It isn't the Australian dingo which is also known as the Warrigal around these parts attacking me. Nor is it the King Brown snake, which is the most dangerous snake in Australia. It's not the White-tail spider, one of the most poisonous spiders in the country and it isn't the Brown Goshawk.
No, it is none of these creatures attacking me. However, what is attack me is just as unexpected and not any less requiring immediate evasion actions. I am being attacked by blowflies. Hundreds and thousands of them.

Now I know you are thinking, "O, come on. What's so bad about flies?" and "Hundreds and thousands, Deon you are exaggerating again."

I tell you what. There is no way I can make you understand just how many flies there are on me right now. They are climbing into my nose, into my ears, into my hair and all over my face. They are even trying to climb into my eyes. I later heard that these flies truly do try to climb into the corners of your eyes as they are after the moisture. I try to scream and swallow a couple of them for my effort and quickly close my mouth again. Soft juice dips onto my tongue as I had just snapped a fly in two closing my mouth. I spit the wiggling, dying fly's front half out to join the other half of its body in the dust and go on the offence trying to swat them away. This is not working too well and does little to chase them away, but rather just encourage them to try harder to eat me.

Images of the 1980's film "The Fly" is the final straw. I swat away as many of the flies as I can then put my helmet back on. I open the face to spit out the other fly that is still in my mouth and quickly close the face again. Now there are three inside the helmet buzzing around and one finds its way into my nose surprisingly quickly. I open the face again and try to get the fly out of my nose. This was the break the others who were left outside is waiting for and now there are at least twenty flies on my face again. By now the irritation is turning into mild panic. I manage to get the fly out of my nose by doing a pretty gross nose blow into the road and shake my head around wildly to get the flies out of the helmet. Snot hangs from the front of my helmet and I cannot imagine being any grosser. This in combination with the three or four times I smack myself in the face manages to buy me a few seconds though. In this single moment I manage to slap the face of the helmet closed. I stand dead still for a moment just making sure there are no flies in my helmet.

Nothing...

Oh, the relief. Then I look down and my jacket, my gloves, the bike, everything is covered with flies. I can feel them crawling around on my neck. If I had to guess I would have say that on me and the bike there were at least a thousand flies. I know it is tough to believe, but I am honestly freaking out at this stage as I have never experienced anything like this.

I decide that I will just get going and ride slowly until Darryl catches up. At least the flies will not be able to get to me while I am riding. This is the theory anyway.

I climb on the bike and try to pull it upright. Now to understand my predicament, you need to understand how bikes work. On the left hand side of the motorbike is the side kickstand. One end is attached to the bike's body in such a way as to allow it to swivel. In the "up" position the other end is flicked back and is neatly folded out of the way. When you stop, all you have to do is push it down and it will swivel down clockwise. Then you let the bike tilt sideways until the weight of the bike is all on the kickstand. Normally this is about a fifteen degree angle at the most. This allows the bike to stand securely.

However, on this fateful day, in this remote place with no one around I had managed to pull over to the side of the road and when I rested the bike over onto the kickstand, it came to rest of the gravel on the side of the road, while the tyres are still on the tar. The gravel is about three centimetres lower than the tar road so this means that the angle the bike is standing at is now quite a bit more than the acceptable fifteen degrees.

Now again for the relevance of this small fact to mean something to you non-bikers, you have to understand two additional relevant concepts. The first is the height of the bike. The BMW GS1200 is a pretty high bike. So basically this means the distance between the seat and the ground is quite a high to allow off road riding. I can reach the ground on both side of the bike at the same time, but only just with my toes. The second thing is the weight of the bike fully loaded. The BMW's are known to be very heavy bikes and with all the gear I have loaded on it, it is now not pretty heavy, but rather bloody heavy.

So to bring all of this together to my predicament next to Stuart highway, I cannot get the bike up. I push as hard as I can but I just cannot get it up. I switch to jerking the bike but that makes absolutely no difference. In this time the flies have not missed the opportunity. I am now just about pitch black, covered with a blanket of flies. They have wormed their way into my helmet through the small spaces in my neck and are now again going after my nose and eyes. I try to give a feeble scream, but this just allows me to add another fly to the one slowly being digested in my stomach.
Of course the fact that I am sweating like a pig at this stage is sending up a flare for all the flies in the area to find their way to me.

The mild panic of earlier is now turning into blind panic. I decide to get off the bike and try pushing the bike upright while standing next to it and then try to climb on. Now this might sound a tad simpler than it is in real life. The weight and height comes right back into it.

To push the bike up, I have to stand on the lower gravel. I will not be able to pull it up from the other side. I push the bike upright and as I lift my leg to try get on, the bike starts tilting to the other side and I have to grab and pull it up again. The fact that I am also now standing on the gravel makes the getting onto the bike a lot tougher as I already have to really stretch to get on in normal conditions and now I have to get my leg up even higher.

So, here is the planned process to get back on the bike:

Step 1 – push bike upright until balanced
Step 2 – lift right leg to the height of the seat
Step 3 – give one small jump closer to the bike
Step 4 – climb onto seat
Step 5 – ride away and leave the flies behind

The problem is that the process seems to be more something like this:

Step 1 – push the bike upright
Step 2 – pull bike back as it is falling over to the other side
Step 3 – push the bike upright again
Step 4 – put the bike back and open helmet and spit out fly
Step 5 - push bike upright again
Step 6 – lift right leg
Step 6 – Realise I am only raising leg knee high and try higher
Step 7 – Catch bike as it over balances and go back to step 1

Look, this carried on for a good five minutes and I wouldn't want to bore you any further. Eventually I get steps 1 to 4 done and give a scream of laughter. I sit forward to start the bike and then see that I had left the key in the top box. That is like leaving the key in the keyhole of the boot of your car. I now know how the Jews must have felt when they realised Hitler was going to try wipe them out. I am in a black moment where I almost give up and let the flies take me away.

Luckily I manage to work out a plan while chewing the two flies that has come to replace the two that has come before. I let the bike roll back a bit so that the wheels are also on the gravel and the angle now back to the norm. I get off and get the key and I will not repeat what I was saying at this stage. I think I might have overdone the swearing a bit, but the moment was too much. I lock the top box and get back on the bike. The angle is much better now and I manage to get back on the bike and get it up pretty easily. I start the bike and get going.

Eventually Darryl catches up and I speed up. Now I am wondering what the chances are of us camping at all? I had these visions of camping somewhere in the Outback just down some dirt road between nowhere and nowhere. However, I cannot imagine even stopping for five minutes again, never mind camping. Reality can be a bitch.

Eventually my mind comes to the kangaroos or 'roos as they are known in Australia. We have been told that there are thousands or kangaroos in Australia and that this will be one of the highest risks we will face on this trip. I can most certainly agree that if I was to hit a 'roo at hundred and twenty kilometres per hour my loved ones will have a very small chance of burying only one piece of me. I will be spread out over a decent section of Stuart highway.

The point here is that to have these animals as risks requires there to actually be 'roos. I have seen and smelled quite a number of road kills, but not seen any sign of a living 'roo. Every time I mention this to someone when we stop, they assure me that I need to watch out on the next stretch as there will be hundreds of them all over the road. I had expected to have to fight them off, but so far not a single live 'roo.

I am beginning to believe that live 'roos are just a myth. I wonder if perhaps there were many 'roos at some stage, but they might just have been eaten alive by all the bloody flies!
This turns out to be a day of discovery. Firstly I discovered the flies own the Outback. The next thing I discovered is that the Outback is the test grounds for road signs. As we ride through the middle of nowhere, and trust me this is the middle of nowhere, a road sign claims:

"Mini Market 300m on left"

I have pretty decent eyesight. My eyes are very sensitive to bright light and if someone else's eyes are hurting, mine will start tearing in sympathy. I claim not that I have strong eyes, only that my eyes can see further than 300 meters and certainly in this flat landscape, I can safely claim that I will be able to spot a market a few hundred meters away. I tell you what, there was not a single thing 300 meters on the left. Not a turn-off, not a fence next to the road, not a rest area, not even trees. Nothing.

These discoveries will in the next few weeks turn into pretty complex conspiracy theories. Firstly that there actually are no kangaroos. My first theory is that they have these two hundred odd kangaroos bred in captivity and when they die they are brought out to the Outback and dropped next to the road as "road kill". Then in the night, they have these other "myth of the 'roo" teams that drive around the Outback and move these carcasses around.

The second theory forming around the 'roos is that perhaps the carcasses we can see and smell next to the road are actually sheep, which they have their 'roo suites they dress them in and leave next to the road.

"What, you haven't seen live 'roos? Well have you seen the dead ones next to the road? Yes? Well then there must be lives ones somewhere."

Now you see what I mean!

The other theory is about the road signs. I believe they test road signs in the Outback. Before a sign is approved by the Road sign Acceptance commission for release for public use they first test them in the Outback. Here they can be safely exposed to the few old-timers, truck drivers and really cool bikers without risking the sanity of the general population. If they are well received, then they get the nod for being available for use in small towns. Then finally if approved they will have it released to the cities. Next time you see a sign for the zoo or the hospital, remember that it was initially tested here in the Never-never for months.

The employees of the road works department, especially the civil engineers who planned the Stuart highway did a very good job, as it is in very good condition considering the large number of road trains. However, they are not the most creative people. The road is now this long, straight line stretching out in front of me as far as I can see. The road disappears in the distance in the heat waves. I lazily sit back against my tent, which is strapped onto the back seat of my bike, giving me a nice back rest. I let go of my left hand and now sit back quite relaxed. Moby is humming away in my helmet and I am starting to feel the roadie feeling. Knowing there is still weeks of riding ahead and many, many miles of road to cover so nothing to worry about I feel my mind going into a kind of Zen moment.

I am rudely jerked back to reality by a ghost wind. There is nothing to my left or right except flat planes, no vehicles anywhere in sight in front of behind me except for Darryl and he is a couple hundred metres ahead of me so he could not have anything to do with this. It feels like a road train that had passed, but there was nothing. I sit forward again and hold on properly. With the adrenaline still pumping through my veins I can see a tower ahead. That must mean that there is a town ahead somewhere.

After another ten minutes we get to Coober Pedy. This is our stopping point for the day. It has been a good day's riding and I am already crazy about the Outback. The flies are a problem, but there is nothing to do about them. I am sure we will figure something out. We pull over at the information centre. As I get off I see my first aboriginal. She shuffles across the road looking by all account, horrible. Her clothes are torn, dusty and old. Her hair is dirty and tangled and I can smell her from ten meters away. I can assure you she did not smell peachy. Then she screams at her friend, or maybe her enemy, I am not enlightened enough to know her feelings towards the other and certainly cannot understand what she is screaming, but it reminds me of the coloured people of the western cape on a Friday night. Loud, drunk and better left to themselves.

I light a cigarette and watch as the Coober Pedy "Days of our lives" plays out between the woman who had just arrived whom I named "Thlunku" who had last night had an affair with the boyfriend of the larger, less sophisticated "Bumbam" who has just crawled out from under the bush next to the road. Thlunku shuffled up to Bumbam and screamed into her face and then Bumbam opens her mouth as far as she can and for a moment I think she is going to try biting Thlunku, but then starts cackling.

Then Dingo, the man who had been mislead by Thlunku sits up from his slumping position against the wall and also say something. Both women look at him and start screaming at him. Luckily my cigarette is now finished so I don't need to see where this sorry story goes. We go into the Information centre where the aircon not only helps cool me down, but also the absence of flies is refreshing. The lady at the information centre is friendly enough and gives us a few options for accommodation. The Opal Oasis is cheap and has a swimming pool, which I am now looking forward to. It is also just down the road, so it seems to fit our requirements. After the expensive rooms in Port Pirie I am keen to sleep in a bit cheaper places otherwise my budget will not make it.

With that we head back outside where the drama had fizzled out as Dingo had passed out and Thlunku and Bumbam had settled down in the dust under the tree, staring out into the distance. Well, what did you expect? You want better drama, go to Hollywood.

We ride down the main street and after a few blocks and get to the Opal Oasis. Here I get to see my first of what is the standard "Budget accommodation" in the Outback. Pretty smart idea, I have to admit and actually I quite like it. What they have done was to buy a bunch of shipping containers and divide it into five rooms. So, they have put divider walls into it, cut doors into the one side and slapped in an air conditioner unit into the other side. Then put a bed in there and there you go, you have a room to be rented out at $65 a night. We unpack our bikes and then go to the swimming pool. The pool is inside a round room. It is pretty dark inside and the pool is about five meters in diameter. I jumped in without another thought, just trying to get away from the flies and to be able to cool down a bit. As I hit the water I realize why it is in this room. Outside in the sun the water in the pool will evaporate within a few hours leaving you with a sad, dry hole. There is absolutely no moisture in the air here. In this room however, the water is not heated up at all and any evaporation that does take place just drips back into the pool from the roof. The water must be about 5 degrees Celsius. I try to catch my breath as I came back up, but it is just not possible. I use the momentum to get to the other side of the pool, but hyperthermia is setting in. I am within reach of the other side of the pool when I feel frostbite taking my left foot's big toe and I am now wondering if I am going to make it. Wouldn't be ironic to drown in ice water in this dry, hot place?

I finally get to the other side and with numb hands push myself up. I manage to get up into a standing position shivering and just stand there for a moment to make sure I did not lose any limbs. Darryl walks in and asks,

"How's the water?"

I use every bit of will power I have to keep my voice under control. "Yeah, pretty nice. Good to cool you down a bit." Clearly I want him to jump in as well so I can at least have a laugh at myself as well.

Darryl is not stupid and know me way to well to just trust me and first feel the water. "Fark. That's freezing!"

Dammit. Shows you that with age comes wisdom! He does get in however and then out as quick as I had. Not the most enjoyable swim I have had in my life, but I do feel cooled down and refreshed. Now it is time to go get a beer. I go and put my towel back in the room and grab my wallet and sunglasses. We walk out back towards the centre of town where we are sure to find a watering hole. On the next corner there is a shop called the "Underground cafe and Didgeridoo shop". They have the VB sign out front, which means we will find a beer there. Hopefully food as well, but I can go for a while before eating, but need a cold drink some time soon.

I slide open the door and walk in. It looks pretty deserted and the ten didgeridoos standing around looks old and dusty. We walk up to the counter and then a short, stocky man walks in from the back room.

"What you want?" he asks in a strong Eastern European accent.

"You open? We are looking for a cold beer." I reply.

"No, we closed. You can go to Opal bar. You not go to Pedy Pub. They too expensive. They ask too much for beer." He gives us advice as he sheppards us out of the shop and when we are outside the door he slides it close and flips to "Open" sign around to now show "Closed", waves at us while nodding and then turns around and walks back into the dark room.

We walk away processing what just happened.

"Well, I guess if I was a Czechoslovakian war criminal this is where I would come to hide. You can be sure that you wouldn't be found here in a million years. Shit, but what a place to end up in!" I joke.

We walk on to the Opal bar, which is just a couple of blocks further. When we get there we order a beer and sit down. I feel a pretty strong headache starting up. Then a man walks in and I kid you not, I cannot remember ever smelling a person that stinks that much. I come from the Eastern Cape of South Africa where the people can smell pretty bad, so trust me when I say that my eyes watered from the smell of this man. He looked almost as bad as he smelled. Luckily he finds a seat closer to the pub, but the smell now fills the room. We are now keen to drink up and get out of there.

Then the cops walk in with their dogs. They stop anyone from leaving and let the dogs sniff everyone. I feel sorry for the dog having to have to go and smell that man in the corner, but so we all have our problems. The dog gets quite excited when it gets to a man sitting quietly at the table next to us. The policeman taps him on the shoulder and they walk to one side of the pub. He empties his pockets and them the cuffs are slapped on him.

Darryl has a chat to the barman when he gets the next round of beers and apparently they do this two or three times a year. The cops drive up from Adelaide and cover all the small towns in the area. They will also be checking the motel rooms and restaurants. Luckily I left my two pounds of cocaine back home!

My headache gets worse and worse and I am keen to head back to the rooms. I need to get some legal drugs into my system and I have some headache bombs in my bag. We then head back to the cabins and I swallow a couple of the pills. I take the time to catch up with my writing to make sure I remember all these precious memories. Darryl takes a nap and then later on we head back out to get some dinner. On the way back from the pub we had seen a pizza place that looked well, dodgy, but at least open. I must say, I am not thinking about Coober Pedy as one of top five places to live next. In fact, it is a dump. The flies are mind boggling. Surely there can't be that many flies?

When we walk out to the pizza place the flies seems to have gone to bed. However, all that has done is made space for the mosquitoes. We make our way to the pizza place and order a couple of pizzas and beer from the brother of the Czechoslovakian warlord we met earlier. His daughter (I will just believe it was his daughter) came out and I wonder how a beautiful woman like that could end up and be happy in a dump like this. But that is not really fair. Why should ugly people be happy in a shitty place and beautiful people not. Just brain washed to think that way I guess. I think I will blame all those romantic comedies my wife keeps renting.

While we sit and wait for the food sucking down a couple of beers, a man stumbles in. He is a pretty big fella and not someone I would want to get too close to due to the smell. What is it with these small town people and bad smells? Anyway, he walks over to one of the machines where you put money in and then you have a few seconds to position the little claw and when your time is up, it drops down and if you had placed it correctly it will pick up a soft toy and drop it in the tray. This big tough man is really taking it seriously. He would put the money in, then be twisting and turning, up on his toes and trying to look from all angles as he position it in the few seconds and then as it drops, then he goes down on his knees, pushing his nose against the glass urging it on. These machines are designed to not hand out the four ugly soft toys easily. As the claw comes up empty, he would get up and moan, walk around muttering and complaining. Then he would stand to the one side and then to the other side strategising how the next round should go. A few minutes of this and then he will try again with pretty much the same result.

I am thoroughly enjoying the show but then something else catches my attention. We had not really watched any TV up to now and when the news comes up it is covering the main story of the large storm that has been hitting Victoria over the last few days. This is when I work out that we had missed the storms by half a day and that is why we had gotten so much rain over the last few days along South Australia. Trains are stranded, not able to leave the stations as the tracks are flooded, cars are under water up to the roof and houses are flooded. That is far behind us though as we have had good hot weather today and the weatherman promises more hot days ahead for where we are heading. In fact, from here of on it is going to be mid thirties every day. Great, I am looking forward to the hotter weather.

Then the pizzas arrive and even though it wasn't the best pizzas, I am so hungry I quickly wolf down the pizza, not leaving a crumb. When we both had finished we go back to the container that is our home for tonight. Darryl says he is going to look for 'roos tomorrow morning at sunrise. I will rather sleep the extra twenty minutes. Anyway, so we sit and smoke a last cigarette and then go to bed.

Day 6
Wednesday 13 April 2011
From: Cooper Pedy
To: Kulgera
Distance travelled: 420 kilometres

Darryl did get up early, just before sunset to go look for roo's but I could have told him it is not going to happen. There are no 'roos. Or actually that's not quite true. My theory on the myth of the roos has matured into a more detailed vision.
According to my observations, there were actually two types of roo's. The Grey-ninja roo, which you know is there but will never see and the Brown Japanese Kamikaze roo, which is the ones you would find as road kill in the mornings on the road.
The ninja 'roos are known to exist due to the evidence left behind by them such as dropping, footprint and ninja stars, but has never been seen by human eyes. The slightly larger and less intelligent Brown Japanese Kamikaze 'roo can be seen lying next to the road in the mornings. At night they sit behind trees, small bushes and tall grass right next to the road waiting for the perfect opportunity to reveal themselves. As I have mentioned, they are the less intelligent of the two types of roo's and what had happened was that those sneaky ninja 'roos told the kamikaze 'roos that if they jump in front of those bright lights and shout "potato!" they will get laid more often. Those ninjas are not nice guys.

When I finally get up, Darryl is back and had not managed to capture pics of neither the ninja nor the kamikaze roos. We load up the bikes and then head back to Stuart highway through the town centre. We pull over at the gas station to fill up. Inside I see they have more of the five litre petrol cans and I decide that I will buy an extra can. This will give me a total of ten litres of spare fuel, which will not only help us out if we run out of fuel, but will now become an extension of our range. This is an extra half a tank of fuel, so this also opens up possibilities of alternative routes we could not consider before.

I walk up to the counter.

"G'day" the hill-billy says.

"O, good day. Listen mate, can I go and fill this can up and then you just charge it all together?" I ask referring to the fact that I have already filled up the bike and now want to take the new petrol can out to be filled up as well.

"Yeee. You go right ah head." He mutters.

I take that as ok, so head outside and fill up the can. Once filled I go back inside and on the television behind him the news is showing the floods in Melbourne.

One of the things I am keen on doing on this trip is to strike up conversations with people. I love the funny characters and just getting a glimpse of what people are up to in these strange places.

"Pretty bad those floods down in Melbourne, hey?" I try to get the man to talk.

"O ye mate. I tell ya what. I warned those people about this. But they didn't listen. They are messing with pretty powerful stuff there. A bunch of them went down there to do some powerful rain dances. Now look what happened. I warned them not to mess with such powerful dances." He growls and now gave me a look, waiting for me to respond.

"Well, I guess you will have to head down there and do some drought dances then to help them out." This was the best I could come up with.

"Naw mate. That is not even funny. Then there will be droughts for years to come." He says and this brings the conversation to a point where I figured we do not have much more to say to each other. Better to leave this where it is.

I go outside and while Darryl smokes a cigarette I call home. Elizna is going to go to the doctor for the results of the blood tests and scans of our baby today. We have had two tries before and had never gotten good news from this stage in the pregnancies. I feel the acid in my stomach boil up. I am so sorry to have left Elizna to face that meeting with the doctor on her own. If it is bad news it will be devastating to be so far from her with almost no way of getting back to her. She promises to call me the moment she knows anything and I promise to call her the moment I get anywhere I have reception.

I see that my phone's battery is almost flat so I plug the charger in and when I push the charger into the phone the small little Nokia connector snaps off. Shit. It is now stuck inside the phone. O, come on! Is this really necessary? I fiddle with the loose wires and manage the get the wires pushed into the hole and the phone charging. I will worry about getting this sorted out later.

We saddle up and leave this dodgy little town behind us. I must say, I hope opal is really worth it, because otherwise there is no reason to keep this town on the map. What a dump. I also notice at this stage that my sense of humour is gone and I am strained. I can feel my muscles in my shoulders bunch up and I am struggling with the bike. Just as well it is a long straight road today.

Speaking of today, we are not planning a very long day on the bikes today. We will sleep on the last piece of Stuart highway before we get to the turn-off towards Uluru. Again, I am pretty happy with that arrangement as I am not feeling great. My whole future will be decided today and I am not there to face it.

As we ride out of town it looks like there must be thousands of giant moles on steroids lose in these plains. Thousands and thousands of piles of earth litters the plain. Opal must be pretty valuable stuff. They pretty much rip a piece of earth out and then see if there is any opal in the sides of the shaft they had drilled. It there is nothing, they move on to the next area and go through this process again.

The distances between towns now increase dramatically. The next town we will see will be in a few days time when we get to Alice Springs. There will be only road houses in between and I am not too sure of what exactly we can expect from Uluru.

The road is really exactly as you would expect if you think of the Australian Outback. Long, flat and straight. Every ten or twenty kilometres there is a slight rise or a soft turn in the road and that is the only times that the road does not disappear in the distance in a pinpoint. It is still pretty early so I think we have missed the rush hour.... Bad joke. There is no traffic here, so the only rush hours would be the mythical 'roos running away from the road so we can miss them.

Then, just to improve my mood, it starts to rain. A cloud is right above us in the dry, dessert and pissing down on me. I start screaming obscenities at the cloud for raining on me. I am pretty happy that no one could hear me as I am losing it completely in my helmet. Spit hits my visor and I am seeing red. Luckily the rain eases off quite quickly and then I feel bad about my anger outburst. I apologise to the cloud and the horse it rode into town on and all the other relations of the cloud I swore at a moment earlier. It is the call later today that is freaking me out. I feel really deflated and unhappy as I sit there on the bike cutting across the barren landscape.

As we go over a small hill I can see three motorbikes coming from the front. The guy leading the group is so excited to see us. He stands up on his pegs with both hands high above his head. I can almost hear his screaming in excitement. It is so cool to pass these legends of the road, three guys taking on the long road on their bikes. Man I wish I could do something like that.....
I respond by also standing up and I recon we both had a moment when we considered trying a high-5 as we passed each other, but luckily logic prevailed. We passed and then the two of us headed north and the three of them kept on their way south. For a moment I felt like Dr Livingston must have felt running into Henry Morton Stanley.

We pulled off at a petrol station, and I am keen to get petrol for the bike, a cool drink, smoke a cigarette and try call home. When we pull into the petrol station there are two other bikes there as well. One is a Harley and the other a tourer. The guy on the Harley gets on his bike and in typical Harley rider fashion believes he is too good to talk to us BMW riders. Well, he can go fuck himself. He rides away and then while I am fuelling up, the other rider comes out from the shop. He greets us, but doesn't seem interested to chat. I ask him where he is headed. He says he is heading the up north to Darwin and then while we then head out east, he will be heading out west. Cool. He says goodbye, mounts up and rides off. O, well. Not the same connection than with the lads on the road. I try to call home, but there is no reception out here. I try to find a pay phone, but the place does not have one.

After the rest stop we get back onto Stuart highway and luckily Darryl takes the lead. I am really messed up right now and not enjoying the ride at all. I am seriously desperate to get hold of Elizna to find out what is going on. There is just no way for me to get to her right now. We push on up to Marla, yet another Road house.

First thing I do when off form the bike is to check for reception. Fuck, nothing. But there is a payphone. The payphone does not take coins, only calling cards, so I go to the shop and ask if they have calling cards. Sure, they have $5 calling cards. O, the joy. I buy one and then get back to the payphone. I try calling, but just cannot get through. I go back to the shop and ask if the card can call to New Zealand.

"Ye, I think so." The fat chick behind the counter mutters.

"Well, I cannot get through. Are you sure it can call internationally?" I ask again.

She rolls her eyes and takes the card from me. My blood is one degree under boiling point. I can feel the acid in my stomach bubbling. If she rolls her eyes again, I am going to rip them out of her skull and shove them up her nose.

"Oh, no. It can't" she says after studying the card for a minute. "Sorry, I thought it could be used to call internationally."

The anger boils up again and it takes all self control I have left to just stand still and not rip her fat ears off her fat skull and shoving it up her fat ass. Luckily the moment passes without incident and I now feel sorry about it, she did nothing wrong and does not really have fat ears.

"Ok, can you just throw this in the rubbish for me then? It is a nice waste of fife bucks. Thanks a lot." I say, keeping my voice under as much control as I can. It seems I didn't do too good a job though as she finally actually looks and me and is now frowning.

I turn away and walk out to get some fresh air. Darryl is fidgeting with his GPS and I spot that they have an Internet station in the restaurant. We eat some lunch and then while Darryl keeps working on his GPS, I go and send a mail to Elizna, hoping that she will be on-line. She should be at work right now, so she should get the mail immediately. I send the mail asking if everything is ok and what the news is. I wait and wait and after 10 minutes I have to accept that she is not at her PC right now. Where would she be? Is she in a meeting or just out for some coffee, or did she go home because the news was bad?

I use the remaining five minutes to quickly transfer money into my credit card account and then we head out again. We point the bikes north and continue on our trek up through the Outback. It is nice to be moving as the moment you stop the flies are all over you. They do not let up for a moment.

Strong cross winds are now pushing from the left and is making riding harder. It is particularly hard on my neck, as it keeps pushing my head off to the right and I have to keep pushing my head to the left into the wind. That make my neck feel strained and the stress is just adding to the pain. After an hour and a bits' riding we pull over a rest stop next to the road. This isn't one of the Road houses, just a rest stop where you can pull over and go stand in the cloud of flies. The temperature has risen to 35 degrees. The heat is stifling. Darryl decides it is time for the jacket to come off and I have to admit, I am also keen. I do not easily ride without the full gear, but this is ridiculous. Riding out of the rest stop, without the jacket and the gloves on, swerving as I am trying to swat the flies from me, I stop to pick Darryl's glove up which had fallen from his bike as he rode out towards the highway. Then I am back on the highway. It is quite a bit better without the jacket for the first while, but soon it is pretty much just as hot, plus now the sun is burning my skin as well.

There are quite a few dead kamikaze roos laying next to the road on this stretch. The stench of decay cloys to the back of my throat as we pass all the dead, rotting meat Again I feel glad we are happy not to ride after dark. These things are huge and will be a serious accident if I should hit it.

Chapter 11 – Really far Outback in the Northern Territories

I usually have something good to say about the state before going on to tell you the rest of the story, so let me go ahead and keep that tradition going, as it seems to be working so well.

The Northern territories is by far the least populated state in Australia. The biggest city, or to be honest, the only city in the Northern Territories is Darwin, which has a population of about hundred and thirty thousand people. The population of the whole of the Northern Territories is about two hundred and twelve thousand people. This means more than sixty percent of the population of the state lives in Darwin. Here is something to think about, while we are on the subject of the population. The Northern Territories is six times the size of Great Britain and two and a half times the size of Texas, USA. It is 1.35 million square kilometres. That is mind boggling and gets me to recheck the fuel and water levels before riding on. This is one of the few places in the world where you can get lost for a long time.

As a state it has been through some rough administrative times. It was originally under the administration of New South Wales and then briefly in 1846 it was part of the short lived colony, North Australia. It then became part of South Australia until 1911 when the Northern territories separated from South Australia. The locals were not too impressed with their state's name and considered changing it to "Kingsland", "Centralia" or "Territoria". In the end though it stayed the Northern Territories.

There was a brief period in the 1930s when they had the Northern Territories split into North Australia and Central Australia.

A bit left field, but as part of the Kimberly Plan, the northern Territories were identified as a possible site for the establishment of the "Unpromised Land", the Jewish Homeland. This was a failed plan by a man called Isaac Steinberg who was trying to create a place for Jews to flee to during the holocaust. Unfortunately that did not work out, but he did get a lot of support from the general population of Australia.

I found this little gem for your entertainment. Not too long ago, an Australian judge who demanded to know the name of the "idiot" who granted bail to a serial burglar discovered he was talking about himself.

Justice Dean Mildren conceded privately he was the judge who bailed Tristan Ellis after apparently forgetting. Ellis, 18, was granted bail by Justice Mildren after breaching a curfew imposed by the judge in April. He was ordered to attend a drug rehabilitation programme in Darwin. Ellis was facing 28 breaking-and-entering charges, says the Northern Territory News. Later on Judge Mildren said he was "absolutely staggered" that Ellis had been given bail three times last year after being arrested for breaking and entering. "Who is the idiot who did that?" Talk about putting your foot in your mouth!

Here is one final funny story playing off in the Northern Territories. A drunk driver tried to avoid arrest by leaping into the back of his moving car during a chase in the Australian Outback. Police in the Northern Territory town of Katherine were stunned when they realised the 24-year-old driver had abandoned the controls and jumped on to the back seat with his three passengers in an apparent attempt to fool officers. The runaway car continued for hundred and fifty metres at twenty five kilometres an hour before a policeman on foot ran it down and applied the brakes. Police said the driver panicked when they tried to pull him over for a random breath test. Hahahaha.

After yet another hard ride we arrive at Kulgera roadhouse. As I stop I pull out the cell phone and yet again I am met with a "no-signal" sign. I feel tears boil up.

"If only I had a phone that could get connection out here...." The thought, as it forms draws me back to when we were busy packing the bikes when we got them in Melbourne and the sat-phone was delivered.

"The sat-phone. Fuck me!" I go over to Darryl and ask for the sat-phone that is in his top box.

"Why don't you just use the payphone over there? It will be much cheaper." He says.

"It works with call cards and I can't call internationally with the call cards." I reply almost ripping his panniers open to look for the phone myself.

"You can use your credit card though. Come I'll show you." Finally I get the connection and then dial Elizna's mobile number. It rings a couple of times and then a rude man answers the phone asking who I want to talk to. Fuck, wrong number.

Again I dial and this time Elizna answers. The line is pretty bad, but I get the message. Everything is ok. The results came back good so we do not need to worry. Relief floods through me and the moment is so big I almost start crying. We chat a moment longer but I am not able to say too much. Darryl congratulates me and again I am so glad to have such a good friend with me on this trip.

I am totally bushed. The stress has used up all the energy I had. We decide that we will just sleep here tonight. We book some rooms and then unload the bikes yet again. Once unloaded I head straight to the pool. Darryl is already there and as I jump in I am caught with my heart in my mouth. Dammit, I need to feel the temperature before jumping into the pools. When I get out I do feel quite refreshed. Darryl says he is going to take a nap and I decide I can now do with a drink. This had been a tough day and I need some alcohol in my system.

"Can I get a XXXX Gold please (pronounced "Four X gold")." I ask for a beer.

The woman behind the counter, "Ye want a tinny or a skin."

I am pretty sure I asked for a beer and I am pretty sure she must have heard me, so I guess it has something to do with the beer.

"A pint?" I say, tentatively.

"A skin. Yeah, no worries. Four dollars fifty." She fills a pint class with a skin of beer.

I sit down at one of the tables and catch up with my writing. I then sit back and look around the pub. It is pretty cool, with a lot of dead little creatures in glass bottles. I swear the things in those glass bottles are the inspiration for movies like "Aliens", "Predator" and the likes. And these things are cruising around outside.
When my beer is done the woman who had served me the beer is not there, but a man is standing there. I spot the opportunity to fit right in and use the local lingo.

"G'day mate. Give me a skin of XXXX Gold." I ask and knowingly nod my head. I luckily stopped before the knowing wink.

"A what?" he asks in a strong English accent. O, come on! Really?

"A pint please." I ask and he then gives me the beer.

We are now in the Deep Outback and I have been waiting to see what type of characters we will meet out here. Sitting in probably the only watering hole in many miles the people coming in looks to be mostly farmers and pretty rough. Not rough as in rude or looks like they want to fight, just rough like in rough edges. These are people who work out in the sun, heat and flies. They speak a version of English I cannot really follow, but they do laugh quite a bit, so I am enjoying sitting there and taking it all in.

A man walks in and sorry if you were never a Looney Tunes fan when you were a kid, as you would not know who I am referring to. It is worth going on line and searching for him. The man that walked in, except that he was grey instead of red, looked exactly like Yosemite Sam. He must be around fifty, but being one of the roughies, he could also have been thirty. He was gruff and when I stood next to him to order a beer and greeted him, he just looked me up and down and turned back to his beer. So basically not mister friendly.

When Darryl rocks up, we go and play a few games of pool. He wins the first and I do the second and then hunger becomes more important than games. We go back to the bar and study the extensive menu. There is a choice of three types of steaks, chicken schnitzel, beef schnitzel or a meat combo. There was fish on the menu, but it has been scratched out. I take it there are not a lot of fresh fish in these parts considering there is no water out here.

I order a rump stake and Darryl orders the heart stopper meat combo. This is a plate with a piece of each of the three types of steak, a lamb chop, sausages, beacon and an egg. I can see his heart trying to escape from his chest. The food comes quickly as we were the first to order and it really good. I did get a salad with the steak, which is actually quite nice. After dinner I am so tired I am wondering if I am going to make it to the room. The walk seems to last forever, but eventually I am back in my room.

I fall over on the bed and am asleep within seconds.

Tomorrow we go to Red Rock!

Day 7
Thursday 14 April 2011
From: Kulgera
To: Uluru
Distance travelled: 380 kilometres

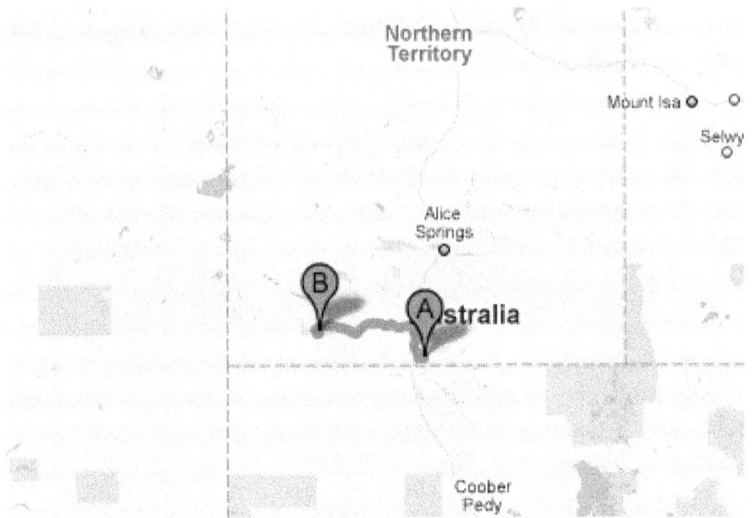

I wake up in the middle of the night to hear a big storm outside. What the hell is going on here? We are now almost in the middle of Australia which is supposed to be one of the driest places in the world and it keeps raining. I am getting pretty fed up with this bloody rain. I am sure the locals are pretty happy about the rain, but I am really, really over the rain now. The storm also brings something else to my attention, not related to the weather at all. Until now that I have been woken up, I could not feel just how bad the mattress is I am sleeping on. Springs are pushing into places where you would prefer not to have springs pushing which is pretty much everywhere. I know for a fact that you are now underestimating just how bad these springs are. There is a spring that when I move my hip left, pushes up into the jugular in my neck. And this is with my head on the pillow. I try to find a position which is comfortable, but after a while just give up. I briefly consider sleeping on the floor, but luckily fall asleep again before I do that.

I wake up later again when I hear Darryl moving around next door. The walls are really thin, so as soon as he moves around, I could hear it. I open my door and see that it is still dark outside. We had agreed last night that we wanted to leave early this morning, but getting up when it is dark just goes against everything I believe in. Last night the bar-sheela said that everything is closed until 7:00 a.m. this morning so we had to fill up last night and will not be able to get coffee this morning. I now get the first opportunity to hook up my butane canister and promptly do this. I pour some of the water from my water bladder into the kettle and juice the flame right up. A bright orange flame lights up the dark morning. I had imagined this so many times while planning the trip and it is just as great as I had hoped it would be.

Darryl joins me outside and when the kettle boils I make myself a coffee and Darryl makes a cup of tea. As we stand there drinking our brews and smoking a cigarette, the sky starts to change to grey and soon it is light enough to see our surroundings. I had expected to see some damage due to the winds in last night's storm, but what I saw had nothing to do with the storm, yet is every bit as breathe taking. I cough up coffee through my nose and drop my cigarette. Gasping for air I finally get a breath in again and finally get the opportunity to start laughing.

Over the last few days Darryl had complained about his hair a few times. He had asked around in Coober Pedy for a barber shop or hairdresser, but could not find anyone to mow his mop. He reckons it is too hot inside his helmet and with shorter hair it will be much better.

That being said, in the slightly increased light brought on by the approaching dawn I can see that Darryl had decided to cut his own hair. I remember what I looked like when I was just old enough to go to school and had once decided to cut my own hair and the style Darryl went for looks quite similar. To make things tougher for himself, Darryl had used a tiny Swiss army knife size scissors to cut his hair.

Through the last few snorts and grunts I finish my coffee and then we start loading up the bikes. I am just about finished packing and dawn is now in the process of happening when I turned around and there stand Yosemite Sam looking down at the wheel of his huge farmer's UTE (4x4). The tyre is flat and he seems to be trying to glare air into the tyre. He looks up and now there is an odd moment. He looks at me, and then looks at the wheel. Then he looks up at the spare wheel tied to the back of the UTE and then back to me. I think he is trying to communicate with me, but I do not understand him. I just never learnt to speak Rude-Australian.

I smile, nod, look down at the bike's tyre, give it a good kick and a nod and tie my sleeping bag to the back seat. Without looking back I go back to my room to get my last few things. He has still not moved since I had gone back to the room. He is grumbling something now, but I just don't really care. I know I should do the "be the better man" thing, but honestly it isn't because he was rude to me the night before, it isn't because he didn't have the decency to ask for help, it isn't even because of all the times he had tried to kill Buggs Bunny. I am not offering to help him because he stinks. Not just the two day sweat kind of smell, the o-my-god-did-you-crap-in-your-pants stink. I know I would not be able to stand to close to him for long and he is already too close to my bike for my liking.

When all my gear is loaded, Darryl is also ready so we start up and ride off. I can see him starting to move in my mirror, having decided that the wheel is not going to fix itself thanks to a mean stare, nor are the young, super cool bikers going to help him. He is just going to have to do it himself.

The morning is stunning, cooled down by the storm last night and with just a few clouds around. There is no sign off rain and with my life being on track back home I am really making up for the lost enjoyment of yesterday. I sing along to Paul Simon and sit back against my sleeping bag watching the world pass. I even have a little hip movement going as a slight dance routine. The warm coffee in my tummy sloshing around and the fresh air is exhilarating and knowing that there is no one out here at the moment, I speed up a little bit. Cruising north on Stuart highway at hundred and thirty five kilometres per hour I feel something start to change. The first few days had been a mad rush with wet and difficult riding. I kept saying to myself, "This is the trip and I must enjoy every second of it." We had not had easy riding along the coast and it had been so wet and cold that it isn't what you would call great riding. Then the stress of the last couple of days seemed to have reset me. That's the best I can explain it. It feels like I had been reset and booted up and now I am really just chilling out. I finally feel the mood inside me settle down and the obsession with trying to enjoy every moment disappear. I am enjoying it and I am not even trying to.

After an hour and a bit we arrive at Erldunda Roadhouse. This is the point on Stuart Highway where we need to turn off west to ride out to Uluru. This is the first road we will have to double back on. There will be a piece of Stuart highway that we will also double back on, but that is later on. Right now we are stopping at the Roadhouse to fuel up and get some breakfast in. Darryl buys a set of razors and says he will be right back. He is going to shave his head.

While he is gone I call home and have a nice long chat with Elizna. With the bad line yesterday and me being over emotional I did not really hear much more than the fact that everything was ok. Now we catch up about where we are and what she has been up to. After the chant I walk around the place and smoke a couple of cigarettes. Finally Darryl comes walking back and again I grunt in laughter. Luckily this time I do not have anything to snort through my nose. He has managed to shave most of his head, save for a few patches. I grab my camera, as this is a photo opportunity I just cannot miss. I snap a couple of photos. Still laughing he says,

"Ok, that's enough now. Now come and help me. I cannot get to all the hair on the back of my head."

It must be due to something that happened to me in my childhood or some horror movies I saw, but I have a thing for touching other people. I can touch people close to me, like my wife and mum and brothers, but somehow I have this moment before I have to touch someone that I have a moment of doubt.

Well, nothing to it, I go and help him. I have never shaven my own head or anyone else's heads for that matter. So the first shave I do, I see a small trail of blood following the blade down his head. I pull my face in that "oops" way and the kid standing next to me at the basin washing his hands eyes go round. He looks at me and then walks out quickly giggling.

"I think I have done well so far. I don't think I have any cuts yet." Darryl says. At this stage the back of his head looks like I have taken a piece of bob wire and scraped it down his scalp. There are a number of cuts, some bleeding more than others.

This puts me at ease as he could not have felt the small cut I just gave him. If he hadn't felt the other cuts, then I am ok. I help him shave his last hair off and now he really looks dodgy. Well, we are bikers so it probably doesn't look too odd.

After the shaving experience I need a cigarette. We smoke and I have a few more giggles about his head. Darryl comes out of the shop with a wide brim hats with a net on. The idea is that the net is secured to the brim of the hat and then hangs down onto your shoulders. This helps to keep the flies from your face. I quickly run inside and buy one as well. What a relief to be able to stand outside without hundreds of flies trying to invade every orifice on your face. I think this is the best money I have spent since arriving in Australia. I honestly cannot convey just what a relief it is to not have flies in my face.
Then we mount up and for the next day and a bit we leave Stuart highway behind us. We are now riding out west towards Uluru. The road is pretty much the same as Stuart Highway, long, straight and in pretty good nick. Just as I think this I see a huge pothole and only just manage to swerve out in time. Wow, that was big enough to possible cause damage to the tyres. A couple of minutes later another big one on the other side of the road. I will have to

remember that one for on the way back. It is even bigger that the previous one. Luckily that seems to be the only section in really bad shape.

Half way down this little detour we come up to Ebenezer roadhouse, aptly named as Mount Ebenezer is clearly visible in the distance. When I first saw it I was convinced it was Uluru, but it is long and flat and actually a mountain, not a monolith. We pull off at the petrol station and after fuelling up I go inside. The girl behind the counter is strikingly beautiful. Wow, how does a woman as stunning as that end up in a place like this? When she talks to me I hear a strong European accent. Darryl reckons she is Swedish. Must be travelling and needed to make some money before moving on. However nice she is, I am still happily married and Uluru is still waiting, so after having a Coke Zero, we mount up again. I take the lead and as we go over a hill I spot two camels next to the road a few meters in from the road. I swerve as I point them out to Darryl. This is the first real wild life we have seen on the trip so for me it is a pretty big deal. I pull over and turn around. I ride closer and then switch off the engine when I am still about fifty metres away. I don't want to scare them away before I can get my camera out of the top box and snap a couple of pictures. I have done a lot of game drives in Africa, so understand that you need to be very careful not to scare them away. Slow movements and no noise is the way to go here.

They are spooked by my arrival and immediately start moving and I blame the Australian government for this. Apparently they consider camels a pest in Australia, so what they do is fly over the herds of camels and bomb them. Nope, I am not making this up. They bomb camels. I wonder if this has anything to do with the Australian's obsession to try impressing the Yanks. The Americans bomb the camel riders up in the Middle East and the Aussies bomb the camels in the Outback. Maybe they are terrorist camels?

However they came to this decision, it was counting against me now. The camels are nervous and are busy running towards the road. I quickly grab my camera and manage to get one picture of them on the hill next to the road and a couple more as the run onto the road and then disappear. All through this, Darryl, who is a professional photographer has been trying to get the right lens onto his fancy camera. I kid you not, the second they disappear he finally has the lens on. Ha ha ha ha. I just have to laugh. He does mention a few words I am loath to write down. Well at least we have some proof of seeing them. With the camels gone the only other thing still around is the thousands of flies, so we get back on the bikes and continue down the road towards the red centre of Australia.

As we get closer and closer to the Uluru area, I see that I am running out of fuel quickly. I am not worried, we have enough spare fuel to take us there and probably back to the Ebenezer roadhouse, but it shows that we have ridden quite a distance. We ride past a turn off for the Uluru Township, but we continue on to the Uluru National park. When we arrive at the gate they say that there is no accommodation in the national park itself. There is no fuel in there either. We need to go back to the township where we will find both fuel and accommodation. I see that the entry fee into the park is $25. Wow, that's a bit steep. I was hoping to do both a sunrise and a sunset at the rock, but at that price, I guess we will do one or the other. We turn back and ride the fifteen kilometres back to the township and stop at the hotel and shopping area. There is an information office as usual and that's what we are after. The thing to remember here, and I did not really think about this at the time is that this is a major tourist attraction. If you think of Australia and the pictures you get in your head, the typical pictures are of Ricky Ponting losing the cricket world cup in 2011, the Opera House in Sydney and Uluru. Just to proof this point for me a Boeing 737 takes off from the airport. Somehow this is not what I had expected.

We ask at the information counter what our accommodation options are and there is a wide variety. Everything from five star Oasis type lodges, to budget camping with no electricity. We opt for the camping option, as we are pretty keen to get a camp in and the prices of the hotels are pretty steep. This is a typical tourist trap. We ride out to the camping area and rent a lawn for the night. We are allowed to pitch as many tents on our lawn as we want, but need to use one of the lawns marked as "No electricity". That suits us fine, as we do not have anything to plug in anyway. We ride up and down the camp ground and find a secluded spot in the far back left hand corner of the grounds. We can see one other tent from this spot and lots and lots of open lawns around us. If sense prevails, we should be left to ourselves for the night.

Right. So now I need to setup my camp site. I choose an area that is right under the large tree that's on our lawn and right against the fence. This feels good as I will be in the shade most of the day and then I can also tie my tent to the fence. Out comes the ground cover and up goes the tent. Setting it up is easy and quickly, just as I had hoped for. Everything works and it looks pretty cool. Right, now I need to get the stuff from my bike that I will need overnight. That includes the self inflating mattress, sleeping bag, inflatable pillow and my clothes. The mattress yet again does not self inflate, but I have been expecting this, so just blow it up myself. Once inflated I also blow up the pillow and then neatly chuck my sleeping bag into the tent. Now who said you have to pay hundreds of dollars to get five star treatment?

There is one problem though. While we are riding my clothes are all packed away in zip lock bags in the side panniers. This helps to make sure my clothes stays dry, but also makes it easier to take my clothes out whenever I need it. The thing is I only packed fours sets of underwear, three t-shirts, three sets of socks and one swimming trunks. We have been on the trip now for a week, so do the math. Some things have been worn more than once. After been worn more than once it is then all placed in a small sealed bag in a very hot box. Opening the bags containing these toxic fumes is a thrilling experience. I see funny colours and shapes until I catch a fresh breath again, then I have a slight headache. I am beginning to think it might just be around about that point in the trip where it is a good idea to do some washing.

Yet, the clothes has waited this long, it can wait till after lunch. We get back on the bikes, this time in shorts, t-shirt and jandles and ride to the shopping centre. It has a convenience store, where I get some chips and six cheese rolls. This will be dinner. Chips on white bread. Students the world over live on this. I get a litre of juice as well, to add to this culinary feast. Darryl manages to secure a bag of ice which is wonderful. This will come in VERY handy pretty soon. We now go to the restaurants and we have a choice of waiting a few minutes for a table in the coffee shop and then being able to order some paninis, or we can go straight into the more formal restaurant and order burgers from their menu. Mmm. Let me think about that for a second while I eat my burger. I order the cheese burger with a large beer and Darryl decided to be a bit different and he ordered the cheese burger and a large beer. I like his style! Good choice I recon. We wolf down the food and gulp down the beers. Amazing how hungry and thirsty riding makes you. I love this. Now, with the feeding frenzy done we need to go do the camping thing. We get back on the bikes and ride back to the camping area. Just before the turn off to the camping area is a road block. I kid you not. There is a road block and the cops are pulling everyone over and doing the famous, "Please blow here...1...2...3, please come with us." Fuck. The first time I have a beer and get back on the bike on the whole trip and there is a road block. I know I said whatever happens IS the trip, but I am also quite determined not to go to jail.
As I approach the road block they pull over the car in front of me and I wave and ride past. Whew. That was close. I turn off into the camping area and then ride all the way to our camp in the far back corner. Now, as I said, we will do the camping thing. Or we will do the camping thing, the way we understand the camping thing to work. We open the bag of ice, open the bottled of Jack Daniels we got in duty free and sit down with our fly hats on and drink whiskey. I must say, I think I am a pretty good camper. I sit there and professionally camp. We talk a bit of rubbish in between, but mostly for the next hour or so we camp.

Then a rude reminder when I open my tent, the washing.... I will need to do something about that right now. As it is I think I might already have contaminated my tent. I did not pack washing powder, but I have been taking an extra soap in every place we stayed. You know, those little use-once soaps left on your bed or in the bathroom of your hotel room. Armed with one of these and my bags of dirty clothes, off I go to the ablutions block. There are washing machines and if I had three dollars on me I would have used that, but as luck would have it I have nada. So, in real third world style, I start washing my clothes in the sink. Eish, I am washing.

After the ten or so minutes when this horrible experience is over, I am back at the tent and now to keep the third world theme going, I use the fence behind my tent to hang all my clothes out to dry. Hehehe. My wife will have a heart attack!
With a job well done and clothes that smells of fresh apple, I sit back down to continue doing the camping thing. We also have a decision to make. Will we go to the rock for sunset this afternoon or sunrise tomorrow morning? $25 is too much to go twice to look at a rock, no matter how far we have come for that. I am a bit too stingy to think of forking out that kind of cash. So, we will go once, now we just need to think which one we will go for.

Well, we have just had a number of whiskeys and a beer earlier today and have already done a lot of riding so will be tired tonight. Plus, we will be well rested in the morning and get up early anyway, so it will not even be too much of a change to our normal routine if we go tomorrow morning. With that all being said, we decide to go for sunset this afternoon. That is logic coming up trumps.

We get ready to go, this time putting on jeans and I put on my bike jacket as well, we head out to the rock. Riding out of the camp area, I see the cops are no longer there, which means they had either left or have just moved to a different location. Hopefully they were called out for an incident of a camel being blown up somewhere out there far away from where we are going. We ride out to the gate where we had to turn around earlier today and then get a pleasant surprise. The $25 fee gets you three days worth of access. Great, so now we can go for sunset and be back tomorrow for sunrise! Wonderful.

I switch on the helmet camera as we ride towards the rock and film most of the ride there. It is amazing just how big the rock is. From almost the moment you enter into the notional park you can see it, yet I see we have done a good ten kilometres and it still does not feel any closer. I see I had lost Darryl, which means he had either fallen or had pulled over for pictures. Considering I had just pulled over to take some pictures I assume it is the latter. I take a picture with me and the rock in the background and then get back on the bike and ride back the way I came. Have a look at the back cover for the photo. A couple of turns later I see Darryl on the side of the road busy taking photos. When he is done we ride on towards the rock and ride pass a parking area sign posted to be the "Sunset viewing" spot. Great, we will come back here later on. We still have a couple of hours at least before the sun will start setting so we ride on past and head closer to the rock.

We get to a circle where you can either go to the cultural village, or head even closer to Uluru. I am keen to get right up to the base of the rock if at all possible. The road twists this way, then that, but the general direction keeps taking us closer to it. Finally we are riding right along the base of the rock and then get to a parking area. Getting off, I feel a slight case of butterflies. We have arrived at Uluru.

Uluru is also known as Ayers rock, named after the Chief Secretary of South Australia in the 1800's by a chap with the handle, William Gosse. It is actually quite an interesting story about this William chap. He lived in Adelaide and was well respected in his community. At the early age of twenty three he had made his fortune selling Russian slaves. He did not sell slaves themselves, but rather he sold things to slaves. The slave business was running rive at this stage in the otherwise quite city of Adelaide. The problem was that he was not a very good business man. He had to take out a large loan from his once school best friend, the before mentioned Chief Secretary Sir Henry Ayers. While this seems well above board, the problem was that his main target market, the slaves, were not really well paid. Well, actually they were not paid at all. So they all bought things from William or Billy J as they called him, on IOUs. Soon he was theoretically a millionaire, but in practice he was bankrupt and had no way of repaying his rather sizeable debt to the man who was once his friend. Soon he had some rather disturbing visitors asking about the money, threatening broken knees and late night swimming with fishes.
He snuck away in the middle of the night and decided to take on the wild interior of Australia and became a pretty well respected surveyor and when he saw Uluru in July 1873, he thought how much the rock reminded him of the shape of Henry's nose, he named it after his old friend.

Well, I have taken some creative liberties with how Bill got to be in the centre of the red desert to get to name this rock, so it might not have gone down quite like this, but I would put more than just a few cents on it that he was out hiding from someone!

The other interesting fact is about its aboriginal name, Uluru. As most people expect, most traditional names given to places has a meaning in the relevant language. If you take the Maori name for New Zealand for instance, Aotearoa, it means "the land of the long white cloud." Uluru however, means nothing in Aboriginal language. There are those who claim that it means "Great Pebble", "Meeting Place" and "Waterhole", but that's all just as much rubbish as my story about Bill. It is one of those names that is truly just a name. I actually found that pretty refreshing.

Be that as it may, the rock is huge. Standing next to it, I can now believe that it is just less than three hundred and fifty metres high. It is almost ten kilometres around the base of the mount and the colour is as implied by the name, red. Standing there looking up at this magnificent view I cannot help but feel the mythical power of the hill. The other thing I feel is flies. I forgot to pack my fly hat and now have to deal with the hundreds of flies crawling all over my face. Darryl walks one way to go and take some photos and I walk the other way. I am pretty keen to get to a quite place and have a silent moment. This is one of my mum's life dreams to stand here, which adds some weight to how special it is to be here.

I walk off and get my quite moment to say a prayer to the people in my life. I walked about a hundred meters to one side where there is no one around. I climb over the low fence and kneel down on the ground next to the mountain. I put my hand on the base and as I start to say my quick prayer I even manage to ignore the fly trying to bore its way into my nasal cavity.

Unfortunately the reality of the place now reared its ugly head.

As I mentioned before, there are basically two globally recognised landmarks in Australia. Those would be the Opera House in Sydney and Uluru. What this means in practice is that there is going to be a number of tourists around. I admit, I am also a tourist so don't get me on that wagon, but there are different types of tourists. To be fair I will use myself as an example of a tourist. Then compare that to the other type.

I smell relatively good as I showered this morning and used deodorant so I do not smell too bad. I have just smoked a cigarette, so admittedly that is not the best type of touristing. However, I am quite and respectful to the places I visit and do not litre or cause problems. I spend some money, paying for accommodation, food and drinks. Even though I do not buy a lot of touristy stuff, I do have a post card in my bag of Uluru and a fly hat. So out of ten, I would give myself a good six and a half or seven out of ten. Not the greatest tourist on the menu, but let me describe my competition and you be the judge.

Standing on my knees with my hand on the base of the rock, thinking of special people and onto the scene come Mister Jim J Jones. Fresh from Tennessee and sounding every bit the cliché:

"A te ya wa. A weel clim dis gaaahd daaaam mountin if A wana." He drawl. Translated to: "I tell you what. I will climb this goddamn mountain if I want to."

He looks back at the fat family following him, the teenage pimple faced son with his large earphones on, not listening to his father and the fat daughter talking on her mobile phone rolling her eyes. Then there is the bottle blond wife with the very plastic boobs and large cleavage tripling after them with the high heels and the red nails.

"Yes dear" she says while waving the flies from her face.

"Eeets jus lak those gaaahd daaam injins a tell ya. Theeee jus caaa eet holi groun to be able to chaaage ye $25. Then theeee seh yaa caan clim the gaaahd daaam mountin. Fo $25 I wheel climb the gaaahd daaam mountin.

Again, translated: "It's just like those goddamn Indians. They just call it holy ground to be able to charge you $25. Then they say you cannot climb the goddamn mountain. For $25 I will climb the goddamn mountain."

They wobble on past the large sign asking people please not to climb Uluru and start climbing up the mount. It is a pretty steep climb and I am sure it would have been thoroughly entertaining seeing them tumbling down, but back to the rating system. As tourists I guess they do get the points for being a family travelling together. But, before you give them the points, first think of sitting next to the father in restaurant having to listen to him boast about how great America is and that everything is always better and bigger in America. That is of course strait after abusing the waiter for being to slow for his liking. Or how about sitting next to the wife on a sixteen hour flight complaining about how her husband doesn't pay any attention to her anymore even after she had the fat sucked out of her ass and fake tan sprayed in places she will show you in the toilet if you join her, wink, wink. No, I am sure you will not be giving this family much more than a measly two. Standing there looking at all the people climbing up and down the mountain like ants I reflect on how this should have been a really special, holy place and now it is being trampled by us travellers. We just have no class. That's basically it. A sadness deep inside me feels really sorry for how we just cannot respect things. I wonder how those people would feel if they get to their church on a Sunday and I am half way up the steeple and then start charging people to run up and down the pews. Not so nice if it your life being trampled on.

Anyway, I am now getting fed up with the flies as well. When back at the bikes we ride back to the cultural shop, but once there I leave Darryl to walk through and go shopping if he wishes, but I have to ride back to the camp ground to get my fly hat. I had promised my mum that I will do a meditation at sunset at Uluru. There is no way that I will be able to sit still for more than a couple of seconds with all these flies. So I have to ride out to the camp site, grab my hat and get back. Now this is becoming a race against the setting sun. I ride as fast as I can considering that the speed limit is fifty kilometres an hour. I do push it a little higher than that though, as the sun is getting lower and lower. Ok, I did push it to just over hundred kilometres an hour, but it was an emergency says the tourist rating himself a seven.

I get to the camp site and now instead of our camp being in the far remote corner of the camp grounds, there is a group setting up comp around our lawn. There are pieces of tents all over the place is various stages of being erected. It looks like Lawrence of Arabia and his entourage has just pulled in. I am not in the mood, nor do I have time to really think about this now. I am back on my bike with my fly hat tucked into the back of my pants and off I fly. I race back pretty quickly and arrive at the sunset spot to find the parking lot filled up. People are milling about as if AC/DC is about to come up on stage and there are back packers with their stuffed up vans drinking and shouting. Kids are running around screaming and hoons are racing up and down. Oh crap. Well, I setup my video camera and record the sunset for my mum. I will dub over the terrible sounds of the crowd with some nice didgeridoo music before I send it to her. Once the sun has set I pack up my camera and we ride back to the camp in the traffic streaming out of the park. I am pretty irritated by now, as it has not been the experience I had imagined it would be. My own fault I know, but still I really did want a spiritual moment here.

My mood is not improved when we ride into the camp. There are six trucks parked around our camping area and a number of tents. We park to the side and when we get to our camp, the group that has moved in around us has setup their kitchen tent next to my tent. They have about twenty seats packed out, a fridge running, enough lights setup to light Wembley stadium. I growl at them as I walk past, not in the mood to even say hello. Darryl has better manners than me and still chats with them and tell them its fine when they apologise for moving in around us.

I start up the little battery powered lantern and we sit at the table outside the tents and smoke a couple of cigarettes and drink a few Jack Daniels. I then decide it is a good idea to turn in early. We will get up early so that we can be at the gate at 6:00 a.m. My thoughts on this is that there will be less people willing to get out of bed early morning and stand outside watching the sun come up than there were at the sunset. So, I might still get my quite meditation at the rock. With that in mind I am happy to go to bed early and then get up early.

I climb into my tent and find that when I had done my tent test in the back yard all those months ago, the cats had played on the inflatable mattress with their sharp nails so it is now deflated. My pillow is also deflated, so I blow both up again. I then lie down and rest my tired head on the soft inflatable pillow and then relax my neck. As I do, my head slowly start tilting on the rolls of the pillow and my nose end up squashed in the pillow. I move my head slightly backwards and then relax my neck again. This time my head rolls slowly backwards and now I am looking up at the top of the tent. I move forward and backwards until I have my face just balanced not to roll off either way. Now, if I can just not move at all during the night I will be ok. With that thought less than a second old my head tilts forward and I end up with my nose squashed into the pillow again. I let loose with a few rather rude words and to then top it all off, one of the women in the group sitting in their lavish lounge tent starts cackling. It is one of those real "witch of the west" cackles. I grab my torch and look for my zip lock bags of clothes, then remembering that it is still hanging all on the fence behind my tent. FUCK. Ok, so I get back up and get all my washing from the fence. At least it is dry, so there is one positive point for me. With my washing gathered I get back in the tent and have to listen to the witch cackle away again. I know she is probably a very nice person and being mean to someone who is clearly just having a good time and laughing is just wrong, but right at this moment I am not in the mood to feel sorry for the people who I am pissed off at.

I get back in the tent and can already feel the mattress has deflated somewhat. I stuff my clothes into the ziplock bags and use that as my pillow. As I want to roll over I realize plastic is not the best thing on hot sweaty skin. The pillow is stuck to my face. Grrrrrr. I take out one of my t-shirts and wrap it around my pillow and try again. Man, this is going to be a long night.

I finally fall asleep and wake up some hours later. I had somehow rolled off my pillow and the mattress is totally deflated. So far the camping thing is not going too well. Thinking of the deflated mattress makes me think of my cats back home and I do fall asleep with a smile on my face.

Day 8
Friday 15 April 2011
From: Uluru
To: Alice Springs
Distance travelled: 479 kilometres

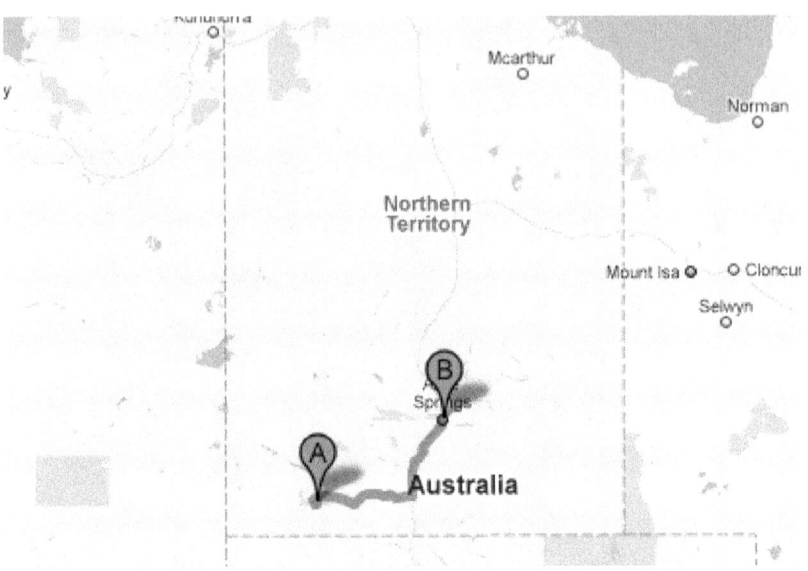

As consciousness fights its way through the dreams alarm bells are going off. These alarm bells have nothing to do with the alarm I set on my mobile phone. Many moons ago when I was still young and sporty I played cricket and seriously injured my neck. I had struggled for many years to get my neck back into a semi normal state. Since then if my neck is just slightly sore or stiff I am worried. The pain I feel in my neck as I open my eyes is not good. I realize I am sleeping without a pillow and my mattress is completely deflated. My shoulders are sore as well and my left arm, which is pinned underneath me, is all pins and needles. Good way to wake up.

I scratch around for my mobile phone and when I find it I see there is ten minutes left before my alarm is going to go off. Well, I will not be able to sleep any further anyway and I am so uncomfortable I would rather get up and get the coffee going. When I get out of the tent I am greeted with a wonderful view. There are millions and millions of stars, as you can only see in remote places. As I stand there looking up at the busy sky, I stretch my neck and it feels not as bad as I initially thought. I am a bit stiff, but it is hopefully not going to cause too much trouble. Already feeling better I start humming to myself and setup the kettle. I then start whistling just loud enough for my noisy neighbours to possibly hear me. I hear one tent's snoring stop, which must mean that their sleep is disturbed. I feel that mean streak in me wanting to make more noise, but I just cannot do it. I get the kettle going and then go and kick against Darryl's tent.

"You awake?" I ask innocently.

"Well, I am awake now." He grumbles from inside.

"Cool. I am making coffee. Want some?" I am still feeling very chuffed every time I make coffee.
"Yes please." It is amazing how quickly he goes from sleeping to being awake. It takes me many hours to get up to speed, he takes less than a minute and sound like he is pretty much wide awake.

I make us some coffee and we stand blowing the steam from our coffee quietly. It is still very quiet and absolutely dark if I switch the lantern off. Not hearing any cars I am pretty hopeful that there will be less people at the sunrise and people will probably be less energetic and hopefully less drunk than they were at the sunset. When our coffees are finished we get on the bikes and ride out. Once we get to the main road, there are a couple of other cars and one bus right in front of us. That actually suits me fine as I do not want to ride in the total darkness. The bus and cars are lighting up the road ahead and if someone is going to hit a 'roo, it will be them, not me. I think a bus hitting a 'roo is going to end better than a bike hitting the 'roo. Except for the 'roo that is. Darryl is riding behind me and since yesterday his headlight had stopped working, so he has to ride with his high beam on. He keeps well back though, which helps not to blind me as well.

On the twenty minute ride to the sunrise spot the light is steadily increasing into a dark grey and by the time we get to the viewing point the outline of the rock is clearly visible. I wanted to start recording in absolute darkness, but the small number of people around and the quite atmosphere is getting me into an elated mood. We walk out to one of the viewing platforms. I choose a point on the highest piece of the deck and setup my tri-pod for the video camera and start the recording. It is still pretty cool, so standing there quietly has me almost shivering, but it is not quite that cold. The fresh air is amazing and the light is increasing the sky to grey now. I take a deep breath and feel myself starting to relax and I will be able to go into a semi meditational state soon.

And then it happens. A rumbling noise is swelling from the parking lot. I look out that way and seven busses pull in one after the next and a steady stream of screaming and running masses ooze along the walkways towards the viewing point. They mill about and within moments someone is standing right in front of my video recorder screaming at her boyfriend to: "Nimm mein bild hier. Dann kommst du und stehe hier und ich werde dir zu nehmen."

The anger boils up again and I am actually getting fed up with myself for getting so angry. They have just as much right to be here and do this as they wish, but for crying out aloud. Which they of course do.

While there is still space right at the front of the platform I move there. I cannot use the tripod here as it is too low, so now I have to hold the camera in my hand. At least no one can come and stand in front of me. Not that that stops them from trying to push me to the side to get more people into their four thousand's picture, this time with granny next to Stan and gramps on the other side. Now change over so that gramps can stand next to granny. I feel something break inside me....

The only thing keeping me standing there is the fact that this is for my mum and I WILL record the whole sunrise. I will never be here again in my life, so I have to make this count.

When the sun finally hit the rock thirty minutes later I am half frozen, very grumpy and ready to leave. I pack my stuff up and growl at Darryl that I am leaving NOW. He packs up as well. I think he was expecting this kind of scene and of course he managed to get a lot of good photos of the sunrise, so his mood is much better than mine. The ride back out to the camp site has me humming to myself to try cool my temper down. The riding does the trick and I am even in a slightly good mood by the time we get to the camp. The bunch that had taken over around us are up and shuffling around the camp. I start up the kettle again for another cup of coffee.

We sit and have a look at the map and decide that we should really get going. We have had a few shorter days on the bikes and need to catch up on some serious mileage. One of the neighbours walks over and asks us where we went so early.

"We went to the rock for sunrise" Darryl replies.

"O, you guys really scared me this morning on your way out." She says and for a second I am really not sure what to say. Ten minutes ago I would have growled at her that she bloody well better be scared of us, but I had calmed down and only laugh. Shame, poor woman.

"Oh, ok. Well, we are packing up so you can have this space now as well." I say.

"Oh, that's wonderful. Bye" she says and heads back to the group to inform them that they have managed to scare us off I'm sure.

We pack up the camping stuff and I chuck my inflatable pillow in the rubbish bin. I will need to get a real pillow if we are to camp again. Finally everything is packed and we are ready to go. We ride out of there now heading straight east as the sun sits right in our eyes. The first few kilometres are pretty busy considering where we are, in the middle of the Outback, but then we pass the turn off for the airport and now there is no traffic. The fresh air and the start of yet another day on the bikes are cheering me up quickly. I am actually singing along to some South African music. I had recently discovered an Afrikaans artist who I am actually really getting hooked to. His name is Theuns Jordaan and I like his voice and he really sings deep, strong songs. Cool.

Too soon we arrive back at the roadhouse where we had stopped on the way in where we saw the Swedish chick. At the petrol pumps is another hot chick that is activating the pumps for people to use. We have a brief chat while I fill up and I tell her where we have been and going. She is friendly enough and then I head inside and there is the other hot chick as well. Wow. What are the odds? We decide this is a good place to have breakfast.

Breakfast is a race against the flies. After trying to figure out how I am going to keep the flies form my food long enough to eat it, I theorise the best approach will be to have a sacrificial piece of food. The theory is that I will take a piece of the egg and put it to the side of the plate and not chase the flies from the piece. They can have that and it will leave me with the rest. Well, it was a good theory with one fatal flaw. The flies did go for that piece, but it was not the same flies that were going after my portion of the food. Those flies are still very actively fighting me for every bite. I managed to get to a point where the hunger is less than the willingness to share my food with the flies. And I give up. I will eat again later at some stage. This will hold me for now. All fed and fuelled up, we now have about hundred and fifty kilometres till we get back to the Stuart Highway and a few minutes into this stretch the emotional and spiritual moment I had been hoping for at the rock caught up to me. Thoughts of my wife and the stress we have been through the last few days lead on to the sad memories of losing our other two children. I think about the issues my brother is having with his health and the stress that is putting my mum through. This is of course a slippery hill to be on and soon I am bawling my eyes out in my helmet. I cannot really see much of the road, but it is just going straight ahead anyway. Every time I think it is over, it just crashes over me again.

When I see the sign for the Erldunda roadhouse thirty kilometres ahead, where we will be back on Stuart highway, I start pulling myself together again. I ride with my helmet face open and the fresh air helps me calm down. By the time I get to the road house I am back in control and actually feel like e new person. I can feel how am detaching from a Deon who was and becoming a new person. The calmness and freshness is so amazing.

We stop at the roadhouse and fuel up again and get ready to head on further north. Seeing Stuart highway again is like seeing an old friend. It feels good when my bike rides up onto the highway and there we go, on our way to the centre of the country, also known as Alice Springs. The ride is pretty cool as I am feeling like a new person and this is where I had hoped to get on this bike trip. The other great thing is that we still have two more weeks of riding ahead of us. So much had already happened and we are only one third of the way through our trip. What an amazing feeling. The heat picks up rapidly and soon it reaches thirty five degrees. The road is quite and the bikes are humming along nicely at hundred and thirty kilometres per hour.

We arrive in Alice Springs and ride to the town centre looking for the information kiosk and find it right in the middle of the town. It is a pretty lively place. It is a relatively big town. Not anywhere close to a city, but just a nice sized place. We ask for directions to the YHA, or for those who do not know what that is, it is a youth hostel group. I know we no longer officially qualify as youth, but luckily that's not really a requirement to be able to stay at the hostels. Darryl is an YHA member so will get discount if we stay at one of the YHA group hostels. We get direction to the YHA and then also for backup to two other hostels. We ride to the YHA, but when we ask for rooms they say just about full. They have one room with two beds left, but we will have to share with eight other people. We are not too keen on sharing, but then he adds that it is the Russian contestants for the Miss World bikini contest on here tonight. They had been complaining that they need some strong hands to massage oil into their bodies before they go on stage.

Nope, not really. They are full up and so we head to the other hostel. They have space and the added extra of a swimming pool. Good stuff. We will have to share a room, but that's ok. It cuts down on our costs a little bit, so we say ok to that. We unpack and then Darryl heads into town to go and look for a motorbike shop that sells headlight bulbs. He will need to have that replaced and this is the last place we can hope to get spare parts until we get to Darwin. While he is out to town I head to the swimming pool. There are a lot of young women lying around in the sun with very little clothes on. Man this is unnecessary. I dive in and have a good long swim. I really do miss swimming in New Zealand. It is to cold most of the time for swimming and swimming pools are very rare anyway. I had grown up with a pool and love swimming. I hear Darryl's bike come in and now the breakfast feel long ago. I think I can feel my stomach starting to chew on my spine. I head back to the room and suggest we go find some beers to stop the worse of the hunger.

At the room I find Darryl who is struggling a bit. He had tried to put the bike's light bulb in, but the little peg that keeps the light in place had fallen into the light cover and he cannot reach it now. We grab my tool bags and head out to the bike and struggle with it for a while. Eventually Darryl has it just about right. We cannot reach the peg, so had made some alternative plans until something worked. The light is working and just about in place, so good enough for us. With that done Darryl goes for a quick dip in the pool and then we head out to the town centre. We find a pub and settled down outside for a few beers.

The crowd next to us are pretty lively and loud, but the atmosphere is good and the afternoon heat is now pleasant after the swim and a few cold beers in front of us. We sit and chat and soon are talking about how we ended up here. Darryl tells me how he ended up doing working with me at Deloitte and I tell him my story. We have been working together for a few years and never really knew the others' story. Darryl is still talking about working for Oracle in Ireland and then stops mid sentence.

"Hey mate. Sorry to bud in. I couldn't help overhearing you mentioning something to smoke. Any chance of hooking us up?" he asks one of the guys at the table next to us. The two of them fall into a long chat and it ends with him promising to see what he can do and he will give Darryl a call if he can get something for us. While this is going on I am more interested in the rest of the people at the table. These are now what you would expect in the middle of nowhere. The one guy has only the very back teeth left in his mouth. That is the last two at the top and the last two at the bottom. How the hell do you eat with those four teeth? The other one looks to be somewhere between a bread and a clay brick on the IQ scale. He brays like a donkey every time everyone else laughs and soon I am laughing with them as this is just so cool. They are pretty cool people and Darryl really likes this place. Real Outback people in a real Outback town.

After five beers I am feeling slightly unsteady, and we decide to head back to the hostel. Once there we sit outside our room while Darryl works on getting is GPS sorted out. He had bought some pins to see if he can pin the cable onto the GPS, which is putting tension on the connection and forcing the connection allowing the power to get through to the GPS. It seems to be working and while he is focusing on that I see a large man stumble his way towards us.

I have named him Rudolph on account of him not introducing himself and of course the large red nose. And it is not a sunburn red. This is a man who consumes a lot of alcohol and he had consumed a fair bit before getting to stand here before us. As he stands there swaying he finally manages to focus on us he starts talking.

I am not someone who mind the occasional swear word thrown into a conversation to make your point or if the emotion is really high and needing to be expressed properly. I do however believe there is a line not to cross. Never swear at someone while angry, that will get you saying things you will regret a lot later on. Never scream a swear word. If you get to that point it is much better to just walk away. You are too angry then. Never swear at a woman. They are beautiful creatures and do not deserve being sworn at. It is however ok to swear at cyclists.

The other line is which swear words are generally ok. The shits and fucks have plenty of impact and should be able to cover the majority of situations. There is really no need to go any worse than that. This lad however had other ideas of swearing. I am not going to repeat what he said word for word, which should give you an indication of just how rough it was.

"Are those bikes upfront yours?" he asks

"Yeah." We both reply.

"Yeah, just wanna know how those c..... ride off road?" he asks and smiles a drunk smile.

"Well, those BIKES are too heavy for proper off-roading and we are not doing any off road riding on this trip. We are mostly keeping to...." Darryl did not get further than this.

"Whaaa? Those c.... can ride off road. Weight has nothin to do with it. All ya have to do is burn the c.... of those c.... Then if you feel ya going over ye just burn the c..... harder." He says and by now both our faces are pretty sour.
Firstly this drunken imbecile has no idea what he is talking about. Weight has a lot to do with off road riding. The lighter your bike the better for off road biking. Big heavy bikes are difficult to control and make manoeuvring very tough. You will fall if you do off road riding, I can guarantee that and picking up the heavy bike could be close to impossible in rough terrain. Secondly he is overstepping his boundaries with us. He is making himself a pest and is really it necessary to swear that much?

"Well, weight has a lot to do with it. If you slip you will not be able to keep it up. We are doing a sealed road ride." Darryl says and takes his stuff and walks off. The conversation is over as far as he is concerned.

I feel I should at least give the guy a few more minutes to see if he has anything useful to say, although I seriously doubt it. I do want to speak to locals and well, he is a local. He keeps trying to convince me that you should just go faster and then you will be able to slide further instead of falling.

"Right. Ye, I am sure you can slide these heavy bikes, but I cannot. So we just keep to the sealed roads."

"Yeah man. Ya gotto go bronco ridin man. That's real ridin. Ya ride those c.... right after the broncos, chasing them across fields. I don't give a f.... I will fall and then just get up and chase those c.... until they are tamed.

"You chase broncos. Like in the horses? On a motorcycle?" I ask him now starting to get a little irritated with his horse shit. Excuse the pun.

"Ye mate. I even chase them right through fences. I don't give a f... I just ride right through the fence and then slide and then I'm back on it."

"You ride a bike through a fence?" I ask dumbfounded that he thinks I am that stupid.

"Ye mate, ye ride those c.... then when ya have them all too tired to run, then you can f... those c...." he says while imitating his intentions after catching a wild horse. He seems to want to mate with it. Well I guess you need all kinds of people in this world, but I have now had enough of this dumbass.

"Right. Gotta run. Cheers." I say and then close the door in his face. He just stands there looking at the door. I hope he just pisses off. To make sure I don't have to worry about what he does next I close the curtain and leave him and his horses outside. It is still pretty early afternoon and I need a rest before going out tonight. Darryl is keen to go big tonight, so to keep up with him I will need to take a nap. I lie down on the bed and take a half nap. It is one of those naps where you never really fall completely asleep, but you are not really awake either.

Later hunger gets me up and we head back out to town. There are two pubs in town which we have been told are the places to go if you want a night on the town. They will either both be busy or one of them will be the main party for the night. Before we do that however, I need food. We walk to a couple of restaurants and then see one place that has Kangaroo steaks on the menu. As I have not seen one after covering almost half the length of the country, I reckon I can now just as well eat one. That decided, we get a table and order some drinks and the food. The meat is good, but I wouldn't say that it is great. I much prefer beef over Roo. It wasn't a very big portion either. Darryl had ordered a pie of sorts and could not finish his food. I take over the cleanup duties and finish his food for him.

With a full stomach I am ready for the night out. We walk down to the street where the party is supposed to be. When we get to the two pubs it is clear that one is doing a bit better than the other tonight. In the one pub there's the bar tender and the bouncers standing outside and loud music playing, but not a single person in the place. In the other bar the people are standing queues to get to the bar for drinks. Ok, so that seems to be the place to be. We go in there and walk through to the back area where we can have a smoke. The guy we met earlier today and offered to see if he can fix us up had not come back to us, so no funny tobacco. Just the normal stuff. We grab a seat outside and sit and have a beer. Darryl goes online onto Facebook or send email and I sit and do some people watching. They seem to be pretty much normal people in a normal pub. Sitting still does nothing good for me, as I now have a full tummy and the riding does tire me out. With my emotional morning I am pretty exhausted now. We have another drink and then agree that we are not going big at all, so it might be better to call it the night. We walk back to the hostel and the walk does me fine. The food gets some opportunity to get the digestion process going and then we are at the hostel.

After a quick call home to say good night I am in bed and asleep almost immediately.

Day 9
Saturday 16 April 2011
From: Alice Springs
To: Dunmarra
Distance travelled: 848 kilometres

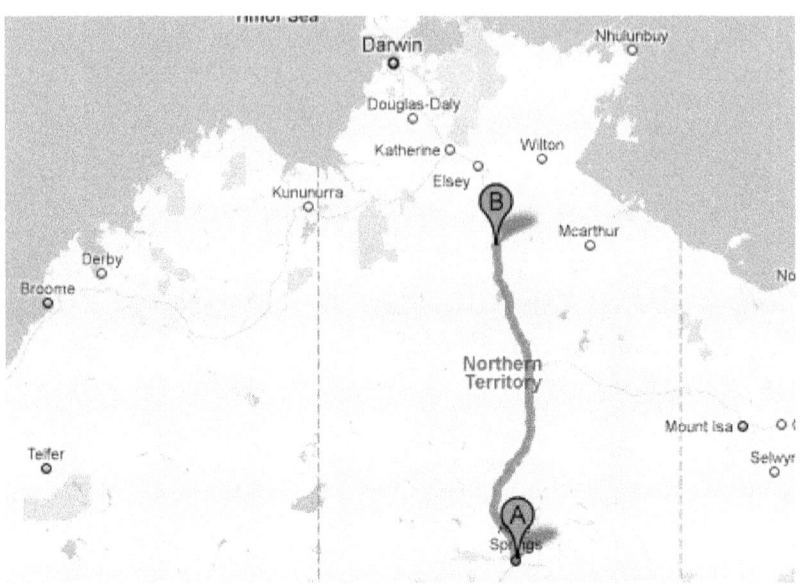

"We have had way too many short days. We need to put some serious riding in today."

"Absolutely. Let's try get to Elliott. I know it is a long way away, but now that we are in the Northern Territory and past Alice Springs, it should be quite roads." Darryl says while looking at the map on his GPS.

We sit and consider the seven hundred and sixty kilometres that will be the day's riding. The longest day we have done so far on the trip was five hundred and forty kilometres. And that was the longest day on a bike ever. We are now planning to do more than two hundred kilometres extra. Well, the only way we can do that is if we get going.

Darryl goes around to the front of the hostel and rides his bike to the back where our room has a door. It will make it easier to load the bikes. I go and get my bike as well. There are a lot of people in the voyeur, all with their bags packed and ready to go. They are all booking out and heading off somewhere today. They are probably going out to Ayers rock. They all seem excited and keen to get going. There are a lot of smiles and excited chatting in a multitude of languages. I work my way through the group to get out the door and outside there is a different scene. Standing outside are two young lads causing trouble. They had obviously gone big the night before and are still pissed. They are standing there shouting rude comments to the girls sitting outside having a smoke. The girls are trying their best to ignore them, but you can see they are pretty uncomfortable.

I walk past them and they both look at me and one comments something I cannot hear properly. I just walk on and leave them be. I am not going to get into trouble here. I decide not to pull any of my world famous Bruce Lee moves, it is still too early in the morning for spilling blood. I get onto the bike and ride in to the back of the building. Thank goodness we have this access, walking past those guys ten times to load everything onto the bikes would not have been very good.

We load up the bikes and when done we head upstairs where the kitchen is. There is some bread left so we make a couple of slices of toast each. There is only butter to be found, the jam had been finished by the large group of people who had just moved through here. That's ok though. I make a nice cup of coffee and sit outside on the balcony after finishing the toast to have a smoke. Just below the balcony where we are now sitting in the early morning air, the two drunken boys are still causing trouble. It sounds like they have found someone else who seems to be keen to join in on their morning activity. The voices are getting more aggressive and I am sure fists will be flying any second now.

I hate violence and feel quite upset about this crap. That's no way to start your day. I hate it if people cannot handle their drink and then get all aggressive with other people. I head down the stairs to go finish up for the ride today and as I reach the bottom of the stairs, storming in from outside is none other than Rudolph the Bronco rider.

"Come with me. I need a witness." He says and I can smell the booze and sweat from a couple of metres away. He wants me to join him outside where I reckon he intends to have a fight with the two drunks.

"No way man. Fuck off." I reply and walk away. I am not interested in any of that.
Back in the room I suit up and by the time Darryl gets there I am just about ready to get on the bike and ride. For a change I am ready before him as I am keen to just get out of here. We ride up to the front gate and now the two boys are busy fighting each other. I have a moment where I think to flip them the

bird, but then think about the rest of their day. The sun and heat, in combination with the punches where they do manage to get each other, added to a good hangover will be punishment enough for them. Have fun dip-shits.

We ride down the road to the petrol station and fuel up. The next town is two hundred kilometres away, so we need to make sure we fuel up to the brim. We are now riding the bikes a bit harder, so our fuel economy is way down. Not that it bothers me, it is awesome to be riding in the Northern Territories. With the speed limit up to hundred and thirty kilometres per hour, we can easily push it up to hundred and fifty. The roads are quite and we haven't seen any trace of police on the roads since around Port Augusta. The exhilaration of the higher speed is brilliant and after having spent over week in the saddle, riding is now so part of what I am, it is hardly something to think about.

With a bit of riding done the clock is on 9:00 a.m. and the temperature gauge shows it is twenty six degrees. This looks like it is going to be a hot day. There are no clouds what so ever, so I am pretty happy. I don't really mind the heat that much and have coped pretty well with it so far. Darryl is less comfortable with the heat, but with his sporting new hairstyle he is doing better.

One of the nice things of Stuart highway is the roadhouses. We pull over at the Aileron Roadhouse, having done our first hundred and fifty kilometres for the day at just after 9:00 a.m. we are happy to get a coffee. While standing outside drinking the coffee a huge road train pulls into the stop. It stops right next to the road and I estimate it must be at least eighty metres long. Wow. We will now have to start passing these monsters. An old man comes walking from behind the truck. He must be close to eighty himself. Surely he's not driving that thing. He walks up to me and starts chatting about the bikes.

"They are the BMW GS1200s. Lovely machines." I reply to his question about the bikes.

"Whe ya rding fro? I am starting to get the hang of Aussie speak. All you really have to do to sound like an Aussie is to pinch your nose closed and then drop the last letter from the word. Then you are well on your way to sound like them.

"We are coming up from Melbourne. We rode along the coast to Adelaide and then now we are heading up to Darwin." I reply. "Where are you heading?"

"We a headin up to Kakadu paaa." He replies.

Kakadu National Park is right up north close to Darwin and we also plan to go through there on the way back from Darwin.

"Ah, that's great. We are also heading up that way. You driving that thing?" I ask pointing at the large truck. He had motioned towards the truck when he was saying that they are heading up north.

He looks back and then laughs. "Na mate. We aa driven aa UTE with a boat." He says. The truck had pulled in front of his UTE.

"Ah. So you going fishing there?" I ask.

"Naw mate. We goin crock huntin." Time slows down as he says this. I count down the seconds. Any moment now he is going to pull a large hunting knife from behind him and say, "That's not a knife, this is a knife."

No knife was produced and time sped up again. So these old timers are heading up to the north to go crock hunting. Pretty dam cool if you ask me. He wishes us well and limps to the shop. I wonder what the croc looks like that gave him that limp?

We get back on the road and I see the temperature has steadied out in the high twenties now. Maybe it will not become too hot today. The ride is great and we do get to pass a couple of these monster road trains. They are amazing. They steam ahead at hundred and thirty kilometres per hour and have no intention of slowing down or stopping for anyone or anything. There is a whole science on how to pass these babies. I worked this out the hard way, so you can now learn and one day when you are out there and see one of them, you know what to do.

Firstly let's look at the process for passing them from behind. I'll talk you through my experience of passing a three section trailer. First thing is to spot it on the road ahead. With the land being flat you can see them from quite a distance. At this point, you try to figure out if the truck is coming towards you or away from you. Of course at this distance it might just be an old-timer in a large camper van. If it is a camper van, you give them a wave on the way past and that's the end of it.

If it is a Road train, well now we need to figure out if it is coming or going. There is a different method to pass them depending on their direction. First off, we have a Road training heading in the same direction as I am. It is travelling at hundred and thirty kilometres per hour, so catching up to it takes time. While I am still a good five hundred metres behind it I can feel the turbulence in the air. It tucks and pushes at random at me, trying to get me unbalances. At this point I keep my speed to around hundred and forty so that I can catch up, but with every metre gained the impact of the road train increases. As I get to about hundred metres from it, the turbulence is getting really strong and it is tough to keep the bike under control. This is now the point where it is important for me to keep my shoulder loose, so that the turbulence that is pushing my body around is not affecting the steering or the bike. When I am fifty metres behind it I have reached the boundary line and I cannot get any closer to the truck safely. This is the point where I have to move out from behind it into the oncoming lane. This makes it over hundred and thirty meters of rumbling truck I have to pass, which is still travelling at hundred and thirty kilometres an hour. With the land being so flat and the road stretched out straight in front of us, I can easily see if something is coming from the front, in which case I just slide back into the turbulence and wait for it to pass. If there is nothing coming, it is time for the business end of this little transaction. I twist the throttle fully open which causes the bike to jump forward. It is a strong engine so the bike picks up speed very quickly and I am up to hundred and seventy within no time. By the time I am up to this speed, I am next to the truck. The noise is incredible next to these monsters. The whole game changes now that I have moved into the space next to the truck. Here next to the beast I now to adjust from the turbulence to being pushed over to the edge of the road. I have to lie in towards the truck to stay on the road. This changes rapidly when you get to the gaps between the trailers. These gaps try to suck you in. So, as I get to the edge of the trailer, I have to change to pulling away from the truck until I am next to the next trailer. Keeping the speed up and zigzagging past the trailers, I move past the truck pretty quickly and finally as I get to the last metre a final blast of turbulence pushes me to the side where the truck is breaking the air in front of it. Now I move back into my lane and bring the speed back down to hundred and fifty.

This sounds pretty hectic and trust me it is, but it holds nothing to meeting these babies from the front. Once I have identified it as one coming towards me, I immediately start going through my routine:

Ok, relax shoulders. Still have time. Just stay cool.

What's behind me? Ok, nothing. Not that there has been anything behind me for most of the day anyway.

What does the road look like ahead? Ok, same as it has looked all day. Long, straight and in pretty good condition.
Ok, now the truck is getting closer.

Relax the shoulders. Focus.

Move all the way to the very left hand edge of the road.

This all happens as part of the preparation and as it gets within a few metres from me, the action begins.

I push my right shoulder down, duck my head down and lay in towards the truck. The wave that hits me feels like those big waves that picks you up and crushes you on the sea bed and you wonder if you will ever get back to the top and then get swirled around head over heels all the way out to the beach. Yes, we have all been hit by one of those. Well, this truck is something like that. The bike is heavily loaded but is still thrown to the side like a toy.

This is the initial hit and even by laying into this it manages pushes me back to the edge of the road. Now as the rest of the rushing monster passes by me I need to sit back up and drag the bike back to the middle of the road. The noise is intense and then before you can say shooza kabooza it is gone. The last jerk is feeble and that signals the end of the experience. Until the next truck. The fun starts when these monsters starts gang banging you and you have to pass them in close proximity.

The impact of the truck is also stronger or weaker, depending on the wind direction. If the wind is coming from the left, the effect is negated somewhat and it is easier to get past these from the front. It does however complicates the passing them from behind. If the wind comes from the right the truck from the front is a coffin riding straight towards you. It is so cool to be doing all of this at hundred and fifty kilometres an hour miles and miles from anything or anyone. We are certainly getting our money's worth of riding experiences.

As we ride in Tennant Creek I am keeping my eyes open for a Dick Smiths or other electronics store. The high speed riding is increasing the wear and tear on the electronics. My cable that is hooked up to the headphones in my helmet have some technical difficulties causing the right hand side's speaker to have malfunctioned. The left is still ok, but with only one side working I can barely hear any music. I need to find a new cable that I can hook up to my I-pod.
I pull over and tell Darryl that I am looking for a tech store and he says he is also looking for one. His helmet's built in speakers has also stopped working. Man, we are really going through some gadgets!

Well, I tell you what. Let me give you some really useful advise, no extra charge. If you ever get to Tennant Creek, looking for some high tech gear, the best advice I can give you is to keep going. The only shop we can find with anything that is higher tech than what Columbus had on his boats is a store that has three very friendly, but very low tech ladies. Trying to explain to them the cable I am looking for is like trying to explain calculus to a chimpanzee. I show them the cable that has stopped working and now they are pretty sure that the cable they have is almost the same and might work. The only difference is that the cable they have is a RCA cable and they recon if I only plug one of the cables into the I-pod it should work. Before you ask, a RCA cable is that cable plugged in the back of your television with the red, white and yellow plugs and again before you ask, no it cannot work on an I-pod.

Darryl seems to have more luck and manages to get a set of earphones for $15. I will just have to listen to the single speaker or just stop listening to music for a while. I have tried it over the last few hundred kilometres and it was actually very nice to just listen to the road flying past, the sound of the tyres on the road and the engine running. Very nice indeed and not a bad second prize.

Now that we have kind of sorted out the technology, we need food. We ride through the town centre looking for somewhere to find food, but honestly I could not see any place that I would park my bike in front, never mind eat at. The places that seems to serve food also doubles as pubs and gabling places, so lot's of drunk, smelly people hanging around. I see a place on the left side of the street which has a sign that says they have fresh food. We pull over and can park under a big shed in front of the shop. A lady has a table setup with Tupperware that she is selling. She smiles at us and it is nice to see someone so friendly. How do people stay so positive in a place like this? If I stayed here I would have moved long ago or gone totally crazy. I walk into the food shop, but as I enter I know this will not work either. There is an "off" smell to the place and the lights are off except for the lights at the counter. Unfortunately it is the exact light I would have left off if it was my shop as the two lonely pies, with a greenish tinge to it are clearly visible.

I ask the guy if there is somewhere in town we can get some proper food, while giving his pies a frown.
The scary thing is he isn't even offended by the remark and directs me to the Red Rooster further along the highway just at the end of town. We can't miss it, it is at the petrol station as you exit the town.

That's great news. I back out of the place and we ride out to the Red Rooster which is exactly where he said it would be. For those who have not been to Australia, a Red Rooster is something like a KFC. The difference is KFC is the five star version of the two star version which is the Red Rooster. It is still the best food in town, so I am not complaining. I order a chicken burger and Darryl orders a ¼ Chicken. While eating he rips apart the headphones and build it into his helmet. He tests it out and only one side is working. I almost choke on my food as I laugh. We are really funny. We have been planning this for ages and have tested all this technology so many times and never had any issues. Here we are in the remote centre of Australia and one part after the next of our gadgets are failing. Still, that's what this trip is about. Just rolling with it.

After lunch we get back onto the highway and head further north. And finally get to Three-ways. If you get to Three-ways, there is absolutely nothing top the place. There is a road out to the east and a petrol station on the corner. There is nothing remarkable at all. It is special to us however. This is the point where we turn towards the east coast in a few days time on our way back from Darwin. When we pass the turn-off to head further north, it is the start of the second piece of road we will double back on for the trip.

The other reason why this is such a special place is how instrumental it has been during the planning stage of our trip. We have discussed this point so many times and it has been one of the key points of the trip. This is the point we have to decide if we will have enough time to get to Darwin and back and then have enough time to get to Cairns. It is one of the only two places where we have the opportunity to take a shorter route if we are running behind. Stopping there we don't even have to discuss the choice. We have made such good time we can easily get to Darwin and even have time to do the extra stretch through the Kakadu Park. So the big question we had pending on what we will do here is easily answered. We will go to Darwin.

We get Renner Springs Roadhouse and take stock of where we are. We have done six hundred and forty kilometres for the day now. That is about the same as the day we rode to Coober Pedy and is now officially a "long day" on the bikes. Yet, it is still early and we both feel that our bodies are ok to do a bit more. We look at the map and see that Elliott is only a hundred kilometres further. That should take us about forty minutes or so. Why not? We have nowhere else we need to be. With a smile I get back on the bike and we ride on. What a good call. The next stretch of road has this amazing perfume smell in the air. There are blossoms or flowers on some of the trees, so it must be that, but whatever it is the smell is intoxicating. The smell intensifies as we carry on and I am so glad we decided to keep going. My body is still doing well and I feel as if I can just keep riding. But like all good things, it must come to an end and before I know it we have to slow down when entering Elliott. Elliott is not what you would call the highlight of the Outback. It is a tiny place with maybe thirty or so houses. Officially there are three hundred and twenty people living in this town, but I'll be a legless frog if I saw six. There is a petrol station, but when we knock on the door we get no reaction. The place is closed. We ride through the four streets in the town and stop at the other petrol station.

Next to the petrol station is a gate leading to the only type of accommodation in the town. It is the camp ground and as we are about to find out the only place in town that offers any type of accommodation at all.

A princess with red head walked over and gave Darryl a look over. I was about to make a comment, but then he explains that the camp ground is closed for repairs and will be closed for the rest of the year. That must have been one hell of a party to cause enough damage to close a camp ground for a year.

"So, is there anywhere else to stay around here?" I ask.

"Yeah. Sure. There is a road house just down the road a bit." He replies half irritated by me interrupting him checking out Darryl.

"Oh, that's great. We didn't know there was a roadhouse close by. The only one we know of is the Dunmarra roadhouse." This roadhouse is another hundred kilometres further.

"Yeah, that's the one" he replies and runs his hand through his red curly hair.

"Right." Without another word we are ready to move right along.

We ride a bit down the road and then stop and decide that there is nothing to it, we will just have to ride on the Dunmarra. So, with that decided we ride out the shitty little town and push on. Somehow the fact that we have done so many kilometres today has not taken its toll on me. I am feeling fresh and good and keen to just keep going. The beautiful vanilla perfume is still in the air and the late afternoon is stunning. The road is not too challenging and I am really enjoying riding without music for a bit. The sound of the tyres on the tar is hypnotic and really soothing. What a stunning day's riding. This is exactly what I had hoped it would feel like being out here.

Then suddenly there are thousands of dragonflies all over the place. I feel them hitting me all over my body and soon my visor is covered with dead dragon flies. The smell of grass fills my helmet. It seems like the juice from the dragonflies smells like freshly cut grass. It is like the essential oils, this being a concentrate of the smell of mowed grass. I think about what I would brand it as and then I feel one hitting me right on the unprotected Adam's apple. I go into a rough coughing fit and finally after what seems like forever I can breathe normally again, although swallowing hurts.

A few minutes later we seemed to have passed from out of the swarm of dragonflies. Then I get this sharp smell of grass in my helmet again. The smell is so strong I can almost taste it. Wait a second, I can actually taste it. It seems like the juice of the dragonfly that hit me on the throat has slowly seeped through my beard and finally got up to my mouth. What a bizarre taste. I think with a little bit of garlic butter and fresh coriander it would actually taste not too bad. Well, much better than some other food on this trip!

As we get within ten kilometres from Dunmarra, I mentally calculate that when we get there, it will be only a hundred and sixty kilometres short of a thousand. Should we perhaps push on and get to that milestone? When will we have the opportunity to get to a thousand in one day again? With that though still in my mind we pull over at the roadhouse and the first thing that comes out of my mouth is:

"Dude, it's only another hundred and sixty to go to get to a thousand." We look at each other for a few seconds taking stock of our bodies and how much more we think we can do today without it being too risky. Fatigue is what I was worried about at first, but when I looked at the time my next worry was that we would be approaching sunset and I am not keen on meeting those large animals that get killed every night by the large truck I am not too keen on meeting either. So, after considering it briefly common sense prevailed and we get off the bikes and let it rest on the foot pegs. We had covered eight hundred and forty eight kilometres for the day and that is plenty enough. Well worth a beer I believe. We had been on the road since 6:45 am and it is now 4:30 p.m.

The manager says they don't have single rooms, so we will have to either book a double room each, or we can share a double room. With the high prices for accommodation we decide that we will share a room tonight. Walking out I can still smell the perfume in the air and I stretch out. What a lovely afternoon. It is quite amazing how good I feel after such a long day. I get back on the bike, with the helmet over the mirror and ride the bike to the room. As I stop in front of the room I realize there is a very thick layer of very loose gravel right underneath me. The bike slips and I just manage to get my foot out in time to stop it from falling. The angle is precarious, borderline between high enough to be pulled upright again and to low and the weight is going to pull it down anyway. I push as hard as I can to push the bike upright again and as I feel my foot slip in the loose gravel, I have just managed to get enough done to stay upright. I quickly get my grip again and push the bike all the way up. Wow, that was close. I get off and let the bike rest on its kick stand, but this just sinks into the gravel and again I have to fight to keep the bike up. Eventually I have it upright again, this time standing next to it. I push it forward, but with the loose gravel I am not making any progress. I start the bike up and kick it into gear and then walk it forward. That is much better. As soon as I am out of the loose gravel I stop again and let the bike rest. Well, now I am bushed. All the good energy I had left less than five minutes ago is now used up.

I unload the bike and all that is keeping me going right now is the thought that as soon as I have the bike unloaded I can go jump in the pool and then go for a beer. I go through the daily routine of unpacking. First the Camelbak I have strapped that on top of the stuff on the back seat. I have found that if I have the Camelbak on my back, I am not sitting that comfortable as it is in the way, plus the weight of the water in it starts being a pain after days and days with the extra three kilograms on your shoulders. Once that is off, I can unhook the bungee cords that hold the petrol cans in place, which is standing on top of the side panniers. This then gets carried inside. Next I can unhook the cords holding the inflatable mattress and tent in place. Then carry these items in. Then back outside and now unhook the cords holding the sleeping bag and travel bag in place. I can now also get to the ground cover so these items are now carried in. Next I can unlock the two side panniers and carry them in and finally I can get my top box off and bring that to the room.

After all of that I am really exhausted, but get my shorts out and on and head out to the pool. I now understand how people say camels and horses can smell water in the desert. I can smell the pool's water and feel my nose flair.
Walking up to the gate I am stopped in my tracks. There is a sign on the gate saying the pool is closed. AAAAAAAAHHHH! I can see the sparkling blue water on the other side of the fence. This is so cruel. I need to get into the water.
It is now time for me to make one of those decisions that can change your life. In the heat of the moment I think,"Fuck that, it's easier to ask for forgiveness than it is to ask for permission. I feel sorrier about that which I did not do than that which I did!" Cornier saying comes to mind, but a soft voice deep at the back of my mind whispers a warning.

"Deon, you are very far away from the closes hospital." Says the little voice of reason.

I start getting the shakes and know I will need to make the decision quickly, or my head will explode.

"SHIT!" I growl and walk to the reception. Outside is one of the trees I have smelt the whole day. Wow, what a stunning aroma. It is somewhere between vanilla and perfume. If I could bottle that, I can retire.

"Heya mate. What's with the sign at the pool? Is it OK if I take a swim?" I ask the owner behind the counter.

"Sorry mate, the acid levels are all out. We have had a lot of rain lately and I had to pour a lot of acid into the pool."

Bloody hell. That would have been terrible. I could have been burnt to a crisp. Thank goodness for the small voice! I am so happy about the small voice I offer to buy it a beer.

So, instead of going swimming I sit down and have a couple of 'skins' of XXXX Gold. While sipping on my second beer I catch up on my writing. We have no mobile reception here, but there is an internet kiosk. I go over and slot in the $2 it requires to be activated. $2 buys me half an hour worth of Internet time. Wow, that's not bad and it is pretty quick as well. The technology is not half bad considering how remote this place is. I email Elizna and while I have the extra time I update my Facebook and email all the rest of the people who said they were interested in following our progress.

I also do the scary part of internet surfing. No I did not go into dodgy websites, or click on advertising material claiming I can increase the size of my willy. I went into my bank account to see how I am doing. I am pleasantly surprised with what I see. I still have more than I thought I would have after the expensive accommodation we have had so far. I transfer money between my accounts and once that is done I THEN go and see how I can increase the size of my willy. Well, actually I went to order another 'Skin' and pulled out my Stephen King book. I am just about finish with it, so will need to get a new book once we get to Darwin.

After about an hour of me sitting there sucking back beer and reading, Darryl pitches up. He has had a snooze, making the most of being on holiday. He is bitching and complaining about fleas in the bed though. Ha. I hope he has sweeter blood than I do. I am starving and order the lamb chops with lots of veggies. I order carrots, potatoes, pumpkin and peas to accompany the dead lamb in my plate.

Darryl mentions that he also had to chase mozzies in the room. Well, I am so tired I think they will be able to drink me dry tonight and I will not even flinch. I order another skin, to make sure that if the mozzie and fleas goes for me, they will get pissed as well. Have to make it worth their while!

After dinner we walk out and have a last smoke. Standing outside with the sun setting, the air smelling like perfume and a full tummy, I can only be content. What a privilege to be able to experience something like this!

I stagger back to the room and have a quick shower. Then I check the bed for fleas, but am to drunk, tired or just blind to see any and fall over in bed. I think I might have been asleep before I hit the bed though.

This was not the end of this long day though. Sometime in the night I wake up to Darryl's snoring. I tell him to turn around, but no joy. Well, that can't work every time I guess. What it does do is getting me wide awake. To pass the time I try to copy his snoring. First attempt it way to highly pitched. I try again. After a few minutes I have it pretty much spot on. Then it starts getting old and I remember my earplugs. It is in my bike pants, so I find them and pop them in. This brings the snoring down to a low rumble, which is ok. I slowly slip back into a deep sleep from which I only wake up again in the morning.

Day 10
Sunday 17 April 2011
From: Dunmarra
To: Darwin
Distance travelled: 631 kilometres

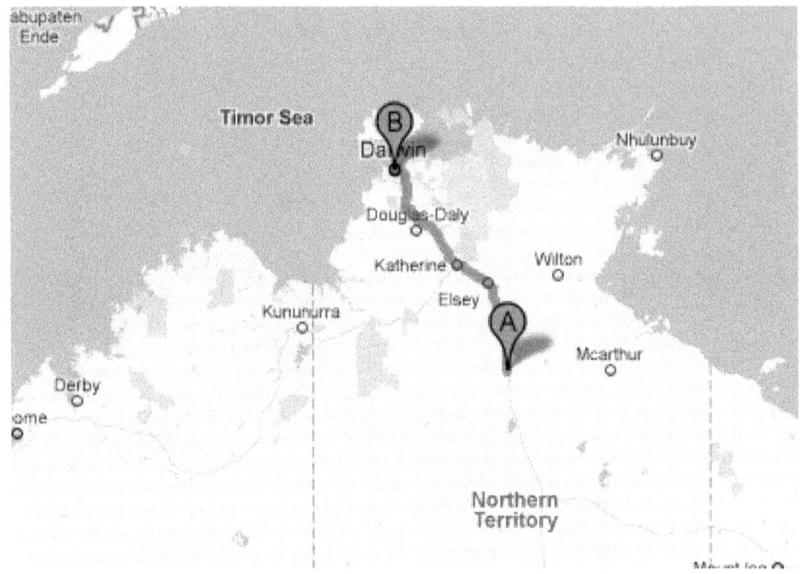

As is the norm for the mornings, I wake up from Darryl's movement. He is up and gets in the shower. One of the benefits of being so tired at night is that we go to bed really early, so we can get up pretty early in the mornings and still be well rested. I get up and make coffee. Darryl complains about the mozzies keeping him awake, but the only thing that kept me awake was Darryl's snoring.

"Well dude, you have a pretty good snore yourself!" he says when I mention it. I am well aware of the fact that I snore, especially if I have a few drinks and smoke. So, I know that I must be waking him up as well. And he is actually doing me a favour in sharing accommodation. It is my budget that is tight and he is just sharing with me to help me out. Good man. I make him a cup of coffee and even give it to him at 5% discount. Ok, that's just a joke. I don't give discount.

We have enough fuel to get up through to the Highway Inn Roadhouse, so we get onto the highway and ride on northwards. We have just over six hundred kilometres to do today to get to Darwin. I am so excited I can barely hold myself in. When we get off the bikes this afternoon, we would have travelled from the most Southern part of the mainland Australia, to the very north. I know there is still landmass further north than Darwin, but this is as far north you can get on sealed roads, so for all practical purposes we have reached the end of the road. We would have done the whole north to south. That is just so cool. Riding out this early in the morning is stunning with the sun just cresting and the chilly air waking me up properly. I still keep my I-pod off as the sound of the road is just so magical. I hum away in my helmet and soon we get to the roadhouse. We pull over to get fuel and also to get our second cup of coffee. They only have instant coffee and I force myself to sip a few drops of it before I chuck it. Yuk!

We walk to the back of the station where there is a Harley rider standing talking to a man with a nose that must have been broken fifty times. I swear to you I have never seen anything like it. It is as if the rest of his face just turned on his nose and beat the living day lights out of it. It is difficult to look at him without looking at his nose. I turn so that I cannot look directly at him and now I am looking directly at the Harley rider.

"Ye lads be well off if ye keep a keen eye on the road up north. The rain has ripped the road apart up the road a bit." he warns us.

Later today we will see what he meant with the road being ripped to pieces, but for now we say ok, then say goodbye and ride on. Riding out I make sure I take the lead. Up front is a place I want to stop. It will mean a slight detour, but this is one of those detours I need to do and will be well worth it. I have a very good reason for it, so just bare with me. A few miles down the road is the turnoff I have been waiting for. I signal to turn off and Darryl pulls up and asks where we are going.

"I gotta go check something out here. Just follow me." He nods and we turn off left off the highway and ride down the few kilometres to Daly Waters.

"Where?" you might ask. "Daily waters?"

"No. Not Daily waters. Daly Waters." I would reply if you were to ask.

Let me explain, as we pull over next to the landmark I am so keen to see. As I mentioned a few chapters ago, there were some people who inspired this trip. There is our Kiwi friend Twisting Throttle and then there are the two fellows Ewan and Charlie. After the trip these two did around the world, they did the trip down Africa. After this trip, Ewan went back to work on movies and Charlie had gotten very, very sick. Not with some kind of obscure virus he picked up in the middle of Africa. Not with some illness that will make him suffer and die, but he was bitten by the bug. The bug to keep travelling. Soon after he was back home from the Africa trip he did a trip from the UK to Sydney and produced the movie and book called "By any means". This is one of the books I am busy reading and it is lying next to my bed back home. The photo on the front cover is Charlie sitting right in front of the Servo station of Daly Waters. And here I am. Standing in the tracks of a great traveller. I get my camera out and ask Darryl to take a photo of me standing at this iconic site.

With the photo taken and my need to get to this place satisfied, we get back on the bikes and head back to the highway. Now Darryl takes the lead, I guess he didn't want me to start pulling over for photos of every book I have read. Suddenly he is waving wildly and pointing to something off to the left of the road. As I pass where he was I look, but can see nothing. Later on he will tell me this is where he saw the dingo. This is monumental, as the only wildlife we have seen were the two camels just before we got to Uluru. Dammit and here I go and miss one third of all the wild life. Well, if we exclude the half a billion flies we saw that is.

I am rudely brought back to the moment as the road just disappears in front of me. For a moment I think I must have dosed off as there just isn't any road in front of me, but there are still the road markers on the side of the road though. I decelerate fast to try get down on my speed before I hit the gravel and rocks. I manage the get the bike down from hundred and fifty kilometres per hour to about 80 when I ride off the end of the road onto what I will call the road to hell. Queue up Chris Rea.

Basically the road had been destroyed by the rain and then they started working on the road by ripping it to pieces. The next step would be to scrape all the loose gravel, rocks and ground off and then tar the road again. Not that that would do us much good as that is months away from now. I force myself to focus on keeping the bike up right while slowly decelerating down to about fifty. I feel the bike slip and accelerate again. This carries on for the next fifty metres and finally I am back on the tar. My heart is beating in my throat and I can feel the adrenaline pump through my body. Wow. From here of on the potholes starts popping up more and more and some places it is pretty cool to be on a bike rather than a car. All you have to do is weave through the holes and keep to the pieces of the road that is still intact. This gets easier as we ride on and soon I do not even slow down for the potholes, but just swerve through them in tight s-curves at hundred and fifty kilometres per hour.

While focusing on the road, time flies by and so does the road and when I look up to see why Darryl has now slowed down, I see we have arrived in Katherine. This is where we would have stayed over tonight if we did not do such a big day yesterday. We will ride through here today and then sleep here on the way back from Darwin. Now it is still pretty early and breakfast is the order of the day. I am starving and almost ready to eat road kill if we cannot find something better in town. Katherine is a bit bigger than some of the towns we have been through over the last few days. We pull over at a petrol station and luckily they also do breakfasts. I order beacon, eggs, toast and a coffee. Darryl seems to be less hungry as he just orders a pie and a milkshake. Well, to each his own.

I go outside and call Elizna while the breakfast is being cooked. We have a chat while Darryl seems to have made some new friends in the outside area of the restaurant. When I see my breakfast coming out I am quick to end my call as one of Darryl's friends have a dog with him and this mutt is looking at my beacon as if he is going to have some pork this morning. When I get out there I see why the dog is so excited. Around these parts when you order beacon, what you are actually saying is, "kill a pig, slaughter it, slice the whole thing up and put it on my plate". Wow, that is really a lot of beacon.

And so begins the charm. Move closer a little bit and give the old puppy eyes. Not too long, just a moment and tilt the head to the left. Smile and then look away and give a big sigh. Now wait a few seconds, then lie down, making sure this bring us just that little bit closer to each other. Then look up, making sure to make eye contact and again flash those pretty puppy eyes. Now time is of the essence, as the dumbass boss has started talking.

While the dog is going through the tricks of the trade to make sure he gets some beacon and doing a dam fine job as well, his boss is about to start working against him.

"Jip, he is such a good dog. Aint ye boy?" he says when Darryl pats the dog on the head.

"Jip, he really hates those bloody Abos. He'll chase them fuckers everywhere, won't ye boy?"
Darryl stops patting the dog half way through a stroke and stand up. That is the quickest way to get him pissed off. He gets up and leaves and during all of this I can see how desperate the dog has now become. Am I going to take offence and not give him some of the beacon? Well, I decided that I will not give his boss any beacon, as he is a racist asshole, but I am sure the dog is not really a racist. I eat my fill and then throw him the last two kilograms of beacon.

He chomps away at it happily while his boss keeps trying his best to make the dog sound like the racist.

As soon as I have thrown the last piece of beacon to the dog I get up and also walk off. When I get to the bike Darryl is still muttering rude stuff about the racist remarks. We get on the bikes and cruise down the main road of the town, but as it is Sunday I have no luck in finding an electronic store where I can get a cable for my I-pod. Not that I was looking too hard. As I have mentioned, the sound of the road is doing it for me at the moment so I am happy without the music for now. I can see that I will need the sound fixed again at some stage, but right now I am fine.

I must say, yesterday's hard riding is catching up to me now. My ass is totally used up and finding a comfortable sitting position is tough. It is amazing how creative you can get with how you sit on such a small seat. I start to divide my ass into zones. If I lie forward onto the tank I am sitting on Zone One. Zone One is the top part of my legs and the start of my bum. The problem with this is that I need to put some weight onto my legs, so it is not a very comfortable position. Then from this position, I will move all the way to Zone Four. Zone Four is the very top of my bum, almost part of my back. This position is quite comfortable for a short while, as I then sit as if I am in a Lazyboy leaning against the gear strapped onto the backseat. It gets tough on my lower back after a while though, so the next switch is to Zone Two. Zone Two is the area between where Zone One ends at the start of my bum and the middle of my bum. And then of course I would finally switch over to Zone Three. Which is the remaining piece of my ass. Then, every time we have to slow down for a town or road works, I would stand up on the pegs. When we started off, I would only stand up if I am on less than sixty kilometres per hour but with me getting so used to the bike and spending so much time on the bike, I am now able to stand up at hundred kilometres per hour without any issues. This helps giving my ass a rest and gets the blood flowing again.

It is still a good three hundred kilometres before we get to Darwin, so shifting around on the bike, I lean into it and get into some hard riding. This is where the men are recognised and the wussies go home. We are now doing serious riding. There are a lot of big Road trains around here and it is now pretty tricky to get past them. The road quality has become progressively worse as we head further north, as this is where the heavy rains had damaged the roads the most. Now it is a case of dodging the potholes and pieces of the road that has disintegrated completely, while also keeping out of the way of the large trucks.

While doing this I also notice how the plant life has changed over the last hour or two. The trees now all have large leaves and I can even see a few palm trees popping up every now and then. The heat is also increased, now reaching thirty five degrees Celsius and the humidity is way up. For the first time on the trip I am really starting to feel the heat as a problem. I am cooking in my helmet. I pull over at the next rest area and get my water bladder from my side pannier. I run water over my head, which is amazing. It cools me down well, even though the water itself is not cold. I run water over my shirt as well and now I will cool down well.

We get back onto the road and push on to Darwin. When we get to Plimerton we have to slow down to hundred kilometres per hour. Wow, amazing how slow that feels now. It is still a good fifty kilometres to Darwin, so the rest of the ride today will be slow. I sit back against the gear on the back seat and lift my legs up onto the petrol tank. It feels so slow I am almost tempted to try steering with my feet, but just sitting back like this is moving my ass to a new zone, so I am feeling much better. This is not a recommended position to use for riding by the way. It is only because I have been on the saddle for such a long time now that this seems like a good idea.

We drive past an area where cars are parked next to the road by people trying to sell them. I keep one eye on the road ahead and one eye out to the side of the road to make sure some dumbass doesn't just turn onto the road in front of me. Unfortunately the dumbass manages to get onto the road behind me and the next moment races past me. It is some kind of Ford that has been through the whole nine yards of being punked up. It roars past me at probably two hundred kilometres per hour, cutting in real close to me. I almost fall over, having my feet up on the petrol tank does little for balance. I also almost soil myself and I scream a bunch of obscenities at the dumbass. If there is any justice in the world there will be a speed trap up ahead and he will be caught.

We finally come over the last hill and wind our way into Darwin. The city riding is a bit of an adjustment after being out in the sticks so long. I keep checking my mirrors and all around me. It feels as if someone is going to cut me off any moment.

Riding into Darwin is stunning. As we enter Darwin, we ride past a marina where lots of fishing boats are moored. It is hot and humid and the sun is shining. It is a small city and as far as we go I just fall more and more in love with the place.
We ride to the centre of the city and look for the Information kiosk. We ride a while before we find it, but once there they are again very friendly and give us a few options on where we can stay. We choose one of the backpackers, at last one of the backpackers for which Darryl has a membership. It is still pretty expensive, but we decide we can now book separate rooms and once we have

rooms booked, we ride to the back of the hostel. Again I go through my normal routine of unpacking the bike, only this time I have to carry everything up two sets of stairs. By the time I have everything up there I am sweating like a pig and immediately get my shorts on a head down to the pool. Darryl is already down there and the swim is one of the best I have had in my life. After the swim Darryl heads up to his room for his traditional snooze and I head to the pub to grab a beer. I get a beer and go sit in the sun next to the pool. I manage to use this time to catch up on my writing and checking out the girls next to the pool. Sitting there in the sticky heat I have a real holiday feeling about me. I sit for a while then jump into the pool and then back to sipping my beer. What a tough life.

While sitting there writing a young Asian couple come and sit at the same table I am at. With them, they have a pot with a couple of bowls and when they dish up it is a fowl smelling noodle stew of some kind. Then he starts eating it and I swear he slurped so loud I could feel my appendix shrivelling. For the next ten minutes he would slurp away until I decide that this is enough, grab a cigarette and light it. He gives me a dirty look and slurps another mouth full of the sludge. This battle becomes the whole of our universe for the next ten minutes. Clearly one of us will have to crack first. I know it is rude to light a cigarette if someone is eating, but bloody hell I was sitting here quietly not disturbing anyone and he came and upset the peace.
His girlfriend gives up and says something that if I could understand it I would have been offended. I am however not too concerned about her, it is all about him and his noodles and me and my filthy smoke.

Eventually I win, not by him giving up, but by him slurping up the last of the noodles. He had eaten the whole pot. That must have been at least six bowls full of noodles. He flinches when he moves and I can see he had kept eating just to not be the one to give up. He is squinting at me, but to be fair, even if he was just looking at me normally I would be thinking he is squinting at me. I feel the pain in my lungs as I deeply suck on the fourth cigarette being chain smoked. Even though the slurping is done and the smoking just about, neither of us can stop now. We have invested too much into this. Then he settles it by giving a loud and very smelly burp and stand up as if he hadn't just eaten half a ton of food. He turns away and jumps in the pool leaving the pot and the bowls on the table. I am tempted to ash in his bowl, but I have already lost and should now just move along and put this behind me.

I put the cigarette out and feel slightly light headed of all the smoking in such a short time. I open my book and read a few sentences and then from the corner of my eye I can see him getting out of the pool. He stands there, built like Bruce Lee and then barks something loudly and within seconds his woman

comes out of the kitchen with a couple of bowls of ice cream. As she approaches he looks back at me and smiles. I open the packed of cigarettes and take another one out. I don't want to smoke it anymore than he wants to eat the ice cream I am sure, but the situation has just escalated. I sit there with the cigarette in my hand and the lighter in the other and his girlfriend stops. She looks at the cigarette and says something to him. His smile wavers and we break eye contact as he talks to her. He is pretty keen to come and sit here and slurp away his ice cream, but I think he has just been out ranked. He looks at me again, then at her and then walks to the table and takes the pot and the bowls and walks off without another word or a look. Man, this is one tough son of a bitch. Thank goodness he didn't call my bluff. If he could see just how badly my hands were shaking I would have been in trouble.
Thankfully I put the cigarette away and give a cough. I get back into my book and then Darryl comes to join me. We grab an extra couple of beers and sit and talk nonsense for the rest of the afternoon next to the pool.

When it starts getting dark   I go and put some other clothes on and we head out to the city centre to get some food. A Thai restaurant was recommended to Darryl by someone and we are pretty keen to go and find the place. It will be nice to get some really good food. On the way down the main street we pass a number of small groups of aboriginals sitting on the sidewalk knocking sticks together. They all have sores on their faces and very spaced out look in their eyes. They are begging for money by knocking the sticks together and when you get close to them they would point the sticks to you then to the bowl in front of them. It is pretty sad to see how bad their condition is.

We finally find the Thai place and go sit down. The waiter comes over immediately and fills up our water glasses. We order some drinks and then the wait starts. Finally the waiter comes around again and fills up our water glasses. I am pretty thirsty so do not mind the water, but after the third time he comes to fill up our water glasses, I ask about our beers. He goes away and comes back with our drinks and when he wants to fill Darryl's water glass again he has had enough.

"That's enough water now." He says and gives the guy a look.

Finally our food arrives and it is pretty good. The meat is tough, but the sauce is magnificent. There are also a lot of very hot whole chillies in my dish. I love chillies and I must have looked like a horse in a corn field the way I worked my way through the chillies. I am burning from the tip of my lips, my whole tongue, my throat all the way through to my tummy. Yum!

When the food is done I am also pretty tired. We pay and walk around to have a bit of a look at the nightlife in Darwin on a Sunday evening. I am sure you have ever seen those TV programs which play off in Miami where the scantily dressed people sit around in the middle of the night in the warm air and partying. It is that exact scene. This is the coolest city I have seen in Australia. I am crazy about the place, but I am also very tired. We head back to the hostel and when I get to my room I get a nasty surprise. Somewhere I have picked up thousands of miniature spiders. My bike pants seem to be the source of the spiders. They are everywhere though. My pants had been lying on my bed, so my whole bed seems to be vibrating as the tiny creatures run all over the bed. I pick up my pants and to try get rid of the spiders I give it a good shake. As I do it I realise it is not a good idea. Now I am covered in the tiny spiders as well and they are not only over my bed, but also all over the rest of my clothes and kit in the rest of the room.

I go for a swim as it is still twenty six degrees outside and very mucky and also to get rid of the spiders crawling all over me. Back in the room I try to get as many of the off the bed as I can and then just pass out on the bed. I know I am supposed to be careful with stuff like spiders in Australia. What if these little fuckers climb into my ears and lay eggs or into my nose and get to my brain? The other worrying thing is that if there are that many babies, where is mummy? With these thoughts in my mind I fall asleep.

Day 11
Monday 18 April 2011
From: Darwin
To: Katherine
Distance travelled: 548 kilometres

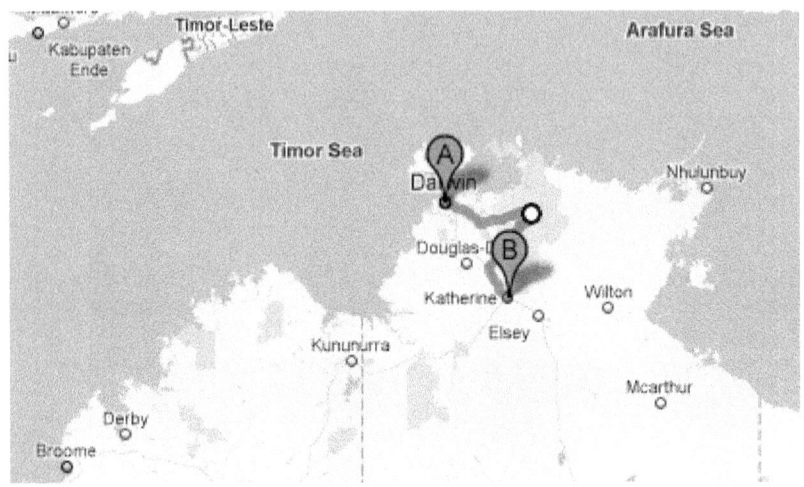

With this being the last day we will have in a city again for a while we have decided to make the most of it. It is also Monday morning, so we will be able to find shops to replace the gear and gadgets that has stopped working. This morning is the first time we have decided to sleep in a bit as shops will only open up at 9:00, so there is no rush. That being said, the thoughts while falling asleep last night is the first conscious thought this morning. It is just after 7:00 a.m. and I cannot sleep any further. I have to do something about the spiders. I get up and switch the light on.

The naive hope that the spiders had moved out through the night is dashed as I can see there are still hundreds of them all over the place, including me. I brush as many as I can see off myself and shake my shorts and t-shirt out. I dress and go outside. It is already hot and the humidity has not come down from yesterday. It is a stunning day out here and I feel sorry for the people who have to go to work today. What a nice day to be off.

I walk down the road past the restaurant where we had dinner last night until I get to the supermarket. It is in the shopping centre where the electronics shop is we want to come to later this morning, but I need to get bug spray now to sort these spiders out. Luckily the grocery store is already open, so I get a can of bug spray and walk back to the hostel.

Once back I spray the whole can out into the room and into and over all my stuff. I hold my breath as long as I can while spraying and then when my lungs are burning I head outside and shut the door.

"Eat that suckers!" I mutter as I go down stairs to the pool. I jump in and have a swim. While floating around in the pool the Asian couple of yesterday walks out of the kitchen with their pot and bowls. Our eyes connect and I burst out laughing. He does not even break a smile. I decide to just let that go and get back to my room. This guy will not break and I am now willing to let him be the winner. Darryl is also up and on the go now and is busy packing his bike. I put the aircon on full blast and leave the door open while I quickly dress and get ready to go. I can see the spiders all over the floor, but none alive, so now shake out all my clothes and then get all my stuff packed as well. We are now ready to go so ride down the road to the shopping centre and head inside. It is still half an hour before the shops open so we have to hang around the centre for a while. We sit down to drink a coffee and have some breakfast and Darryl finally gets the poached eggs he has been looking for through the whole ride through the Outback.

After breakfast we go back to the Dick Smiths and wait in front of the door for them to open. Ten minutes to go and I realise I have a serious problem.

Generally I have a pretty good sense of humour and don't really think the Eddie Murphy farts and toilet humour is funny, but I had to laugh at myself. I only laughed afterwards, but it was funny.

As we sit there I feel my tummy grumble. Just one rumble and then it's quite again.

People talk about bullets being fast, light which is even faster. But I tell you what. If you eat a plate of super hot chillies tonight, some time tomorrow you are going to be fine one second and faster than the speed of light your situation will be quite desperate. In less time it took me to register that my tummy had rumbled I went from nice and relaxed to sweating and in danger of shitting myself in front of the Dick Smiths closed doors.

Only by using the example of my Asian friend's inner strength do I get some type of control over my bowels and I work my way down to the other side of the mall where the toilets are. I see the gate where the toilet entrance is and when I get there, just in time, I realise it is locked. I need to stand still for a moment to just try get back in control again. By now sweat is pouring down my face and back and I am in serious pain. The pain is so intense I actually start

seeing flashes of coloured bubbles popping in front of my eyes. I shuffle back to the desk where the security guard is sitting and groaningly ask him if he can open the toilets for me.
He looks at me and quite rudely says I have to wait till 9:00 a.m. The toilets are locked till then. For a moment I think I am not going to be able to hold it in and as this man is so rude, maybe I should just let it go right on his desk.

I hold myself together and shuffle to the side, standing next to the jewellery store, half way between the mall doors and the supermarket, or in my case half way between hell and an even more painful hell. For a few seconds the cramps flair up and I groan, then they settle down and I have to stop my body from trying to get rid of the problem causing me so much pain. All through this I am sweating terribly and to be honest my t-shirt can do with a wash, my bike pants are really dirty and if you wear a helmet your hair doesn't look too kept.

I only realised just how bad I must look when a mother and her small boy walk past me. He looks up at me and when she sees him looking at me she pulled him away. This is still processing through the fog of pain when a beggar walks past me, smiles and greets me. Now I realise just how bad I must look standing there.

I see a man walk up to the toilets and think, shame he is also going to have to wait, but instead of turning back he goes in. How had that happened? While I was looking at the beggar walking past, the gates must have opened. I shuffle towards the toilet and growl at the grumpy guard as I pass him and then make my way into the toilets. There are a couple other people in there, but I rush into the toilet and blessed relief.

When I walk out, there is no one left in the toilets, I do apologise, but it was an emergency.

I do feel like a new man now and can function normally. I walk back to Dick Smiths and Darryl is already talking to the people there to have his GPS looked at and also he has managed to find better earphones. I find the cable I need and then we sit outside while drinking a coffee he breaks the earphones apart and then build them into his helmet.

Once this is done we are ready to leave Darwin. I feel sorry that we have to leave so quickly, I really liked the place. It is such a beautiful city and for anyone who wants to see the best of Australia, I would highly recommend coming here. Well done Darwin. I am a fan. I should go and see if I can become a Facebook friend of Darwin!

It is stifling hot and I follow Darryl's example and ride without my jacket and gloves on. It feels strange as I always ride with my jacket on. It is just one of the safety things with me. I guess it is because I have been through a couple of accidents I just feel so much more comfortable with the jacket on. The jacket is so well made with the vents that I am actually feeling warmer without the jacket on and the sun baking on my skin. Just before we turn off Stuart highway to head into the Kakadu National Park, I pull over at the petrol station, fill up the bike and put my jacket back on. It feels much better even though the temperature has already reached thirty two and it is only 10:00 a.m. Today we will be cooked alive! I pour water all over my head. If I am to be cooked alive, I would prefer being steamed rather than baked. I believe it is healthier.....

As we leave Palmerston we turn off the Stuart highway onto the Arnhem highway and it's a short ride until we just have to pull over. It is marchlands all around us and the only way I can describe it is the purest green for the bottom half of your vision where the green grass stands in the pitch black water, with deep blue sky filling the rest of your vision. The colour is so absolute that it looks fake. It is mind bending and I have to blink my eyes a few times to get used to the stunning scene. I feel a slight case of vertigo as the landscape is so precise. A car slows down to see if we are ok and when I point to the scene to the side of the road the man just nods and smiles and drives on. He must have seen this many times, but could still appreciate that we just had to stop and take it in.

Darryl takes a bunch of photos and then we ride on. The marchlands pans out to stretch to the end of my vision and now the big sky effect is also added into the scene and it feel like I want to cry it is so beautiful. I have Enigma playing in my helmet singing one of the stunning songs. Wow, what an amazing experience. It feels like I am on drugs, it is so bizarre. I would not have been surprised to see Alice and the Mad Hatter sitting down for a cup of the in the middle of the road.

We keep pushing on and slowly the scenery starts to change and soon the marchlands are left behind and now woodlands have moved in all around us. I am amazed at the absolute change as the trees are now almost on the road and then it happens. After just over 4300 kilometres of riding through Victoria, South Australia and a fair chunk of the Northern Territories without seeing any roo's I see a Wallaby standing next to the road. A Wallaby looks like a miniature roo, but technically it isn't one, so I still have not seen a roo.

The little bugger is just sitting there next to the road on the grass line. I am actually amazed that I saw it, it blends so well into the colour of the dry grass, which is also the same height as the Wallaby.

I pull over and wait for Darryl to catch up. I open the face of the helmet and call out to him,

"Did you see the wallaby?"

"Did I see the want-to-be what? He calls back over the noise of the bike engines. Talking while the bikes are running and we have helmets on is not always the easiest thing to do.

"NO, NO. DID YOU SEE THE WALLABY? SITTING NEXT TO THE ROAD!" and then I do that thing people do when they ask for the time and point at their wrists. I bring my hands up to my chest striking a T-Rex pose and then do a hopping motion. I have to laugh at myself, but at least Darryl gets the message.

"What, no. Where?" He asks and looks back. The thing is pretty small and a bit behind us, so we can't see it from here, so we decide to ride further. We keep going deeper into the national park and finally get to a roadhouse. Here we stop to fuel up again and then a Harley rider pulls up.

He parks off to the side and walks over to us. He is coming from the front, were we are heading so we have a chat about the road conditions. He reckons the road is ok, just a few patches where you have to swerve to get around the potholes. It is due to all the rain, we hear once again.

"You guys are lucky, last week this time is was pouring with rain." He says.

"Ye, it is just very hot!" Darryl says back.

"Well, it has cooled down quite a bit. It's actually pretty cool at the moment." He says and I kid you not, when he unzips his think leather jacket I can see he is wearing a think jersey underneath. Amazing how the body acclimatise. Here is this man wearing extra layers while we are cooking hot in as few layers as possible.

We say our goodbyes and then head further along the road to Jubilu. We come around a curve and now there is something new I haven't seen at all on the trip so far. The bush is black from fire damage. Large sections of the veldt are completely scorched and when we go over a small bump in the road I can see the flame licking up a tree on the left. I have a moment where I consider grabbing my water bladder and trying to dose out the flames, which does not seem big from here. However, as I am on leave and only a superhero during normal business hours, we just ride on past. Honestly the fire was quite a bit bigger than just a small flame crawling up a tree. Thick smoke from deep in the forest tells a story that warns to not being foolish.

An interesting thing greets us on the next bridge ahead. There are a number of people standing fishing from the bridges. How bizarre. I am used to national parks not allowing people to hunt or fish in the parks. That begs the question, are they fishing here because they are allowed to or are they fishing here because it is so remote that it is pretty unlikely for someone to stop them. That reminds me, this is where the old timers told us they were coming for fishing and croc hunting. So I guess that you are probably allowed to fish here.

Still, standing in the thick heat, on a bridge with a tar road over and cars driving past.... I am sure there are better ways to go fishing. With that thought in my mind we are over the bridge and the next few bridges we ride over also have people fishing from it. It seems to be the thing to do around here. At the next bridge we decide to stop. There is no one here, so it is probably not a good fishing spot from this bridge, but there is a sign warning that there are crocodiles in the water and not to leave the road.

Darryl walks back onto the bridge and I take my video camera out to take some footage of the swamp. As I sweep the recorded across the landscape I see movement in the water only a few meters into the swamp. Surely it is just my over active imagination? Then the croc surfaces and it is a big one. It is less than ten meters away from me, completely side on and drifting closer to the side. I think it is trying to sneak up on me. Suddenly, without any type of warning, Steve Irwin jumps from one of the trees onto its back and screams something about shoving his thumb up the croc's butt and it really going to piss the croc off.

Nope, sorry I lie. There were no crocs and no Steve. There is a sign half covered with mud and you would really need to crawl down the side of the road right to the edge of the water to get to it. The part that I can see has "Croc warning" printed on it. Seems like the crocs are getting smarter and have started setting traps! I guess that will just have to lay there in the mud. No one will be willing to go down there and remove it!

I pour more water out over my head and shirt. It really does help to cool me down a bit, but by the time Darryl is done with his photos and I have my helmet back on, my hair is dry again. This heat is amazing and I absolutely love it. How come I stay in Wellington where it is almost always cold?

Once we reach the end of the Amhen highway, we are at Jabiru. This is the end of the line. Jabiru was originally established as a closed town for the workers of the Ranger Uranium mine, about eight kilometres away. I am not sure what a closed town might be, but it looks pretty open to me. We do not ride into the town or stop here, but decide to head straight down onto the Kakadu highway.

The Kakadu highway runs from Jabiru south west through the southern part of the Kakadu national park and then we will get back to our old friend, Stuart highway at Pine Creek. Earlier on our trip, still down in South Australia, we pulled over at Salt Creek. Salt Creek brings up certain images in my mind to due to the Salt Creek city reference in the States. Cowboys and gunfights at high noon feels about right. I was bitterly disappointed with Salt Creek in SA, and now with Pine Creek is also sparking some western cowboy movie images, the town has to make up for the lack of imagination of its Southern brother.

The ride on the Kakadu highway is great though. It is one fast corner after the next. Nice wide curves not requiring much need to slow down, but I still have to really lay into the turns. It is quite nice to have to think about going around corners after the many, many miles of straight roads.

I spot another wallaby next to the road again, it is small and I really just saw it by accident. It by the time I look back to see if I can see it, it has blended into the grass so well it seems to have disappeared. Well, I am getting more hopeful now that I might still see a 'roo.

We pulled in at the Mary River roadhouse, thirsty and hungry. Breakfast is long ago and the heat really has died me out. I keep drinking water from my Camelbak, but every now and then I need something else. I walk into the shop and for the first time since we have become regulars at the roadhouses, the shop is not air conditioned. It is stifling hot and smells a bit off inside. A sweaty and tired looking woman stands behind the counter staring into space.

"Hi." I say as friendly as I could, trying to breath only through my mouth so I don't have to smell the sweat.

"Mmmm" she almost replies, but at least her eyes move towards me and then seem to focus a bit.

"Do you guys do lunch?" I ask, not sure I want her to answer. I have not had "bad" food so far on this trip and do not want to get food poisoning now.

"Hey hon. We have some pies over there and some pre-packed salads over there." The pies are in one of those cabinets that is suppose to keep the pies hot, but the power seems to be off for this cabinet and when I touch the glass it is not hot. Everything in the shop is hot except the pies! The salads are standing on a shelf on the side of the counter. Even if it was packed this morning, it has been standing in this stifling heat the whole day. The lettuce looks more like cooked spinach.

"That's it? I ask, hopeful that they do not have anything else.

"Well, we have a couple of sandwiches." She says, but while she mentions it, she also starts frowning.

I do not know about you, but if someone frowns when they refer to food they want to sell you, I have the tendency not to feel too positive about it. Making one of my snap decisions I thank her for her help and walk out.

"Foods no good in there." I tell Darryl and we decide that as Pine Creek is not too far away, we can be there within half an hour or so and then get some food there. We ride on and with a tummy full of water I am actually not feeling to hungry anyway. I had also run some cold water over my head from the tap outside the roadhouse, which has cooled me down a bit. The ride is still fun, but it is really hot now. The steam inside my helmet requires me to ride with my face open, which now feels like someone is standing in front of me holding a hairdryer in my face. The valley seems to have caught all the heat of the day and just hanging on to it. The onboard computer says it is 37 degrees.

We come around a corner and there is Stuart highway ahead of us again. We slow down and have to turn back towards Darwin for a few hundred meters before we get to the turn off for Pine Creek.

Officially there were six hundred and sixty five people living in Pine Creek in the 2001 census. As we ride into the town, I see nobody. It looks like a ghost town. It was a mining town and then became an important town when the over land telegraph lines were put up in the 1800, but it seems its prime years are way behind it. Rumour has it that it is still a notable tourist stop, but when we stop at the petrol station, I have my doubts. The doors are locked and the petrol pumps not. I place the nozzle in my petrol tank and pull the lever. A single spurt of petrol sloshes out, but then stops. It registers 0.13c on the pump. I walk back to the door and knock, but there is no reaction. I owe them thirteen cents and am a bit apprehensive due to too many small town movies where the hero accidently sets off the mass murderer. I take out a twenty cent piece and put it on top of the petrol pump. Better safe than sorry! And they can keep the change, so I am even one ahead of them.
We ride through the rest of the town, which takes us to the crossing, the only crossing in town, and look to see what's in this street.

Luckily there is a petrol station and a pub. Good. And there are even people walking about. Not a great many, but the three people crossing the road allow me to believe that there are still some kind of food available in this place. We fuel up and then walk across the street to the pub. The guy at the pub says this is not a restaurant, I can go to the other door, where they can give me food. I go there and Darryl and I stand there and look at our options.

"Sorry guys, we are not cooking anything today, so nothing from the menu. Only what you see here." The woman behind the counter says.

Here are our options:

3 x sausages on sticks, deep fried
4 x deep fried chips
2 x sausage rolls
2 x pies, unknown filling
1 x something

I have never and will never eat one of the sausages on a stick. It looks disgusting. The four lonely chips look old and greasy and I truly have absolutely no idea what the other thing is left to the side. I would not have said it is fit for human consumption, but what do I know. I look out through the front window at the sign in front of the place where it boldly claims:

"Quality food"

This brings my attention back to the food available. Maybe the pie will not be too bad, at least it is warm. And even though I do not eat sausage rolls often, they are nice every now and then. That makes up my mind and I decide to leave my cynical view of the food outside and trust the sign. I buy one sausage roll and one of the pies. Darryl gets the same.

Honestly, in some parallel universe I guess the pies could have qualified for food. Not good food, not even ok food, but at least you would be able to get the argument settled that it is indeed "food that might not kill you". But there is no way that anyone, anywhere, anytime can call that sausage roll food. If I went outside and scraped together all the road kill on the highway and left it in the sun to get nice and ripe. Then boiled it for four days in bovine urine and then spiced it with baboon shit, I would vote that the better tasting meal of the two. It is sickening. The sign outside, even though not claiming what type of quality food it is being sold in here should have an emergency number on there as well and instructions on how to resuscitate someone after eating here. Even as hungry as I am I cannot eat the sausage roll and the bite I did take makes the acid in my stomach boil up. It must have pulled the emergency switch in there and all acid on deck!

Darryl laughs at me for the face I pull when walking out of there and even though the chocolate milkshake does help with both the taste in my mouth and the acid, it does not make me feel any better. This was by far the worst meal of the trip..... so far. We still have to get to banana bender country, so there is every possibility that there might be something worse upfront, but I doubt it. My advice is if you ever pass by this piece of the earth, just keep driving. The time spent hungry while waiting for the next place to eat is much more pleasant than the time spent driving away from there with that crap in your system. YUK!

We get back on Stuart highway and now head down south. We will push on till we get to Katherine which is about a hundred kilometres away. Then we will sleep there tonight. I did like the look of Katherine on the way north, so I am glad we will be sleeping over there. At the very least there is bound to be medical help close by if the lunch tries to kill me.

While attempting to digest the shit in my stomach I see movement ahead. Up front in the road I see a small snake crossing the road. It must be about thirty centimetres long and is really moving fast. At the speed I am going we will just miss each other, but I do slow down a bit to make sure it can get across my path before I get there. Then, just as I am almost next to it, it rears up as if it is going to strike me.

Going at hundred and fifty kilometres per hour, with bike boot on, with bike pants pulled over it and being on the high BMW, I do what nature dictates you do when a snake is going to strike at you.

I scream like a little girl and at the same time jerk my legs up.

The bike swerves, but I manage to keep it under control. Now I start laughing at myself. Adrenaline is pumping through my system and the pathetic shriek I gave is making me howl. Man, it is good that I am alone on the bike and Darryl far behind. I am so happy no one will ever know I can be such a wuss! Well, just like Indiana Jones, I do not like snakes. And very unlike him, I scream like a little girl when I have a snake seemingly getting ready to strike at me. I am now just happy I managed to keep my bladder from letting go.

We get to Katherine shortly afterwards and I can feel my body is really sore today. I am ready to get my sore ass off the bike and go for my daily swim and grab a few beers. We ride into town and spot a caravan park advertising cabins and a swimming pool.

Can I get a Hallelujah my brothers and sistas, we have seen the promised land.

We pull over and get off the bikes slowly. When I am sure I can still walk we go and ask if they have any availability. Can I have another hallelujah please, they have a cabin for us to share if we want it. My body is too sore to worry about looking for something else so we take it and go and unpack. I just don't have the energy to unpack the whole bike and leave the panniers and top box on, just taking the loose stuff from the back. I get my shorts and am in the pool in no time. Darryl joins me and he finds a button that switches on bubble jets in one part of the pool. I have found a new pleasure in life, bubbles on a sore butt. There is a restaurant next to the pool and when we later on go and eat something, I end up eating the best meal of the trip on the same day that I had eaten the worst.

I ordered gnocchi which is perfectly cooked and the blue cheese sauce is stunning. Good end to a tough day. We talk about our ride for tomorrow. We intend to have a long one, again stretching it close to the eight hundred kilometres. I will need a bit of sleep and even though it has just started to go dark, I know I will be able to sleep soundly within seconds from touching down in bed. I feel the need to take a shower before bed, needing a good night's sleep. Interestingly the shower is a building just outside the cabin. I switch on the water and when I get in I am surprised to find a small frog on the wall. It is sitting there just about the height of my privates.

I carefully watch it as I start soaping up and the hot water must have gotten it spooked so it jumps straight at me. Again I shriek like a little girl and jump out of its way. It is now on the shower curtain and is watching me just as carefully as I am watching it. I laugh at myself again for being such a wuss then almost choke on my laughing as it jumps again and again I shriek while jumping the other way. After the third jump/shriek I get out of the shower and then shake the curtain roughly trying to get rid of the fucking frog. Sorry, but my sense of humour is now failing. I am tired and not feeling very manly after this. Again I am glad that there is no one around to see this and that no one will ever know about it.

When I look into the shower the frog is now gone. I did not see it going anywhere, but it is not anywhere I can see. Hopefully it somehow washed down the drain. I rinse of while carefully watching all around me and then go to bed. I am asleep even before I have reached my bed and the last few metres just happened by accident.

Day 12
Tuesday 19 April 2011
From: Katherine
To: Barkley Homestead Roadhouse
Distance travelled: 824 kilometres

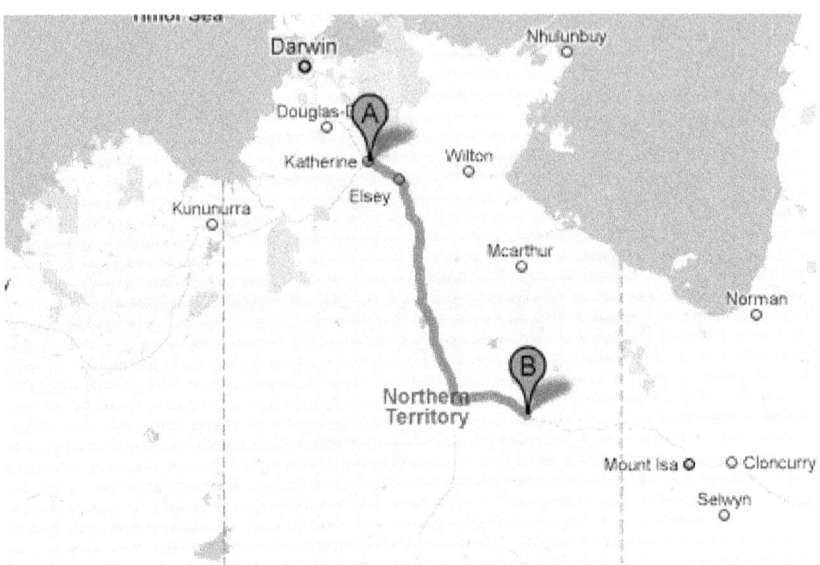

This morning we get up at 5:30 a.m. as we feel we want to cover a lot of miles today. There is no real reason why we feel this need to do the extra long days except that we can. It is so cool to think we can ride as far and long as we want and we will not run out of road.

Riding out of town with the sun just cresting it is pretty tough on the eyes as the sun is shining through the trees on the roadside causing a strobe like flash. There are quite a few potholes on this stretch of the road so I focus mostly on the road ahead of me. We plan to ride down to Daly Waters and then turn off Stuart highway onto the Carpentaria highway. When we sat with the maps in my lounge so many months ago planning the trip we looked at this piece of road and said it would be nice to ride this, but due to the fact that there is no fuel for four hundred and fifty kilometres, we decided we cannot ride this route. Now that we have an extra ten litres each we should easily be able to reach the Barkley Homestead Roadhouse.

However, before we get there we still need to do a few miles this morning. It is very beautiful out here this morning. Mist hangs between the trees and with the sun still low in the sky it is turning everything orange. It is also absolutely still except for the grunt of the bikes. This is one of the most amazing things of being out here. We are truly just two lads out here in between the Never-never and the Ever-ever. I can highly recommend find a place like this!

We arrive at Mataranka still pretty early in the morning and pull over to get some coffee. As part of a national drive to help drivers stay awake and alert on these long lonely stretches of road, the government sponsors free coffee for drivers. I have freely admitted that I am a coffee snob and the powder coffee just will not do it for me. I grab a mug of hot water and one of the Dutch coffee filters. That's more like it. With a shake of his head, Darryl asks if I am happy now.

"What do you mean am I happy now?" I ask a little confused. "In the general sense of the word, yes I guess I am pretty happy. We are on a once in a life time journey, I am riding motorbike, I have good coffee. Yes, I guess I am pretty happy."

"No, I mean are you happy that the roo's are real and not just a conspiracy?" he replies.

I am caught out with absolutely no idea of how to respond. Is he pulling a prank on me? Did he actually see some 'roos? If so, were they ninjas or kamikazes? And if so, why did I not see them? A very scary thought pops into my head. Is Darryl involved with the conspiracy?

Finally I manage to respond. "What? Did you see roo's? Where? When?" I am no longer mister happy.

"I waved and pointed at them! They were just a little off the road hopping around." He says looking a bit disappointed that I did not see them after all the trouble he went through to point them out to me.

"I guess I was concentrating so much on missing the potholes and the strobe flashing of the sun through the trees." I say.

When we ride out of Mataranka I feel kind of odd. It is strange feeling of being disconnected from myself. Unintentionally I start having a major introspective analysis of where I am in my life and who I have become. I guess being stuck in such close quarters with myself is taking effect on me. I also realise I am really missing Elizna today. I just want to give her a hug and hold her for a few minutes. I am sure a couple of minutes would make all the difference, but I can also now feel just how far away from her I am.

When we pull into the Highway Inn roadhouse I am quiet and not too keen for chit chat. We sit down and have some breakfast and just sitting there chilling and sipping on a hot coffee makes me feel ok. However, as soon as we get up I am keen to just get on the bike and be on my own. I just do not feel well.

This is the point where we are planning to leave Stuart highway to get to the Barkley highway. There is a cop car at the turn off and an electric portable traffic sign saying due to the road conditions, this road has a temporary speed limit of eighty kilometres per hour. This will not do. We have a look at each other and with a shake of the head we turn around and head further South on Stuart highway.

With me being back exclusively in my own company, stepping back from myself it is actually quite amazing to see how my experience of the trip is constantly changing. Back in South Australia I was frantic to make sure I enjoy every second and later in the Northern Territory I was relaxed and with no conscious effort managed to really enjoy the experience. I am sure I will feel better and what better to improve a mood than riding a few hundred kilometres on a cool bike.

While going through this psychoanalysis I reckon I have a few life changes to make. I am generally an easy going person, but I do get wound up about stuff not worth the anger. I need to be more accommodating with other people and not judge people so harshly. I promise myself that I will work on myself and be a better person every chance I get.

Even though it took you only a few seconds to read this, it took me hours of going through things I have done and said, knowing how I felt sometimes when I just didn't say anything and generally just being tough on myself to get to this point. Feeling that I have made a breakthrough start pepping me up.

I am jolted back to the here and now when I rapidly approach the disintegrated piece of the road we went over a few days ago. I am still on pretty high speed, as in my daze I did not heed the "Slow down – Road Hazard" sign. I manage to slow down to about fifty and then I am on the deep, loose gravel. The relaxed state I am in and the slight disconnection with myself keeps me pretty lose and I manage to keep the bike upright and pull out of each of the slides. Just as I feel myself begin to tense up I can see the end of the gravel and I open the throttle a bit as my tail slides out. I feel the jolt on the steering as I ride back onto the tar road and have a look back to see how Darryl is faring.

He still has about twenty meters to go and then slides and loses control. The bike jumps to the left and he goes over the side of the road and into the ditch next to the road. I see his knee hit one of the signs next to the road and I wait for the inevitable fall. I guess it is the amount of time we have spent on the bikes that is the key here, as he manages to push onto the ground just at the right time and keep the bike upright until he has it stopped. That was so close. I pull over to the side to get off and go back to help him back onto the road. It might be easier to walk the bike out from where he ended up, but then he will need help to keep it upright.

Then I feel ice cold fear run up my back. We had passed a high speed road train a few minutes ago and as Darryl rides over the hump back onto the gravel road the truck is on the start of the gravel. There is nothing I can do, but I call out to Darryl anyway, knowing he cannot hear me. I don't think he has seen the truck yet and it is not slowing down at all. Not that it would be able to stop from that high speed in time anyway. Darryl turns the bike strait and is now right on the side of the road, but at least not moving for the moment.

The truck speeds past him and I can see him being pushed by the rushing air, the truck missing him with about a metre spare. That's all I can see as the truck then rushes past me, with not too much extra space for me either, but at least I am off the gravel. Rocks are shot up and smacks against my helmet and body. Man he is going fast. Then he is past and the dust settles as Darryl slowly rides onto the tar as well. I am sure my eyes are just as big as his right now. What a scare. We have a smoke to calm the nerves and give him time to make sure he did not hurt himself when he hit that sign. Luck is on our side again and he is fine.

When the shaking stops we ride on and soon we are back in the lovely dump called Elliott. Man what a rubbish place. At least we manage to get a cool drink. I need both the sugar and the coolness. It is just after 10:00 a.m. and way over 30°C. The sugar does do me well and I run water over my head. I am starting to feel a bit better, but not my sparkling self. We still have a long ride ahead of us and so after finishing the drink, we ride on further South. Soon we arrive at Three Ways. Now we will turn off Stuart Highway for the last time and I can honestly say I have a lump in my throat. It has been such a good friend and such an amazing ride up and down this two thousand eight hundred and fifty kilometre highway.

We will now end our south/north trek and start our ride out east towards Queensland and eventually the east coast at Rockhampton on the Carpentaria highway. We still have a good two hundred kilometres of riding left for today, so with a last fond look up and down Stuart highway, I bid it farewell and thanks as ride off it for the last time. We stop at the petrol station to fill up and have lunch. After lunch I give Elizna a call and she is not having a great day either. She has a nerve pinched in her hip that is causing her a lot of pain and discomfort, Chloe our cats has a bladder infection of some sort and is pretty sick and she just misses me. I think the fact that we both felt a bit down actually managed to help us cheer up. Nothing wrong, just a bit of TLC required.

When we ride off east, Stuart highway disappears in the rear view mirror I am feeling a bit better now so get back into the riding. Having a look around it is actually quite an amazing view. I stand up on my pegs and now I am just slightly higher than a green carpet of trees stretching as far as the eye can see in every direction. All the trees are almost exactly the same height and colour, creating this image of a solid green carpet thrown over the landscape. It is quite spectacular really. On the horizon I can see a number of smoke columns going up and then being swept west by the high winds. The road is absolutely straight and it will be another hundred kilometres before the next turn in the road. This gives me time to really have a look around. Now I can see a dozen smoke columns going up. There are a number of pretty large forest fires up ahead. As we approach one of these fires, the smoke passes between us and the sun, causing the light to become brown. It is like looking through the brown lenses of sunglasses. The fire is not one big fire, but rather thousands of little ones all over the place. None seems threatening to us as we ride through the smoke and luckily the smoke is too high to cause breathing problems. The smell of the smoke is strong though and when we do ride through some smoke my eyes, nose and throat burns. When we pass out from under the smoke, colour returns and then we pass into a large swarm of dragonflies. My taste buds immediately calls out for grass flavoured juice with some garlic butter and coriander and I quickly close my mouth.

After some time we arrive at the Barkley roadhouse, which is the end of the ride for today. We had covered a lot of kilometres today and it had been exciting, emotionally straining and a beautiful day all in one. We book a room and for the first time I can remember the people at the roadhouse are not really friendly. They are not rude, but just kind of short-off. We ride around looking for our room and when I park I decide that tonight will be one of the nights I will not unload the bike. Just take what I need. I am keen to get to the pool and go for swim, while Darryl says he is taking his camera to go and look for some roo's at sunset.

After a swim I head over to the restaurant. Sunset is beautiful as I sit outside the pub with a beer and a smoke, feeling like the Camel man. There are no roo's that I can see, but thousands of dragonflies and even more mozzies. I move inside and when Darryl turns up he also only managed to see mozzies, but no roo's. I order a nice big steak with a salad, to ensure I do get some greens in. As I mentioned before this is the first place on this trip where the people of the roadhouse are actually pretty rude. I hope this is just a once off thing and that the road ahead has more of the friendly Aussies we have had the pleasure of so far.

I am exhausted after a day of eight hundred and twenty four kilometres and when I get in bed, even though still early, I am asleep in no time.

Chapter 13 - Queensland, Banana bender country

Well, to start off with, Queenslanders are known by the rest of Australia as Banana Benders. It is also called the red state. Their rugby team is called the Reds and all this red boils down to one thing. They are the redneck state of Australia. I am not saying they are all rednecks, just that there is a particularly high ratio of rednecks to upscale people in this state.

It is a very tropical place with large banana and sugarcane farming happing here. It is also home to the lovely Gold Coast, which attracts millions of tourist with its warm climate and of course their water parks and Disney attractions.

Queensland is the second largest state in Australia, covering about 22.8% of the country. The far north is pretty remote with sealed roads ending about two thirds of the way up the coast. Any further north and you are on gravel roads only.

I found a very funny fact about Queensland that is worth mentioning. In Queensland, it is illegal to come within one hundred metres or a dead whale. So, just keep that in mind next time you are out there and just happen to be close to a beached whale. It will be well worth your time to make sure it is still alive before you walk up to it and start poking it with a stick while your friend records it on his mobile phone.

Day 13
Wednesday 20 April 2011
From: Barkley Homestead Roadhouse
To: Cloncurry
Distance travelled: 568 kilometres

Yesterday I had to say goodbye to my dear friend, Stuart highway and today I will have to bid my other friend, the Northern Territory goodbye as well. We have about two hundred and fifty kilometres this morning before we will cross the Queensland border and end a stunning piece of the trip. I have high hopes for Queensland as well, but honestly, it will really need to shine to outdo the Northern Territories.

Last night we asked the staff what time they open so we can get some fuel and they said that we can get fuel from 6:30 a.m. onwards. We decided last night that we will get up and be at the petrol station when they open, so we get up just before 6:00 a.m. It is just before dawn and I quickly get some coffee ready and then sit down outside on the veranda and watch the sunrise. It is so beautiful and I feel remarkably good considering the distance we did yesterday and the shitty mood I was in. I am all excited today and feel on top of the world. I am about to get to know Queensland, so am pretty keen to get going.

As they open the doors of the petrol station shop, we are there and fill up. The fact that we have been riding at hundred and fifty kilometres per hour has increased our fuel consumption and currently we get about two hundred and forty to two hundred and sixty kilometres on a full tank. I fill up and then we get going. For the first time the rising sun is a real problem. It is right in front of me, in the centre of the road, on eye level. It is tough to see much and within a few kilometres Darryl pulls over. He puts his sunglasses on under the built in dark visor of the helmet which seems to be a pretty good idea. I copy his idea and this helps a lot. My sunglasses have polarized lenses so the glare is reduce enough so that I can actually see the road.

I am a bit nervous though. Even though I had not seen the roo's, I have seen and smelt the evidence of them being here where they are lying as road kill all over the place. Even if it is a dead one, I still need to be able to see it in time to swerve around it. If I hit one at high speed, I will crash.
Through all this I do find the time to look around and it is quit pretty around here. It is very green, reminding me that they have had a lot of rain in this part of the world. I had expected the Northern territory to be much drier. As to the remoteness of the place, that does not disappoint. We ride for a full hour and a bit before the first road train passes us and we are yet to pass anything else except dead roo's.

We ride past small settlements called Soudan and Avon Downs and both these settlements are just off the highway and have signs saying they have no fuel. As I have ten litres of spare fuel, this does not worry me much, but as we approach the border and my onboard computer claims I have a zero kilometres range left in the tank, I am very happy that I have the spare fuel.

As we ride over the border, leaving the Northern Territory behind us I stand up on the pegs and give a big "whoop!". Goodbye N.T. You have been good to us and an experience well worth it. We have now entered the red state.

If you are not from there, this state is so full of rednecks, my I-pod automatically starts playing "Duelling Banjos" from Deliverance and I do not even have it loaded on the I-pod.

This reminds me of some pretty funny redneck jokes.

You might be a redneck if you have been married three times and still have the same in-laws.

I believe it is a state law in Queensland that if you and your spouse are divorced, you are still legally brother and sister.

You might be a redneck if you believe "Possum" is the other white meat.

You might be a redneck if your dog had puppies in your living room and nobody noticed for three days.

Ok, enough of that. O, wait one more. My favourite:

You might be a red neck if you believe incest is ok, as long as you keep it in the family.

Hahahahaha.

Anyway, where was I.....?

Oh yes. There I am just crossing the border and with the fuel gauge on empty, waiting for the fuel to run out. I have never in my life run out of fuel, so even though I know what should happen due to seeing it happen many times in movies, I have never experienced it. The speed limit is reduced to hundred and ten kilometres per hour, which I assume will be the maximum for the rest of the trip. I think I remember reading somewhere that the speed limit is hundred and ten in Queensland.

With Camooweal in sight, maybe five kilometres away, I feel the bike sputter. It loses power for a second and true as only movies can be, it sputters for a moment. I don't know much about the mechanics of engines, but I have been told it is not good to try running the last few drops of fuel out of your engine. I immediately switch the bike off and let it coast to a stop. Darryl is up front and in a few seconds I see him breaking and turning around.

"I was keeping an eye on you. I am also almost out of fuel and wondered if you will make it." He says when he pulls over. For some unknown reason he uses less fuel than I do. We don't have a huge weight difference in body weight and have roughly the same amount of luggage on the bikes, which are exactly the same. All I can think is I might care a little less about the environment and thus burn a little bit more fuel.
Jip, that one is for all you greenies. If you don't like it, please send your complaint to my email address, I_dont_care@burn_a_tree.com

Anyway so there we go, for the first time on the trip I use the fuel carried all the way from Port Augusta in South Australia. I pour the full five litres into the tank and then start the bike up. No problem, the bike starts immediately and we ride the four point two kilometres to our first town in Queensland, Camooweal.

As we ride into town we pull over at the petrol station and fuel up. We decide that it is also a good time for breakfast and go and order some beacon and eggs. I will miss these roadie breakfasts when I get back home and am back on oatmeal. The food is good and the coffee ok and now I feel ready for a good stretch of road into Queensland.

Outside on the wall is a funny sign:

You have now entered into Queensland
Please turn your watch forward Five years and 30 minutes

Well, my experience of Northern Territories allows me to form the opinion that yes, it is a remote and sparsely populated area where mobile phone reception is pretty poor and no big cities exists. However, almost every Roadhouse we stopped at had high speed Internet connections and Darwin was just amazing. The people were friendly and the long aerials on all the cars and UTEs show signs of technology.

If Queensland believes they are five years ahead of N.T. so be it, but they will need to prove it to me.

The first thing I notice is that the road condition is much worse when we ride out of town, but I decide to be fair to Queensland and not judge anything so early. I had a lot of time and distance to make up my mind about N.T. so will afford Queensland the same.

As we ride away from the town on our way to Mount Isa, the landscape changes to vast grasslands. It looks so much like the savannahs in Southern Africa, where as far as the eye can see, there is just grass. Talking about how far the eye can see, I have noticed that the horizon has been a bit higher than where we are for the last fifty odd kilometres. Every hill we go over has a hill following, but the top of the hill is higher than us all the time. We are doing a slow, but steady assent onto the Great Dividing Range. This mountain range is not only the longest mountain range in Australia, but the third longest in the world. It starts up in the north of Queensland and runs south for more than three thousand five hundred kilometres through Queensland, New South Wales, then into Victoria and turns west until it reaches the central plain Grampians in Western Victoria.

We are now crossing it to get to Mount Isa. As we ride higher and higher the grass plains turns into woodlands. The slow, almost unnoticeable change in the environment is again a testament to the sheer size of the country. It takes hours and many, many kilometres before you suddenly notice that all the grass has been replaced by think woodlands.

Still we keep climbing. With the sun now high in the sky and the road pretty much straight and uneventful, it provides ample opportunity to look around. As I sit and scan the scenery I spot two adult and three juvenile Emus. As we ride past them they run further along the tree line and then disappear into the woods. Great, so now I can add Emus to the list of wild life. My extensive list includes confirmed (by me) sighting of camels, a snake, a frog, forty billion blow flies, half a million mosquitoes and two Wallabies. Darryl has seen kangaroos and a dingo as well, but I can only claim what I have seen.

As we continue to climb, it is getting cooler and the temperature has come down to middle twenties now. This is pretty comfortable, but I have gotten so used to the heat of the last week or so that I feel almost a slight chill. Coming closer to Mount Isa the scenery is changing again, this time leaving the woodlands behind and rocky hills taking over. The road also now starts twisting a bit to get around most of the hills, which is quite nice. It is good to have to lay into turns for a change.

As we approach Mount Isa the road becomes quite busy with large trucks. These have the "Road Train" signs on, but they are not the same road trains that we encountered on Stuart highway. These are mining trucks and not the same length and not doing the same speed. There are loads of these trucks on the road and the road quality which has been poor since getting into Queensland now turns nasty. Potholes are becoming more popular than tar and the reduced speed of hundred and ten kilometres per hour ensures we are now quite busy with the riding, dodging trucks and potholes.

Riding into Mount Isa confirms that this is a mining town. It is dirty and the outskirts of town have loads of mine entries and smoking chimneys. We ride into town and now the heat is right back up there in the middle thirties. We stop at the petrol station as we get into the town centre and fuel up. Darryl has had enough of me having reception with my pay-as-you-go Telstra sim card and him always struggling with his Vodacom card. While he pays for his new card I stand outside and a very pretty woman drives up and when she gets out I am reminded of that T.V. show "My name is Earl". The woman who is Earl's ex-wife is a pretty woman, but really, really rough around the edges. This woman walking past me is very much the same. Very good looking, but the redneck is oozing out of her. I smile as she walks past, mostly due to my train of thoughts, but she must have thought I was smiling at her. To be fair, I have been in the Never–never for a while now with only Darryl as company, so I might have smiled at her.

Her reaction is to give me a good look over, from head to toe and then she smiles back. She walks past me and blows a bubblegum bubble and pops it while looking me in the eye and then walks into the shop. Now I am laughing, as the image of Earl's wife is now complete. With the distraction out of the way I concentrate on what must be done. I need to get to an ATM to draw some cash. This is the first big town since Katherine and I did not manage to draw cash there. I ask one of the people working there where I can find a Westpac ATM and he directs me to it. It is pretty close, so that's easy.

Darryl walks out, closely followed by the chick that had smiled at me earlier, now checking me out again. I think if she got closer to me and smelled the fragrance coming up from out of my boots, she would not have smiled, but would have run away screaming for help. I smile back and then turn back to Darryl.

"I need to get to an ATM. It is just down to the traffic light and then down the street to the right. Follow me."

We ride down the street which is pretty busy as it is the main shopping strip of Mount Isa, but we find parking easily with the bikes. There are four people in the queue waiting for the lady at the machine to finish up. The guy right behind her is looking a bit irritated, but then again he might not be on a three week holiday and probably lives in this dodgy town, so might have ample reason to be grumpy. On the other hand, I am standing there quite relaxed and just waiting for her to finish, so I can get some cash as well.

Proving to be five years ahead of the people in Northern Territories, the lady is really struggling. By this time the guy gives up and storms away, she had had her card ejected four times and by the time I am next in line I have now counted eleven times of retrying.

She turns around and in her tent sized, curtain fabric, rose pattern dress looks at me and asks, "What does 'Insufficient' mean?" Her puffy eyes behind thick glasses look scared and a drop of sweat is hanging on her nose, ready to drop to the dry pavement. This is the perfect picture of a person not coping.

"It might mean that your husband has been to the races again or it might mean that there are not enough funds in your account, or you might be doing something wrong." I suggest.

"Oh, these robots are so complicated. I will need to call my husband to come and help me." She says and swallows hard, clearly close to tears.

Knowing how I smell and not really knowing how it will be taken if I give her a hug and say it will all be ok I just nod and say, "O.k."

She turns and starts walking away which allows me to step up to the ATM. There is a message on the ATM asking me if I would like to perform any further transactions. That's not right, shouldn't the "robot" be asking me for my card? I press "No" and her credit card pops out.

"Excuse me 'mam! Your card! Sorry lady! You need to take your card with you!" I call, but she is not hearing me, still muttering to herself. I run after her and come around to her front. She startles and I back away a bit.

"You will need this again." I tell her and hold out the card.

She gives me a puzzled look, but nothing seems to have registered.

"This is your card. It was still in the AT..... in the robot. You need to take it with you." I say and now she registers.

"Oh, these robots are so difficult. I will need to ask my husband to help me." She says and grabs the card from my hand as if I am trying to steal it from her. She then shuffles away.

Bloody hell. That was bizarre. I turn back and the guy that was in the queue behind me has started on the ATM. The lady behind him has watched the whole scene and steps back and tells me, "That was nice of you young man." And offers me the spot in front of her. She does have a different accent, sounding quite a bit more like the people had up in Darwin.

I gratefully take her up on the offer as there are four people behind her in the queue. I draw my money and when I get back to the bikes I tell Darryl, "Come on, let's get out of here. What a dump."

He laughs at me, "Don't hold back, just say what you feel."

We have laugh and then get back on the bikes.

Riding out of Mount Isa the heat of the day intensifies. We are now heading further up onto the top of the mountain range heading to quite a special place in Australia. The town of Cloncurry, our destination for today is credited with the title of having recorded the highest temperature in Australia. The temperature was recorded as 53.1°C on 16 January 1889. Now I know that was quite a while ago, but it is still the holder of that title and it is one of the two claims to fame for the town. The other claim is also related to the heat. More specifically due to the area's extreme solar conditions, it is due to become the first Australian town to be run exclusively on solar power. Bunch of hippies I imagine. Hehehehe.

On the way towards Cloncurry the heat is extreme and the lower speed limit of hundred kilometers per hour does little to help cool me down. After days and days being able to ride at pretty much any speed I wanted to, keeping it down to a hundred is quite challenging. We keep going for a while, but hundred kilometers out of town I pull over. It is just too hot to keep my jacket on. Against all my best intentions and believes, I just cannot keep the jacket on. I take the jacket and gloves off and tie it on top of my sleeping bag. I pour half a liter of water over me and then we ride on. The first few miles I feel cooled down, but this does not last and the heat feels like it is going off the charts. My onboard computer says it is 38°C and it feels all of that plus a bit more if you ask me.

The road is nice and twisty, which is refreshing and helps with keeping my mind off the heat. Standing up on the pegs with my visor open also helps, but it help in cooling down the same as standing next to a very hot heater and then using a hair drier to cool you down.

We finally ride into Cloncurry and ride through the town centre to the information kiosk. The lady at the counter tells us where we can find budget accommodation, which also has a pool and luckily it is pretty much right across the street from us. Walking outside there are a bunch of kids hanging around the bikes. They are absolutely fascinated with the bikes. I love it if kids are interested in bikes. I feel so proud of them and just want to encourage them to take more of an interest and get into biking. I am sure I have been cursed by quite a few moms around the world after I got their kids interested in bikes. I know, because my mum still freaks out about me riding a bike.

There are seven kids, five boys and two girls, all aged around ten or eleven. They are coming from where ever they were playing and causing trouble, on their way to the next place to cause further trouble and play I imagine. They gather around the bike and ask if I would do a skid or a wheelie. Now this is a challenging situation. I don't do wheelies and a skid with a fully loaded heavy bike is a risky idea. If I try it and lose control of the bike, not only will I look like a total dick to the kids, I can injure myself and also instead of helping them fall in love with bikes, it might scare them off. On the other hand not doing anything fun for them might also make them think that bike riders are dumbasses and boring.

So, to start off with I tell them they can start the bike if they want. This goes off really well and almost causes a fight on who is going to start the bike. And so starts the process of trying to reason with a bunch of wildly excited ten year olds. In retrospect I now know that it is completely impossible, so mostly a waste of time, but I think at the end they were relatively happy.

One of the kids seems to be the dominant one. I mostly know this as he is fidgeting with my key and no one is trying to stop him. I can't believe how quickly these kids have taken over and I had lost control. He turns the key, but of course nothing happens. I tell him to just wait one second, as the bike does not start with only the key.

"You also have to say the magic word." I say and to my surprise this has them all quite. They don't really look like they believe me and honestly I don't know enough about kids to know at what age magic becomes bullshit.

After the few quite seconds chaos again erupts, with one kids screaming out every magic word he knows:

"Abra cadabera, hocus pocus, siem sala biem..." and a few more I can't remember.

The other kid with his hand on the key doesn't look impressed, as it seems he doesn't really know magic words and someone else is bound to get it before him. For a second I sit back and enjoy the chaos, but like all things with kids, it soon spirals out of control. One kid is almost going into spasms as he jumps up and down scream "Abra ca dabra" as loud as he can, going red in the face. He of course jumps onto the little girl's foot, who promptly starts crying. The one with the key is twisting it on/off so hard I am afraid he is going to break the key off.
I give a loud wolf whistle, which again to my surprise brings them to a quite.

"Ok, I will help you by giving you the magic word, and then you can all say it at the same time, which will then start the bike." I say and after a quick look amongst themselves, they seem happy with this solution.

"Ok, so here is how we will do it. If you stop crying little girl, you can press this button for me." I say and it seems to work. She stops crying and presses the ignition button. The bike is in gear, with the foot pegs down, so cannot start.

"Right, now hold the button down until we all say the magic word." She is pretty happy and the concentration on the face is so funny. She is not going to mess this up. She holds the button down firmly.

"Good. Now you turn the key until the lights come on." I tell the kid who still has his hands firmly on the key. He is not letting go. He turns the key to the on position and the lights going on. The one who got so excited earlier is now tripling around as the tension increases. I am really worried about this kid. He needs to chill the fuck out.

So, now I need to get their attention on something so they don't see me flicking the bike out of gear, which will cause the bike to start.

"Ok, so here is what you need to do. I will softly say the magic word to you and then I'll count to three. All of you stand here in front of the bike and then scream it out so the bike will start." They all move to the front of the bike and I have to call the girl back who is supposed to keep the start button pressed.

"Ok, so the magic word is...." I look around to make sure no one is around that can overhear us. "Kangaroo."

The one girl laughs and there are some frowns, but mostly it seems they like it. The nervous one starts screaming it already and before I have the chance to count they are all screaming it except the girl focusing on holding the button down. That will have to do I guess and so flick the bike out of gear. They all jump back as the engine starts up and then they laugh. I have to tell the girl to stop pressing the button and then it is chaos again.

The one who still has his hand on the keys grabs the throttle and refs the bike. Now the nervous kid is running around in circles.

"Ok, got to go now. I will do a wheel spin for you." This is again met with cheers and then I ride to the middle of the parking lot. It is gravel, so should be easy to do a bit of a spin. I pull the front brake and keep the back brake in, ref the engine up and then let go of the back break. The wheel spins and shoots out gravel. The bike slides a bit, but I stop the spin before losing control. All and all I am pretty impressed, but when I look over to see if they enjoyed it they have all run away. The little bastards. Instead, there is an old woman standing there looking at me and shaking her first at me while screaming something.

Fuck. That's my queue to exit! I quickly pull away, without spinning this time and ride away. Now I need to find Darryl, but luckily the place is just down the road. He has already asked about accommodation and is inside the office busy with getting the room sorted. I go in and pay my half of the room and then we head down the dusty road to the "budget" cabin we rented for the night. It is actually not too bad. It has a bed in the front room where the kitchen is and a separate bedroom with a door that can close. Wonderful, we will not be bugging each other with snoring tonight.

I am really hot and it is pretty much as quickly as possible for me to get into my swimming trunks and into the pool. The pool is between the worker's quarters and the old shed and needs a bit of work to get it back to its prime, but the water is cool and wet and does its trick. It is so nice to cool down in a pool after a long day's riding. Darryl joins me at the pool and after a while in the water we head back to the cabin. Darryl says she is going to do some washing and I decide to rather go and find a watering hole. I walk down the dusty road in the trailer park and when I get the end of the lane I am next to the manager's trailer.

I have seen quite a few movies that have those real trailer trash people who sit next to their trailers drinking beer.
This is what I find. The trailer is on bricks, which I believe is a crucial part of being rednecks. You have to have at least one vehicle on bricks in your yard.
They have a number of different coloured ground sails tied together and tied to the roof of their caravan. It is held up on the other side by two pillars of crates. This creates a lovely outdoor entertainment area. To add to the ambiance of the scene, the toothless mummified grandfather is sitting right at the back against one of the crate pillars in a fold up chair and I hope they have check recently if he is still alive. He looks really old and possibly dead. Then it moves, the hand coming up bringing the can of beer up to the mouth. The rest of the family is also there, grandma is just finishing her beer and with a practiced eye, she loops the empty beer can through the air onto a heap of beer cans lying at the open side of their lounge. This is too good opportunity to pass.

"Good day guys. How you doing?" I ask and stand a bit closer. I am not going in there, but I have to have a chat with them.

"Yee a the guys weeth the beeks." The manager says.

Not to sure what he has said I just smile and shake my head and pull up my shoulders.

"The beeks." He says again and this time mimics riding a motorcycle.

"Oh, yes. We are the guys with the bikes." I now understand what he said. "Do you guys know where I can find a pub?" I ask.

"Wecanna funda wha?" the toothless beauty that must be his wife asks while she also loops an empty beer can through the air onto the heap and follows it up with a pretty decent burp.

"Um. Where can I find a bar? You know a cold beer." I reply following his previous example and mimics drinking a beer. That seems to work as the honey of the trailer park let her spaghetti strap drop off her shoulder and then she hits her husband on the shoulder.

"Ah. Ye. Tellem hurny. Tellem whe he can finda beee."

This exchange to get directions takes a while and with mostly hand signals I manage to get the directions to what I hope is a bar. I guess I will see when I get there. I walk out of the caravan park and the heat is stifling here. I am already sweating like a pig. As best as I could understand I have to go right, down the main street for about half a kilometre, across the railway and then when I get to the petrol station I turn right again. The bar should then be on the corner.

Right across the road from the trailer park's entrance is a hotel with a pub. What the hell? I walk across the street and walk into the bar. The side where the slot machines are is dark but the lights are on in the bar. There is no one around, so I ring the bell. In a few minutes a pretty rude woman asks what I want.

"Can I have beer?" I ask, but rude people get my blood boiling quite quickly. If it wasn't so hot outside I would have told her to have an intimate time with herself.

"Do you have a room here?" She asks while looking me up and down in disgust.

Now I know I might be looking a little rough not having shaved for three weeks and might even not be smelling that great, but come on. I am not that bad.

"No, I am staying across the road tonight." I reply and then she says the bar is closed today.

"Fine." I manage to keep my reply to just that instead of the rather graphical things I wanted to say. I walk out and start the walk down the road. Walking down the hot quiet road towards the town centre I am actually quite enjoying the hot summer heat. We have so much cold weather in New Zealand that this heat is exactly what I need. Pretty soon I am smiling again and when I pass a couple walking the other way I greet them. They just nod and walk around me. Man, what happened to the friendly people in the Northern Territory? These people are rude and can go stuff themselves.

I finally get to the town centre and manage to get to the pub. It is a real truckies pub and the guys in there seem pretty rough. As I sit there and watch some of the Aussie rules rugby on TV I try to eve's drop on the conversations of the truckies at the bar, but cannot understand a word they are saying. Their accents are really strong and the slang makes it impossible to follow their conversation.

On the other side a couple of real grease monkeys are playing pool with a real little home wrecker jail bait. She must be all of fourteen and wearing clothes a sixty year old hooker should be wearing.

I head back to the trailer park and when I get there Darryl says he could not find me and ended up buying a roasted chicken and some bread rolls for dinner. We have the food and then I call it the night. That's enough now for today.

Day 14
Thursday 21 April 2011
From: Cloncurry
To: Barcaldine
Distance travelled: 631 kilometres

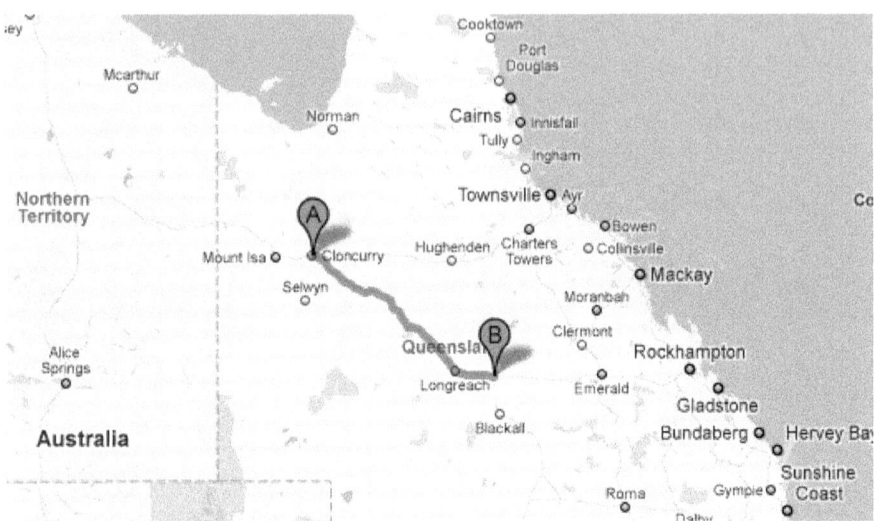

The African people can call up their ancestors to place a curse on people and when I walk out I set all my ancestors to work. Rotten, dirty, filthy, scaly thieves have stolen my gloves from my bike. I had left them on my bike, like I have a few other nights and they are gone this morning. May whoever has stolen my gloves put them on and have their hands rot off. I hope your dandruff gets worse and your breath smells like dog shit for the rest of your life, you miserable excuse for a human.

It is still really early, the sun just up and when we ride out of the little dodgy town I am not too unhappy about leaving this place behind. Inbred Dodgeville if you ask me. I have my warmer winter gloves on, but even now, just after 6:30 in the morning my hands start sweating quickly. The morning is breathtaking beautiful and all bad thoughts are blown away by the rushing air and soon I am humming along with Cat Stevens really enjoying the ride.

After about thirty kilometres we turn off onto the Landsborough highway which will take us closer to the coast. Within half an hour I pass Darryl and show that I need to pull over. I have to get the gloves off. It is just too hot. I don't normally ride without gloves, but with the heat it is just not going to be possible to keep them on. Riding away I feel quite bit better with all my vents open in my jacket and pants and the winter gloves off. I have a real childlike pleasure in the riding this morning. It is everything long distance riding is all about. Riding through McKinlay is just passing through yet another small town I can't understand why anyone would want to live there. I guess it is a special type of person who can live in a small, remote town. I just know that whatever it is that makes you a small town type person, I do not have much of that in me.

We keep riding and as soon as we are outside the town I am back in that almost giggling pleasure of the ride. The road is in shocking condition and it is pretty exciting to dodge all the potholes while keeping the heavy bikes' speed up to hundred and twenty kilometres per hour.
We finally get to Kyniana roadhouse and after filling up a huge truck pulls up. I stand and watch as the truck door opens and a huge slap of meat gets out. I don't know if you have ever watched wrestling. You know that WWF, or WWE, or some WW. There was this one wrestler called Big Show. Do yourself a favour go and Google this name. I swear to you this guy was at least the size of the Big Show guy and looked as if he could have been his twin brother.

This huge man walked past me and I greeted him with a "Good day mate."

He looked me up and down, snarled and then replied in a deep bass voice, "Yeah. OK."

Well, there we go. Yet another friendly banana bender. I walk after him and grab him by his greasy hear and jerk him down to his knees. "That's not polite!" I scream in his face and he starts crying.

Yeah right. He can tell me to go and fuck myself and all I will be able to say about that is, "Thank you sir". I guess he rarely hears anyone telling him he is rude. When I walk out of the petrol station's shop, a bike rider on a BMW pulls in. He nods as he rides past us and parks at the petrol pumps. We have taken cups and hot water and are busy making a cup of coffee. He pays and then walks over to come and have a chat. For a change we get to speak to a friendly Queenslander. He is an Iron butt. He is doing a ride at the moment for the Iron butt club. He has done 1800 kilometres in the last twenty four hours. That's good going. He says he'll do a few more then call it the day and ride back home to Rockhampton. It is so nice talking to someone who has done something like this and be telling him of our ride and having his respect as well. It just emphasises how great our trip is.

It is just after 10:00 a.m. as we ride out towards Winton and it is already over 30°C. It is going to be another hot day. I am also noticing little bumps on my hands. At first I think that it must be a couple of mozzie bites, but at the next stop my hands are covered in small little pumps. These are heat blisters my friends. At Winton we stop for breakfast, again working away two slices of toast, two eggs, two hash browns and ten slices of beacon. The standard breakfast of bikers. Well, us bikers anyway. When we get back on the bikes we need to fill up first. We ride up and down through town looking for petrol, but cannot find anything. We pull into a place that looks like a petrol station, but the pumps are just shells standing there. Dammit, we will need to fuel up here. We ride on a little and soon are back where we started. Darryl pulls out his I-phone and looks for a petrol station in the map. It shows we should ride to the town exit, just before we get back on the highway, there will be a petrol station there. Of course when we get there, there are two across the road from each other. Again, if you have one place in town that is your only competition, why would you open the place right across the road from them? Surely they did not build it at the same time and the others did not noticed until the opening day that there is the only other petrol station within the hundred kilometres right across the street from you? Surely if you built it on the other side of the town you would be sure to get more people stopping at your petrol station?

Never mind I just pulled into the one on the side of the road in which direction we are heading. I fuel up and after having a smoke we ride out towards Barcaldine. The road is in really bad condition. It is truly the worse roads we have encountered so far. Potholes make up more of the road than the good sections. We do find workers busy working on the road every now and then, but they are just pouring tar into the pot holes, basically covering the problem for a few months. The scenery isn't too flash at the moment either, just farms with some cattle and sheep. The size of the place is amazing. The scenery just stays monotone for the next hour or so of riding over and through more and more potholes.

When we ride into Longreach I finally have signal on my mobile again and I try to give my friend Marius a call. They live in Mackay, where we want to stay in a couple of days and I am trying to get hold of him to make sure they will be at home. We had thought that by the time we get to the coast the long weekend would be in the last day or just after the long weekend. Here we are with the long weekend just starting and already getting to the coast. This is now showing that we are actually quite far ahead of schedule. I leave Marius a message as he is not answering his phone. I will just have to call him again when I get signal again. After drinking a Coke Zero and having a smoke we ride on out of Longreach. The ride the Barcaldine is uneventful except for the heat. It was quite hot in the middle of the country and it was very hot up in the tropical north, but this is now really very hot. I hold my head under the tap at every stop to cool down and in a few kilometres my hair has dried out again and I was just as hot again. The heat blisters on my hands are getting quite bad, but there is no way I can put my winter gloves on in this weather. I will need to get some summer gloves as soon as possible.

We soon arrive at Barcaldine and find out from the people at the Information kiosk where we can stay. There is a place with some budget rooms and a swimming pool about half a kilometre from where we are now. My ass is quite sore so that suites me well. We ride out to the place and the guy wants to charge us twenty dollars extra each from what their ad says we got from the information kiosk. When we tell each other that we will just go to the other option that they gave us he drops his price to that of the ad and says he will need to make sure the ad is changed. Well, at least he dropped the price. I was not too keen on riding on right now, but I hate it if people try taking advantage of me.

So, we get a couple of rooms and then into the pool. The pool is a little dirty and lots of dead bugs floating around in it, but I enjoy the swim so much I just could not care. After the swim I ride into town again. I want to try call home from the payphone, as I do not have reception in this town and the guy from the motel says it will be very expensive calling from the hotel. I get a phone card, first asking the woman if the card will allow me to call both internationally and locally. She assures me that it will.

I go to the pay phone and when I try to make a call the phone does not seem to be able to read the card. I call the woman out to come and look at it. She wiggles the card around a bit and finally says that it doesn't seem to work. Amazing. That it only took her five minutes to figure that out after I already told her is amazing. She must be a genius or something.

She also says that unfortunately once the card has been taken out of the wrapping it can only be exchanged if it doesn't work. This seems to be the phone not working, so she can't exchange it for me. My blood starts boiling and I decide to just walk away. I walk past the bottle store and then decide to go in and buy a six-pack of XXXX Gold. I ride back to the motel and call Darryl over for a beer. While sipping on a beer we sit and plan the next few days. We need to make sure of what we are going to try do over the next few days as the Easter weekend is starting this evening and we are bound to struggle to find accommodation on the coast plus there is bound to be pretty heavy traffic.

After planning our ride tomorrow I order a burger as room service and scoff that down. After the burger I am just too tired to carry on. I don't even have the energy to shower, I just fall asleep on top of my bed.

Day 15
Friday 22 April 2011
From: Barcaldine
To: Rockhampton
Distance travelled: 675 kilometres

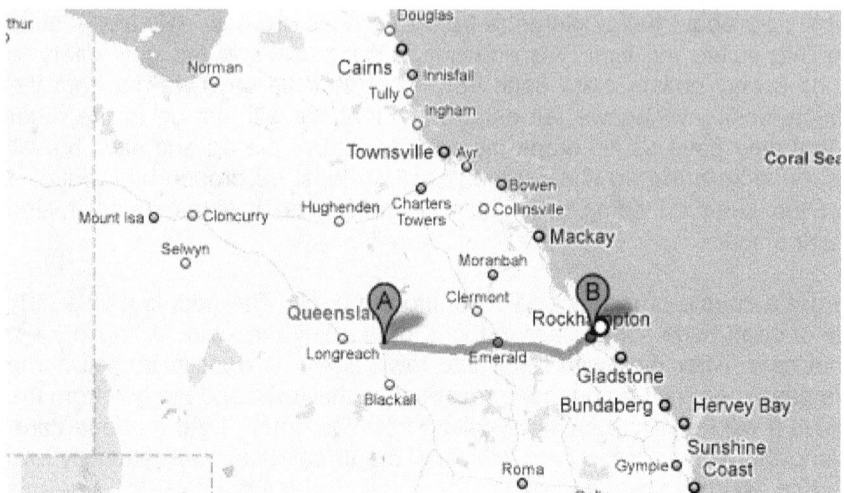

So today we will reach the third of the four coast lines of Australia. We started off at the southern coastline along the Great Ocean road, we then rode all the way up to the Timor Sea making part of the northern coast line and today we will reach the Coral Sea making part of the eastern coast line. The western coast will need to wait for another day and another trip. It is many, many miles away from us.

I get up and take a shower and then make some coffee. In the dark of the room and the fact that I am not quite awake, my hand slips with the amount of coffee I put into my cup. I take my first sip of the coffee and my eye lids opens so quickly it smacks the back of my head. This is very strong coffee. I am suddenly wide awake on an overdose of caffeine. It takes a pretty mean cup of coffee to get me this awake this early in the morning. This together with the shower has me wide awake and I can see Darryl is surprised to find me so perky. He has joked a few times over the trip about just how bad I am in the mornings.

We load up the bikes and get going. The riding east is tough in the mornings as the sun is directly in our eyes. But it does add an extra beauty to the world this early in the morning.

We have travelled about seven thousand three hundred kilometres through the land of the roo and are now in the fourth state of the country and yet I have not seen any live, wild roos. I reflect on this and start to deal with the impending disappointment when I get on the plane and have to admit that I did not get to see any of the roos. Darryl is about thirty meters ahead of me and setting a brisk pace for the early morning.

As Darryl passes a specific point ahead, unknown to me the noise of the bike sets in motion a trap set a while ago. The final stage of the elaborate scheme worked out by these cunning animals is set in action and with my guard down, sun flashing in my eyes and the false belief that these creatures do not exist all finely worked out and now the trap is sprung.

As with the ying so is the yang. Unknown to them I made my coffee too strong this morning which sharpened my reflexes. I had a really good shower this morning where I had closed the hot water and the cold water tap had gotten stuck and blasted me with ice cold water. I had ridden with my visor open and had my sunglasses on under my dark visor, allowing me to see the movement on the side of the road.

My first reaction was to scream in surprise and joy. After all the distance and days of hard riding I finally get to see a wild roo hopping on the side of the road. Even though this initial surprise reaction only lasts a second it is almost my undoing. Before I can grasp the seriousness of the situation, the roo changes direction and starts crossing the road. I quickly react and slam on the brakes. I have to keep the brakes from locking the wheel and causing a slide as this will make steering impossible. Only as a very last resort will I slam on the brake completely. The fifteen odd meters between me and the roo when it changes direction and starts on its way to cross my path is quickly being reduced and I am not stopping fast enough. The other problem is even though I can still steer, I do not know which way to go. Every time the roo's feet touches the ground it hops in a slightly different direction. I cannot avoid it and I will not be able to get the bike stopped in time.
As I make up my mind to risk the locked brakes the roo decides to change direction and try go back the way it came. Unfortunately for it, the gravel on the tar is too loose to allow this. It slips and starts to slide straight in front of my bike. This saves the day for me as I now know where it is going and I let go of the brakes and swerve hard to my right. I had slowed down enough to be able to keep the bike under control as I throw all my weight to the right. As I pass the roo sliding to the left and me almost at the point of falling over to the right my left boot clips its ear on the way past and then we both have to change our priorities to cope with the aftermath of our evasive actions. I pull the bike back

upright and the roo jumps up. I am now down to about twenty kilometres per hour and stop completely. I turn around in my seat and look back and there it sits. Probably just as high on the adrenaline right now as I am and I'm sure if I have a look around I would find that it also crapped itself. It just sits there and looks at me while I just sit there and look at it. I feel the shake setting in and pull over to the side of the road. This is also the queue for the roo to hop out of the road and into the grass. Dam that things was big. I would say I would have had to look down into its eyes if we were to stand face to face, but only just. That thing must weigh more than I do. If I had hit that thing, I would have come off the bike and would have damaged the bike quite badly.

Darryl come riding back and stops in front of me. I tell him about the near miss while we smoke a cigarette. The sour taste of the tobacco mixed with the bitter aftertaste of the adrenaline makes me feel sick. While telling Darryl the reality of just how close it was really gets me shaking. Wow. Bloody things hide for our whole trip and then suddenly try to kill me. At least now I have seen one of the Brown Kamikaze Kangaroos.

When my shaking subsides a little we get back on the bikes and ride onwards towards Jericho. The thick eucalyptus forest is slowly thinning out into farmlands and soon it is one farm after the next, or maybe just one huge farm all around us. The heat and humidity is very high and it is getting pretty uncomfortable when we stop. While riding, with no gloves on and all the vents open on my bike clothes, it is still ok, but the moment you stop, it is stifling hot. When we ride into Jericho we stop for a coffee. The coffee helps to get the sour taste of the adrenaline and cigarettes out of my mouth and I also drink a lot of water. This makes me feel better and after wetting my hair and shirt we ride out of the town.

Shortly after leaving Jericho, I spot some motorcycles pulling up behind Darryl and keeping behind him. I am now leading a train of five motorcycles and set the pace at a hundred and thirty kilometres and hour. We have discussed the speed last night and said as it is now Easter weekend, we should stick to the speed limit. We are not keen on getting speeding fines and do not know just how many cops are going to be out here today. It is not easy to keep the speed down to the hundred kilometres per hour speed limit though. The road is a nice and twisting road with easy corners that you can lay into without needing to slow down at all. It is so nice having these nice corners that I keep catching myself back up at hundred and thirty after a couple of minutes.
Even though I do not see any cops around as expected, the traffic has increased dramatically. I pass more traffic in one hour at the moment than I did for two or three days in the Northern Territories. Lots of mining trucks and lots of people on their way to the coast for their long weekend.

Last night when we discussed our plans for today we thought that we would go through to Rockhampton and sleep over there. The challenge will be to find accommodation in this coastal city. Back when we were still planning the trip we thought that we would only get here on maybe the Easter Monday, which would have allowed us to find accommodation easily, but due to the long distances we travelled per day, we are a few days ahead of the schedule.

Soon we get to Emerald and the bikes that had followed us rides on, while we stop to fuel up. After filling up the bikes we feel ready to fill ourselves up as well. We ride down the main road, but in this little town just about everything is closed. We do finally spot a small corner cafe that is open and order the usual beacon, eggs and toast and go and sit outside in the shade. The owner of the shop comes out and says that we are lucky. Her friend who is helping her out today did not know that they are not serving hot food today, only waffles, salads and pies. But, as we have already paid they will make it for us. She also points out the large sign right next to the shop's entrance, clearly saying exactly what she just told us. Well, lucky us.

The food is great and I go back inside afterwards just to thank them for the beacon and eggs. That was pretty nice of them and I did really enjoy it. Before we carry on, I try to call my friend in McKay again and finally we get hold of each other. They are not going anywhere for the long weekend and we are very welcome to stay with them tomorrow night and the night after that if we want. He has the meat and cold beer ready for us and we will have a nice BBQ outside next to the pool. Yummy! He also says the kids are really looking forward to us getting there, apparently they are big motorbike fans and they really want to go for a ride on the bike.

With a big smile and ready to head out to the coast we ride out of Emerald. The ride from emerald to Blackwaters is uneventful and just a nice easy ride. The traffic is pretty heavy, which demands my full attention, but due to the lower speed, I am actually feeling quite relaxed. The heat is getting heavier with the humidity going through the roof. We could probably have passed through Blackwaters, but the lure of a cold cool drink and water on my head is too great. We pull into the petrol station and find parking in the shade.

There is a grassy section with a few tables in the shade of a few trees where a bunch of travellers are sitting taking a moment out of their journey. When we get off the bikes, a man holding a little baby girl in his arms walks over. He is an ex-biker who now has a daughter and I can see the longing in his eyes. We have a good chat about the journey we have been on and where we are heading. He recommends we do not stay in Rockhampton, but rather ride through the city to a small coastal holiday village called Yeppoon. He says that there is a camping ground right on the sea, you pretty much walk out of your tent onto the beach. That's where he would have stayed if he was riding with us.

Saying goodbye he walks back to his wife who does not look too impressed with us. It must be that biker's sparkle that she now saw in his eyes again. Shame, poor bastard.

Then we finally arrive at Rockhampton. This has been another one of those landmarks on a map for me. This is the point where we start the last leg of our journey. From here we turn north again and follow the coast up to Cairns. I start feeling that deep panic chewing away at my heart knowing we have reached the start of the last stretch. How can that be? We are running out of road.

Rockhampton is again not a pretty place. It is a smallish city with a population of about seventy five thousand people and is known as the beef capital of Australia. It is located on the Tropic of Capricorn and has three hundred days of sunshine a year. As we are planning to camp next to the beach tonight, I am now going to try finding a pillow. I will not be able to sleep without a pillow again. That is of course easier said than done. As we ride through the city centre, we see that pretty much everything is closed in the city. We do find a petrol station, fuel up and then start looking at how to get to Yeppoon. It is about thirty kilometres out of Rockhampton, so we ride out that way. I must admit, my body is pretty sore at the moment and I will enjoy getting off the bike and go for a swim in the sea. The water should be nice and warm and it is still bloody hot.

Saying we are heading out to Yeppoon is easier said than done. We get lost a couple of times and end up at an information kiosk. It is closed, but after looking at the GPS, we think we know which way to go. Eventually we find Yeppoon and it is truly just a holiday village. Even though it is beautiful, it is filled to the brim. There is no accommodation at any of the camp grounds and when we get to the country club with its manicured golf course, we decide that this will not do. Everything is due to be overpriced this weekend anyway and to stay in a place as fancy as this will kill my budget. As sore as we are, we ride back out to the Yeppoon village centre. We see a sign for a few B&Bs and ride down one of the side streets. When we knock on the guy's door and ask if he has accommodation, he looks at the bikes and asks if we are from the Bike around Oz group. This is who we rented our bike from and say "Yes." He then says well, he has your booked rooms ready. Now I am really confused. It ends up that they have an arrangement with Bike around Oz for setting up their bikers and there is another group on their way. So close, but no cigar. I am starting to think we are going to have to sleep on the beach or next to the road somewhere.

Darryl and I stand to one side and now we need to decide what to do. We can ride back to Rockhampton and see what we can find there, or we can try pushing on, but there is nothing bigger than Yeppoon for the next hundred and fifty kilometres. My ass will not make that kind of distance today. I vote we ride back to Rockhampton and take anything we can get there. Darryl agrees and we ride back into Rockhampton. The very first motel we see has a sign claiming they have vacancies.

We pull into the motel and thank goodness yes, they do have rooms available. We book a couple of rooms and as an added bonus they also have a swimming pool. Oh, the joy. They do not serve dinner or breakfast over the weekend due to it being Easter, but that's ok. We will find food elsewhere and as luck would have it, there is a pizza take away, Dominoes next door to the motel. After unpacking the bike I jump in the pool and when I feel my ass will be ok, we go for pizzas. The pizzas are ok, but nothing great and as I swallow my last bite my eyes start falling closed. I am so tired I am struggling to get out of my wet swimming trunks and within minutes I am fast asleep.

Day 16
Saturday 23 April 2011
From: Rockhampton
To: McKay
Distance travelled: 330 kilometres

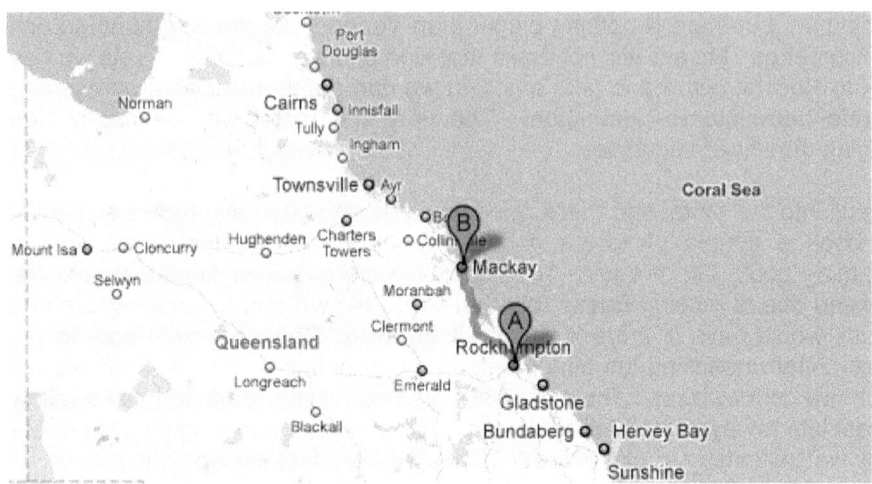

As we have just over three hundred kilometres to ride today we do not jump up too early. I have a leisurely shower and after the bikes are packed, we ride out of Rockhampton on our first morning of riding north since riding into Darwin. As seems to be the norm, it is very hot this morning. It just after 7:30 a.m. and already the temperature is 25°C. The sticky heat is eased a bit by riding with my helmet face open.

Even though it is early, the traffic is already heavy, passing more cars per minute now than we passed per day in some areas in the Outback. The road condition has gotten worse and worse and it is now the worst we have seen so far. I am really disappointed with Queensland so far to be honest. The roads are horrible, the people are rude and the speed limit is low. I am happy with the heat, but I can see Darryl is not enjoying it that much. He is much more of a cold weather fan.

We stop at Marlborough to get some fuel and also some coffee and I take a little time out to check out the people of the East coast. There are a lot of surfers and beach people about. Everyone has good tans and is wearing beach clothes and no shoes. Bleached hair and red eyes seems to be the standard outfits.

As I sit there and sip on my coffee a campervan pulls up to the petrol station and out pours four young chicks. They must be in their mid twenties and real beach bunnies. The one point at the left back tyre and all four of them stand around it and seem to discuss what they will do about the tyre that is a bit flat. So starts a process that for the next ten minutes amuses me. It takes them a few minutes to figure out how to get the pump nozzle attached to the wheel and then instead of inflating the tyre I can see that the tyres is going flatter and flatter. It takes them about a minute to notice this as well and chaos breaks out. They did not connect the pump properly to the valve, so it has been deflating the tyre. I laugh and quickly look the other way when they glare at me. When they finally get it attached correctly, it slowly starts inflating the tyre again. It stops when the tyre still seems pretty flat to me, they must not have figured out how to set the required pressure on the pump. I laugh again, but this time put my helmet on and we ride out of there. I am sure they managed eventually and I know it would have been the gentleman's way to go and offer them help, but honestly they were just so amusing.

We head further north and even though the traffic keeps our speed down we get to McKay quite early and then follow the GPS instructions to my mate Marius and Talana's house. They live in a nice neighbourhood and when we stop there we are welcomed with warm smiles. We unload the bikes and after the first bit of chatting, we go for a swim. Marius takes me out to the shops, so I can buy a few beers and then we settle down at their place. The kids have graciously offered up their rooms for us to use. Thanks guys! I know how it is when your parents' friends come and visit and you have to give up your room. I had to do it a few times so know it sucks. I hope the ride on the bike made up for it.

So, to make up for using their rooms I take the kids for a ride up and down the road on the bike. I give them my helmet to put on, as part of the experience as well as safety, but when the helmet drops onto his head, I am worried that the kid will pass out. I have been wearing and sweating in the helmet for the last few weeks, so it smells less than fresh in there. But, the excitement must have been enough to be able to get over the smell. He does say it feels stuffy in there. They absolutely loved the ride and I hope two new motorbike fanatics got going there. Talana is also happy for me to do some washing, so I get all my stuff into the washing machine and tomorrow I will ride in clean clothes for a change! Wow, it is about time as well as all my clothes have all been worn at least twice since the previous wash. I must admit, the washing machine is much easier than washing it in a basin.

Later on while we sit around the swimming pool, waiting for the meat to braai in the lovely heat of the early evening I bend over the side railing of the outdoor chair I am sitting on to pick up the ball that rolled my way and the hand railing managed to catch me right between my ribs and I can feel it being damaged. The pain is immediately and awful. I know I have more than a thousand kilometres left to ride and we are also going scuba diving somewhere along the coast and with a possibly broken or cracked rib, this is going to be very tough.

Marius says that he doesn't think our idea of going diving in Whitsundays is the best way to go. It is a very popular tourist attraction and if we thought we struggled to find accommodation in the little Yepoon village, we will really struggle to get something in Whitsundays on Easter Sunday. We will probably not get any accommodation and if we do we will have to fork out more than we were hoping to. Also, the dives will be busy and expensive. He then suggests that as we have time once we get to Cairns, why don't we wait till after the Easter weekend is over and then go diving from Cairns? There are lots of diving charters operating out of Cairns on the Reef so we should be able to find pretty decently priced dives.

With this good advice I go and search for accommodation on the internet for tomorrow night and also for the rest of the time we will be in Cairns on a last minute deal website. I find a place that has reasonably priced rooms in Townsville, where we can stay over tomorrow night and then find a true bargain for a three star holiday resort in Cairns. The price for a room is less than what we have been paying for really small dodgy cabins and the place looks amazing. So, with the accommodation sorted, Darryl and I look at diving charters in Cairns. We find a couple that looks to have pretty good deals and send them an email. We only want to go for a dive somewhere in the middle of the week, so no great hurry on that.

We sit outside again with the sweet smell of meat on the coals, good friends around a table and laugh and eat into the night. After dinner we watch a bit of the Super XV rugby competition, but I am not able to make it through the half time break. I am just too tired. I drag myself to the bed and lay down, feeling my rib complain as I try to find a position that hurts the least. Half way through this exercise I fall asleep.

Day 17
Sunday 24 April 2011
From: McKay
To: Townsville
Distance travelled: 380 kilometres

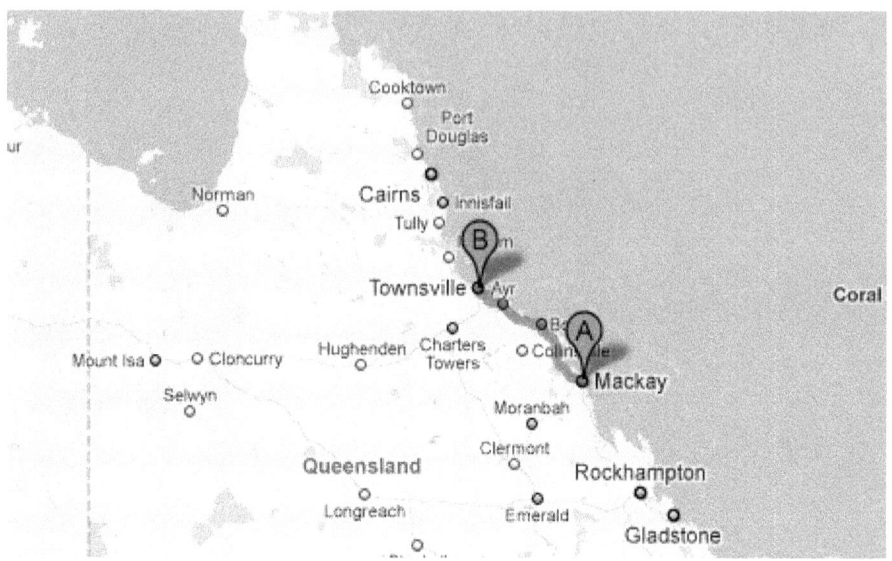

The first thing I feel as consciousness overtakes sleep is the pain in my side. I was hopeful last night that I had maybe only bruised my rib, but the pain is a deep, hard, throbbing pain. This is not good. It hurts with every breath and when I sit up it is bloody painful. A groan escapes my mouth as I stand up. How am I going to do this? I need to cover more than a thousand kilometres, just to get to Cairns. Then we will have a few extra days in which I have a once-in-a-life-time opportunity to go diving on the Great Barrier Reef. Just thinking of the heavy air cylinder on my back pushing down on my ribs makes me groan again.

I get up and take a shower, but I can't even lift my right arm. Where the rib was complaining last night, it is now screaming insults at me. I will need to pop some strong pain pills if I am going to make it to Cairns.
After the shower, Talana has taken out beacon, eggs and toast for us for breakfast. It is so nice to stay with friends. We have only had the one night with them, but it has been magic. While we sit and eat breakfast a heavy shower pours down outside. It is a typical tropical shower, coming down thick and fast and by the time we get up from the table, the sun is shining again. I

imagine we will get a few of these showers over the next few days. The effect of the shower is that the humidity jumps up and I quickly go for a swim. The pool is looking just too good to skip before riding.

After carefully packing everything back onto the bikes, we say goodbye and then ride off. Each bump in the road jolts my ribs, but I mostly feeling ok to ride. I will have to see how bad it gets after an hour or two. The road is now steaming and fogging up my visor. It feels as if I am in a steam room. It is quite incredible really. When we ride out of MacKay and back onto the Bruce's Highway, the jolting gets worse as the road is in terrible condition. Surely they must complain about this and someone come and fix it? Maybe I have just gotten so used to New Zealand where the roads are firstly in good condition and secondly if you do find a road in this condition, one complaint will get something done about it.

I thought that the road would be quieter today as it is Sunday and the middle of the Easter weekend, but the road is very busy and slow. The scenery is interesting though. It is think rain forests all around us, reminding us that we are right on the Tropical or Capricorn. This is also big sugarcane and banana farming country here. Once out of the forest we see miles and miles of sugarcane plantations stretching out in every direction. We are not seeing much of the coast line, although it is just off to our right a few kilometres. We were warned that out in the Outback there are a lot of snakes, but I can just imagine the size of the snakes that must live in these green fields of cane. When I was small my grandparents took us to a sugarcane farm once and the farmer told us about the rats being the size of cats in these cane fields. And that there are also snakes in there that can eat rats of that size. I think I am happy never seeing the things that life in there. I much prefer my motorbike.

We ride past the turn off to the Whitsundays and I am tempted to turn off here and go and see what it looks like. I don't know if I would have the opportunity to come here again, so it might be really worth checking it out. I know it will be pretty busy, but so what? What makes up my mind to just keep going, except for the fact that I have now already passed the turn off, is that I would be pretty upset if we turn off here and get to the Whitsundays and find that it is not too busy and that we could have easily stayed here. I guess it is better to just stick to what we have already booked and paid and just keep going. It is a short stretch from here to Bowen, with lots of traffic and potholes.

As we ride into Bowen, which is about halfway to Townsville, it sparks a memory of earlier in the trip. We were sitting in one of the roadhouses in the Northern Territory when a news bulletin reported that there had been an earthquake in Bowen in Queensland. At that stage I looked at the map and thought we would be going through there in a week or so and here we are. Bowen is where the movie "Australia" was shot. It was that awful movie Hugh Jackman and Nicole Kidman acted in. We did not see them there when we rode through although I was surprised how Tom Cruise managed to catch up to me again.

With the recent earthquakes we had in Christchurch in New Zealand, that pretty much destroyed most of the city centre, I had expected to see a lot of damage here in Bowen, but I could not see any buildings damaged at all. That's good news, as the area from here further north had been hit by a pretty bad cyclone in February 2011. It has only been two and a bit months since that disaster and then they also had incredible floods end of 2010, where Brisbane was almost completely destroyed. This part of the Queensland coast has suffered a lot of natural disasters over the last year. I am glad the earth quake did not seem to have done too much damage.

On the other side of Bowen the sugarcane fields just continue. The sea of green covers most of the landscape and even though there are pretty strong winds out here at the moment, the heat is heavy and thick with moisture. As we get closer to Townsville the wind is picking up quite a bit and by the time we ride into Townsville, I am happy to be in the town. We ride to where we believe the hotel is we have our booking and after a few missed turns, we manage to find it. It is a real roach motel, not the classist establishment I have visited, but we each have our own room, there is a pool and a bar, so who am I to complain.

It is still pretty early afternoon and I am happy to get to bike unpacked. It is a little bit dodgy looking around the hotel, so I decide to unpack everything. The last thing I need now is for something to be stolen from the bike. I can only carry one thing at a time, as my rib is very sore, so after seven trips to the bike and back to the room I have the bike completely unpacked and while Darryl goes for his nap, I go for a beer and a swim.

Later, Darryl joins me and after a couple of beers we head down to the waterfront to get some food. Darryl is keen for some Indian curry and when he mentions it, I feel I am also pretty keen on it. My mouth waters as we walk around looking for an Indian restaurant. The only places we can find are either coffee shops, take-aways or a Greek restaurant.

We sit down at the Greek place and order some food, which is stunning! Really tasty food and hits the spot. I had thought we might need to go out for dinner as well, but this late lunch is big enough to carry me through to breakfast! As we walk back to the hotel, we pass a DVD store that also has internet stations. We go in there to go and check to see if the people from the diving charters in Cairns have contacted us back. They had and will be able to help us on either Tuesday or Wednesday which is great news. We will call them and go pay for the booking when we get to Cairns.

When we get back to the hotel, I have a nice long chat with Elizna. The pressure has been building over the last few days and it is good to have a nice long chat. With the last few days to go, she is now keen for me to finish up on my trip and come home. I am also keen to go, but there is still some riding left to do. And I still want to go for that dive on the Reef. It is starting to scare me that the trip is coming really close to ending!

Day 18
Monday 25 April 2011
From: Townsville
To: Cairns
Distance travelled: 345 kilometres

Getting up this morning is the start of the end. Today I will pack the panniers and load up everything onto the bike for the last time. By the end of today, we will be in Cairns. It is almost unbelievable that we managed to make it so far ahead of schedule. I am pretty sad that this will be the last part of the planned trip today. Carrying the panniers and kit down, one piece at a time, my rib is still throbbing. It is definitely cracked and I need to get some serious pain pills pretty soon.

After loading the bikes up, we use the remaining fuel left in the spare cans we have with us. We will not need extra fuel anymore and it would be good to use the fuel now and keep the cans open, so the fumes can evaporate and I can take the cans back home on the plane. After fuelling up we ride out of Townsville northwards. Today we will see some spectacular scenery. We have seen a lot of variation of beauty on the trip. From the stunning coastline along the Great Ocean Road to the empty beauty of the Red centre. From the tropical parks up in the far north around Cairns to the humid coast line around Rockhampton. But what we will see today is not about beauty. It is about power. Before we get there however we have an hour's worth of very enjoyable riding. The ride this morning is special in a way that only the last part of a journey can be.

The heat and humidity is still here and heavy and due to riding without my gloves on for a few days my hands are covered with heat blisters. I cannot think of having my hands out in the sun today, so have my winter gloves on. This is pretty uncomfortable, but I feel better knowing that my hands are out of the sun. It feels like today might just be the hottest day of our trip and I can feel sweat pour down my body and I have to ride with my visor open to keep the sweat out of my eyes.

The good thing is that the road is quite a bit quieter. I guess it is because it is the last day of the long weekend so the morning should be quite and then the afternoon will get very busy with people starting to head back home. Then we arrive at the scenery I mentioned earlier. In early February this year, Cyclone Yasi hit Queensland. It was categorised as a category five cyclone. I am about to see what happens when a storm of this magnitude hits land. The winds were up to 290 kilometres an hour, accompanied by a storm surge of up to seven meters high.

I have never experienced anything like this and even though it filled our news papers and news programs for weeks when it had hit, there is no way to actually comprehend the damage a storm like this can cause.

The first thing I see is damage to a few larger older trees next to the road. There seems to be a large proportion of these trees that have the majority of their branches lying around it. Here and there I can see a tree that has fallen over, but nothing too bad. As we get closer to Ingham where the cyclone had made landfall the damage is becoming more apparent. It is no longer just the odd tree that looks damaged, but all trees look like they were stripped by some machine that has ripped all leaves and branches off the trees. A shed next to the road looks like a bomb had gone off inside with the roof being blown out. It looks like the cartoon gun after Bugs Bunny had pushed his finger in the barrel and the barrel exploded and peeled back. Now the damage is everywhere I look. Forests ripped to pieces with even small trees ripped apart. I see pretty decent sized trees that look like they were snapped like a toothpick. The only thing I can think of that I have seen on television before that can explain how surreal the scene is, is when they showed the damage after the large tsunami had hit Thailand and the surrounding areas. Kilometre as kilometre this devastation just continues and every corner we go through just opens up on more damage.

It must have been like living through Armageddon to have experienced this storm. I am flabbergasted at the extent of the damage.

When we get to Ingham we pull over at a petrol station and the man behind the counter, without the luxury of his four front teeth, is willing to serve us breakfast. He is a very upbeat type guy, who is probably the friendliest person we had met in Queensland so far. We have a bit of a chat and when I walk out and join Darryl outside, I see the small stage that he has outside at the back of the store. There is a photo of him in his cowboy hat, wearing jeans and a leather singlet up on the wall behind the counter inside. He must do his own shows there. Real country and western, which I assume as Kenny Rodgers is playing and he is doing a pretty good job with keeping up to the song. I am not a real fan of country and western, but I am tapping my foot along as the whole scene is pretty catchy. It is all exactly as it should be. I think if you asked someone to plan and setup a scene like this they would not be able to do a better job.

Anyway, soon he brings out the breakfast and I ask him about the stage out back. He says they do a few concerts every now and then. He reckons they are not really any good but they love it.
"That rocks dude." I say, really enjoying this chance encounter.

"Yeah mate. That's what life is all about..." I get goose bumps realizing I am about the find out the reason for life. I always knew I would find it somewhere remote and unlikely and I guess that is why this place feels so right and almost as if there is electricity in the air. I am about to get the answer to the oldest question in the world, from this man in his leather singlet in the backwaters of Queensland.

"...it's all about having a bit of fun." He says smiling with his toothless grin, gives me a nod and turns around and walks back to the kitchen whistling a tune.

I reckon he got it just about right as well. We toil away day after day fighting to get ahead and make a living and sometimes forget to enjoy that living as well. I found a piece of myself on this trip and now I get confirmation on the reason for life. Cool.

While sipping the coffee and having a smoke I sit and look at the traffic coming past. It has become quite busy out there. It is everyone heading home after the long weekend I guess. We will have to be wide awake out there from here of on. It is often said that the first and last part of a journey is always the most dangerous. People are unsure the first while and complacent in the last part.

When we get back on the road I see that the road condition is pretty much just getting worse. We decided before the trip that we would stick to sealed tar roads as far as possible, but now I am starting to think maybe riding over ploughed fields might be easier. Surely the roads need to have at least some maintenance done on them?

As we come around a long bend in the road, we get to the sea for the first time since Yepoon. We pull over to have a look. The vegetation is true tropics. Palm trees, thick bushes with large leaves and lot's of beach grasses. There are still a number of trees that have been snapped off by the storm and a lot of debris lying around. But the sea is stunning. Long white sand beaches with turquoise water and palm trees. I love this holiday and it will forever be one of the all time greats, but the other holiday I am a big fan of is the Fiji-lay-on-the-beach-and-have-cold-drinks type is also right up there. The scene here reminds me quite a bit of those lovely island vacations.

While we stand there Darryl gives the guys at the diving charters a call. We had contracted them from my mate Marius's house and believed it was all sorted out when we got the email when we were in Townsville, but now they claim the company is closed over the Easter weekend so the deal we found an advert for is not available.

We live in tough times for small companies and as the owner of a small company I would think you would try and make the most of golden opportunities. Now let's analyse this. It is Easter Weekend, which means there will be a lot of people on holiday, so the potential client base is bigger. It is the last long weekend before the winter settles in, so a last push as a diving company before the cold brings business down should be a good idea. The economy had been hit hard in this part of the world with floods and then the cyclone and over the last few weeks I had heard everyone talking about how the economy is just starting to pick up enough for holiday makers to go and do something for the Easter break. And what do you do? You go and pay to have an advert created and published to draw clientele and then close the shop for the weekend. I just do not get it.

The agent says he will call around and see what else is available, so we decide to hang around a bit and wait for the return call. While standing there waiting, Darryl walks off to take some pictures and into the parking lot pulls a RV. You know those large RVs they always have on the movies in America? This thing is immense. The man driving it pulls into a parking that I have no idea how he is going to get out of, but I guess he must know what he is doing. The truck had barely come to a stop and out pours a woman of immense size. She waddles off to the toilets and I have a frozen moment where I think I should react but just can't get myself to move. A small kid is sitting playing in the sand between the woman and the toilet and at the speed she is going I don't think she will be able to avoid trampling the poor kid.

She amazes me by doing a pretty nifty sidestep that would have made any rugby coach smile and then she is gone. That must have been a pretty mean emergency.

When Darryl gets back the guy eventually calls back and we get confirmation that we can go diving on the Wednesday. That is great as that gives us tomorrow off the bikes and all we have to do is lay around the pool, have a few drinks and rest. The off day we had planned finally does come in handy. I must admit, if we had a few more days worth of riding left I might have had to call an off day anyway. My rib is extremely painful and it feels as if the bone might be cracked. Not a pleasant feeling at all. I need to have a day of strong drugs mixed with alcohol to get over this.

It also will leave us with enough time to go for a couple of day trips around Cairns. We are both quite keen to go further north right to the end of the road. Apparently it is very beautiful up there north of Cairns.

With our dives booked, we now only need to ride the hundred odd kilometres to arrive in Cairns. As we get back on the road, the speed limit is brought down to eighty kilometres per hour and then down to sixty kilometres per hour. I cannot really see why the speed limit is dropped, but with the traffic as heavy as it is, all we can do is hang back. Over the next hour the speed limit is set back to hundred kilometres per hour and without exception within the next kilometre it is back to eighty kilometres per hour and then back down to sixty kilometres per hour. I recon who ever have the contract to supply speed limit signs for this stretch of Bruce's Highway needs to be investigated as I am sure they have taken the good people of Queensland for a ride. There is no way that it can be planned to have all these random speed changes.

As we pass a sign that allows us a brief hundred kilometres per hour ride I lay into a long bend to the left. With the increase of traffic I had decided to be extra careful and I am riding in the middle of the lane. This gives me more time to react to any potholes and allows me to go either more towards the centre of the road or the outside, depending on the traffic and the condition of the rest of the road. Just as well, as a minivan coming from the front is drifting into my lane and the guy driving is looking out of the window at something. I lay deeper into the turn and within a second I am right on the edge of the road, almost onto the rough gravel shoulder. Just before passing me the guy looks up and I can see the whites of his eyes as he misses me with maybe half a metre to spare. I hear the car behind me hoot and tyres screeching, but I have to deal with my own situation as a series of potholes has ripped the road on the edge to pieces. I decide to just ride over these holes, as I am already not well-balanced and to jerk the bike around now will be too dangerous. The bike does hop a bit, but the weight of the bike ensures the tyres grip the road and then I am back up and look behind me. The car is a bit further back than it was before, but still coming, so it seems they must have seen it coming and had also moved out of the way. That must have been pretty close as well.

The adrenaline pumps through my body as the close shave with death sinks in. Here we are about forty kilometres away from our journey destination and some twat almost kills me. Asshole!

Then the signs start coming up, we are now thirty kilometres out from Cairns. Of course I need to stop for fuel one more time and we do that at Gordonvale. I tell Darryl that we need to stop at the sign that welcomes us to Cairns, as I would like to have a picture of me standing there. Darryl says that's fine, we will stop if we see the sign.

So, there we go, our last stretch to our destination. We ride off back onto the highway and soon the outskirts of Cairns come up. A fair bit into Cairns we finally see a sign that welcomes us to Cairns and we stop to take some pictures of it. It is actually quite emotional to have arrived here after more than a years' planning, after riding for more than nine thousand kilometres and of course five days early! But, we have done it.

We ride to our hotel and what a pleasant surprise. It has the real colonial look and as we sign in, they tell us there are four different pools, there is a casual restaurant at the main pool and a formal dining room as well. The cost per night here for a large room with a King size bed is less than half what it cost us for the little box we stayed in Coober Pedy! It is truly unbelievable what a little bit of competition can do. We ride around to the back of the hotel, closer to our rooms and my room overlooks one of the swimming pools.

I unload my fully packed bike for the last time and then we head to the pool. The heat of the afternoon is humid and stifling so we spend a good half an hour in the pool. While Darryl goes for a nap I decide to go for a bit of a walk. I walk out and around the block, but then lose interest in the walking. It sounded like a good idea to start off with, but it is too hot for walking around. I go to the main pool and sit down with my book and a beer and when Darryl joins me later we order some lunch. I get a steak burger, which is amazing and very tasty. It has three large pieces of steak on and is cooked to perfection. The large salad with it is also great and with a full tummy and a sore rib I sit and read for a couple more hours until dark and then go to bed. Tomorrow is another day and right now all I need is some sleep.

Day 19
Tuesday 26 April 2011
Off Day – Stayed in Cairns
Distance travelled: 11 kilometres

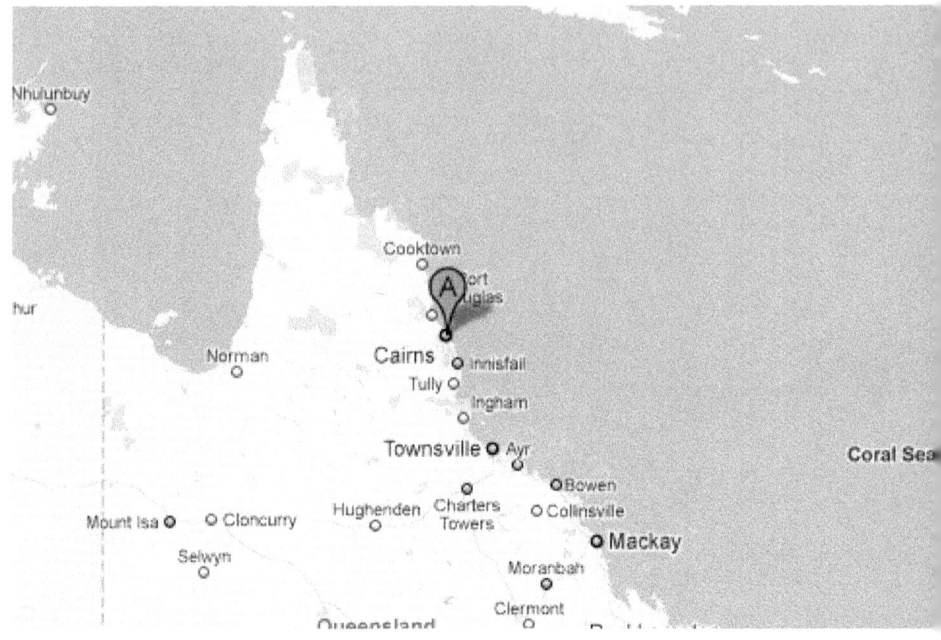

Waking up this morning the first thing I think of is that we are not riding anywhere today. My body is ready for a rest day, for sure, but it is still a bit sad to think that we do not have a bunch of kilometres to do today. My mind is not in synch with my body on this topic. In my head all I want to do is get back on the bike and head towards Darwin, or maybe even Perth.

I have slept later this morning, only waking up at 8:00 a.m. This is not really that late for me as I am a late sleeper, but it is the latest sleep for me for the trip. I don't really have much planned for today. I reckon that if we are going to spend a day not doing anything, we might as well do it properly. The only thing I absolutely have to do today is to get to a pharmacy and get some pills for my ribs. While in the city I would also like to get a new book. I have been reading one of Darryl's books about a guy that tried to smuggle drugs from Thailand. I have done a few stupid things in my life, but mate, if you are dumb enough to get anywhere close to drugs in Thailand, then you should take what is coming to you and not complain.

I have almost finished that book and I intend to lie at the pool the whole day sipping cool drinks and basking in the warm sun, while reading.

I start off with a swim to get me woken up properly and then take a shower and head down the corridor to Darryl's room. We decide to get ready and ride into town now. We can then stop on the way at the dive shop to pay our dives and get that finalised. We get on the bikes and ride into the city centre. Once there we walk around a bit and find a coffee shop that is pretty busy, but the food looks good. We sit down and order some breakfast.

After breakfast we walk around a bit and I find a pharmacy. The woman behind the counter is a New Zealander from the Nelson area. We chat a bit about travelling and then I have some Voltaren pills and a bottle of water and swallow two immediately. Next door to the pharmacy is a book store and I get a trashy novel about voodoo murders in Miami and the cops who are dedicated to find the truth. Groan. At least it is a book and if I do not really concentrate on it, then it is ok as well. At least it is not another story about a CIA agent who is double crossed and need to find the real killer before time runs out. You will not believe just how many books have a plot time pretty close to that.

On the way back to the hotel we stop at the dive shop and pay for our dives. We will do two dives on two different reefs. The weather is bound to be warm with some rain and a bit of wind. Not ideal, but I'll take it anyway.

Then we head back to the hotel and settle down next to the pool. The pills are amazing and soon I am feeling almost painless for the first time since hurting my ribs. I really spend the rest of the day just sitting next to the pool, drinking beer and reading. I can't say much more about this day except that if they say "Do not take pills with alcohol" they have no idea what they are talking about. It gets me pretty woozy and when I go to my room for a nap I do have to retrace my steps a few times to find it. The simple lay out of the place has become a labyrinth of corridors, pools and rooms. My nap is powerful and I sleep easily for the first time since I hurt my rib.

By evening Darryl says he is hooking up with some friends for a few drinks early evening, but I am tired and with the pills working themselves out still sore so skip on that. I scan through the movies in the on-demand list and decide on a stupid movie with Bruce Willis and Morgan Freeman. The movie is almost as bad as the book I am reading, but with the pills swimming in a couple of beers in my tummy I watch is out of focus and know that I will not be able to remember the plot line tomorrow. No great loss I am sure.

Day 20
Wednesday 27 April 2011
Diving Day – Dive on Great Barrier Reef
Distance travelled: 26 kilometres

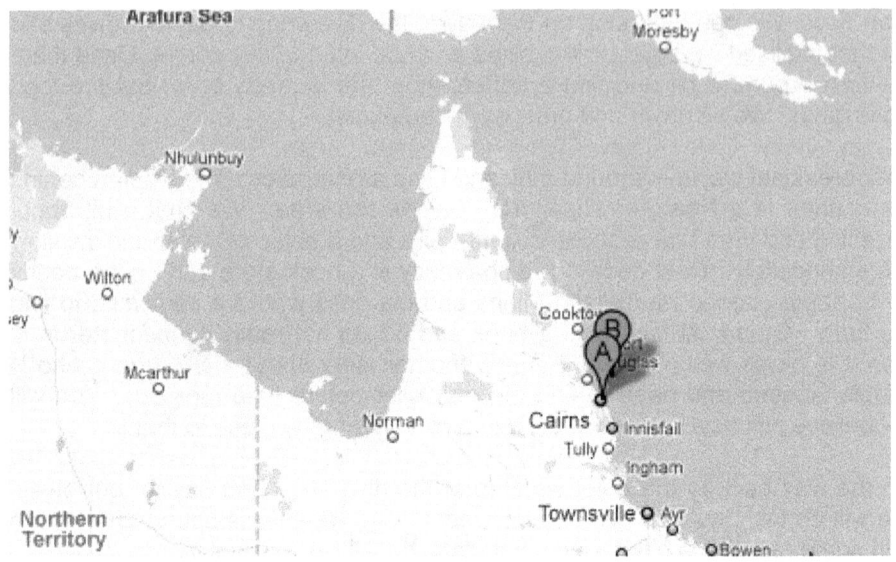

So waking up this morning I know that I will tick off a second item from my bucket list on this trip. The first is obviously doing this trip and the second is to do a scuba dive on the Great Barrier Reef. The Great Barrier Reef as we all know is famous for being able to be seen from space and is the biggest single structure made by living organisms in the world. It is actually a reef system containing over 2900 individual reefs and over 900 islands. It covers a total of approximately 344,400 square kilometres. To put that in perspective, it is about the same size as Germany. The whole of Germany. Basically it is bloody huge. It is also one of the natural wonders of the world.

Did you know that the Great Barrier Reef actually has a postal address? You can send a letter to the Reef.... Imagine doing that postal run. Tough day if the sharks are out and hungry.

Anyway, so up early and off we go to the waterfront where the pier is from where we will launch. We ride out that way and there is quite a bit of wind, but not too bad. It is a warm wind anyway, so I am not too worried. There are also some heavy clouds out over the ocean. For those of you who are not really sea people, rain is not a problem if you are out at sea, if you can just stay dry you will be fine. Wind however has a very different storey. The wind itself is not the problem, but the effect the wind has on the water. It makes the sea choppy and even big boats are pushed around quite a bit. With the wind as strong as it is this morning at the water's edge, I can just imagine what it must be like out there in the open water.

To make sure I give myself the best chance of feeling ok on the boat I need to pack in a large breakfast. But first things first. We need to book ourselves in for the dives. We stand in the queue and there are probably forty people in front of us and within a few minutes another twenty odd behind us. It must be a pretty decent sized boat to be able to handle so many divers. Or maybe it will be more than one boat? Seeing the slow progress and the chaos I am conscious of the fact that there have been movies made of divers being left out at sea. Which means it is possible and with the first impressions I am getting of this diving charter, they seem to be struggling to get going. I will make sure that they know when I am going in and not to leave until I am back on board.

After a while we get to the front and register for the dives. They tell us where we can find the boat and then we head to the restaurant at the start of the pier. I order a full breakfast and Darryl gets a pie. I have never understood how he can eat pies for breakfast. But my older brother can also eat leftover meat for breakfast, so I guess we see morning food differently. Regardless, we have our breakfast and then Darryl heads out to the shop to rent an underwater camera. When he is back we head out to the boat and yes, it is a pretty big boat. Once onboard it is clear that the chaos continues onboard and people are milling about seeming without purpose or direction. Luckily someone eventually takes charge and calls out that all qualified divers must go to the cabin upstairs and all divers needing to do their qualifying dives and people intending to snorkel needs to go to the main cabin downstairs. We go upstairs and it seems that the majority of people are either busy with their qualifying dives or only going to snorkel as there are only about twenty odd people in the top room.

As we cruise out of the harbour the Malaysian man who is our dive master starts trying to tell us about the dive. His English is shocking, although to be fair, my Malaysian is not too good either. He explains that we will do dives on two different reefs, with a possible extra dive on the first reef and one on the second reef. If you want to do the extra dive, you can pay for it when you kit up. The first reef is the Sayon reef and the second one is the Hastings reef. These are both reefs that are way over dived, with quite a few of the larger diving charters using these reefs. We went for the budget dives and will be getting budget dives.

The ride out into the open ocean is pretty rough as I had expected and I am not racially stereo typing, but within half an hour almost all of the Asians onboard, who makes up of almost half of the passengers, are hanging over the sides puking. Sea sickness is no one's friend and soon the sides of the boat have a new colour. The sea was pretty rough so I can understand why people are not feeling well. One of the worst things about sea sickness is that if you get it on your way out to sea, you have a very long day ahead of you, as it will not go away until you put our feet back on solid ground. And trust me, just because you are not feeling well does not mean anyone else cares or is interested to cut their day short.

I feel really sorry for these sick people as the worse is yet to come. While the boat is steaming ahead, the rocking motion is there, but it will be much worse once the boat stops. Then you have to sit with your head down, trying to get your clothes off and the diving kit on and the boat is rocking the whole time. Also once the boat has stopped, you can start smelling the petrol fumes and puke all around you. It is not a pleasant time until you get into the water. Of course, the moment you hit the water you should be fine. Yet while you are puking your guts out, you just cannot imagine jumping into the water.

The dive master explains that for $15 extra, we can have a guided dive or otherwise we are welcome to dive on our own. Most of the certified divers choose to go with the guided dive, while Darryl and I lead up the rough necks that are going to have a go at it on our own. Another woman and man are also keen to dive with us and they are buddied up while Darryl and I will buddy up.
The guy is from some South American country, I think it was either Brazil or Argentina, but I could be wrong, has never done an unguided dive and asks me if he can stick with us once we get down there. I remember my first unguided dive. It is pretty scary at first thinking that you will be down there on your own, needing to navigate and plan your dive in such a way that you do not come up to the surface half a mile from the boat. It is a hard slog to paddle that far once you are on the surface, as the wind and waves will make it difficult and if you are downstream as well, good luck to you.

I agree that he can follow us and so the four of us will have a dive together. There are two other chicks also diving without a guide, but they are not interested in diving with us. The one girl seems to be quite an experienced diver and is taking her friend out. Once the first group has hit the water it is our turn. Kitting up is painful and I cannot wait to get into the water so the weight of the cylinder can be taken off my rib. I just hope that the pressure down there does not do more damage to my rib. I step up to the door in the hull and then with my right hand holding the clasp of my weight belt and my left hand holding the regulator and my mask I step off the boat into the warm water of the Coral sea. I show the guy on the boat that I am ok, then when the others are around me I give the sign for us to descend and down we go.

The two girls who are diving on their own had gone down before us and as I get to the bottom, the one I judged to be an experienced diver swims up to me. She shows me a sign. This is how you can really tell if someone has done a lot of diving. There is no official scuba diving language, although you are taught the important signals like "descend", which is pretty much the thumbs up sign only with your thumb showing downwards. The "ascend" signal is then obviously the thumbs up sign. If something is not quite right you hold out your hand open in front of you, with your palm to the bottom and then swivel it so that the sides of your hand goes up and down. Other signals are for pointing direction, my air is at a specific level and the ever popular "my air is used up", which causes panic I can assure you.

Anyway, the sign she is showing me was not part of any course, but very clear. She put one hand on top of the other, showing a shell covering over the turtle. She then points the direction and starts swimming in that direction. I quickly follow her and as she had shown me, there is the turtle. It is busy eating seaweed from between the coral. What luck to immediately after hitting the water be seeing a turtle? I have seen a few turtles before and it is always special to see how calm they are.

I swim back to where the others are still sitting in a circle not sure of what to do. Only Darryl, who is also an experienced diver has moved and he is busy taking photos. I swim over to Darryl and signal for him to follow me and then swim through the centre of the group sitting there and show them the direction we are going in. They all follow and then they also see the turtle.

I have never done my underwater navigation training, that is part of the advanced diver training and I had never bother to do it. So, now I am swimming in the lead of a group and the only other experienced diver is Darryl and he is not interested in the rest of the divers, he is having fun with the camera. I keep the reef on my right shoulder, as the dive master suggested, but this sounds much easier than it is. The reef is not a defined area, with absolute borders and soon we find ourselves on top of the reef, which is not good. The water is way to shallow and we are being thrown around by the surge on the surface. It is also shocking to see how damaged the reef is here in the shallow water. On the boat I overheard someone talking about the damage to the reef from the cyclone and it is sad to see just how damaged it is. Large sections are just dead coral being pushed around by the current. I work my way back to deeper water and when we finally get to calmer water again, I have no idea of where we are. I decide to just trust my instincts, which of course means we will be going in random directions.

The current is quite strong and the visibility not great. With the cloud cover the light down at fifteen metres is not great, so it ends up being a rather tough dive. I check my oxygen-levels and see that I have used just over half of my air. I stop and then make sure I put what looks to be the main part of the reef on my left shoulder and then swim that way. When I check my levels I am just about at the point where I will have to go up when I see the anchor rope. Can that be? Before I get too excited, I have to keep in mind that it might be a completely different boat's anchor. Regardless, this is where I will be ascending.

Once at the top, the waves are pretty choppy and I get pushed around. Getting onto the boat, which is the correct one after all so I am feeling pretty chuffed with my navigation, will be challenging. The rough water, the sixty other people snorkelling and pushing to get on and off the boat all the time, dodging the projectile vomiting coming from the poor sods who are still feeling the sea sickness and of course the bruised rib all makes getting onboard a challenge. I work my way to the front of the queue to get onto the boat and luckily there is someone there to help me get up.

I am very relieved to be up on the boat and get the weight of the cylinder off my rib. So, there I have it. I have done a dive on the Great Barrier Reef. It was by no means the best dive I have done in my life, but it was special anyway, because of where the dive was. I climb out of the body suite I was wearing for the dive and hang it up and get dressed back into my swimming trunks and t-shirt. Darryl and I sit and have a smoke and excitedly talk about the dive. I think the most spectacular scene of the dive for me was the devastation on the top of the coral reef. I am still quite amazed at the power of the cyclone. I am sure in a few hundred years the reef will be recovered and that this is just a normal cycle of life. I am also glad we saw the turtle.

We move inside and have to step over the bodies laying everywhere. There are a surprising number of people seasick. The sweet tang of vomit fills the air and the dry retching sound coming from various areas on the boat tells the story. Shame, it is still early and we will only be back on land late afternoon. The hell that is this day is still far from over for the sick people. I have been very lucky so far and have never been sea sick. I have become queasy once or twice, but never sick. Once you go past a certain point, you become sick and stay sick until you're on firm ground again. The trick is to fight it as hard as you can so it does not get started.

We go sit inside and join the girl that had dived with us. She has a friend with her that comes from South Australia, actually from a town pretty close to where we passed between Mount Gambier and Port Pirie. She is originally from New Zealand and I can see the Maori blood in her. We have a nice chat and a few laughs as their other friend is one of the victims of the sea. He is crawling out the door to go and feed some more fishes.

My rib is pretty sore so I decide to skip the second dive on this reef and save myself for the next reef. Darryl decides to do the same. While sitting there in the air conditioned cabin, I feel that extra bit of saliva in my mouth and the rolling tummy. I am starting to feel the fringe of seasickness. I get up and walk down the stairs to the main cabin. They have Ginger beer and so I get one of those and go stand outside at the back, in the middle of the boat. If you ever find yourself on the verge of seasickness, this is the best thing to do. The ginger beer will help settle your stomach and the back of the boat in the middle is the point of the boat that moves the least. The mistake people make is to run to the side and hang over the railing looking down into the water. This is a guaranteed barf! Keep your head up and look at the horizon and deep breaths. With all these working together if you are still not quite there, the last thing that will absolutely work is to put your right index finger in your right ear. Trust me if this doesn't work, the last thing I can advise is to find a nice soft place to lie down and find a barf bag as you are about to get very sick.

They serve lunch which is pretty good, but I keep to the fresh salad and veggies. I also don't load too much into my stomach. I see people packing in some serious meals and I hope they don't plan to go diving again. That is going to be a very uncomfortable experience. After the meal the boat starts up and we cruise out to the next reef. Some of the bodies started to move, but they are being lulled into a false sense of believing the worse is over. The brief respite from the death-warmed-up feeling will be over within seconds when the boat stops again.

The boat stops and we are now at Hastings reef. We kit up and this time it will be just Darryl, me and the one girl we had been chatting with. We jump in the water from the back of the boat and as we are just the three we can immediately descend. As we get to the bottom we can see that this reef is in much better condition that the previous one. The surge at the bottom is also less severe and the dive starts off pretty good. There are the usual parrot fish, butter fish, nudibrancs and other tropical fish. Nothing truly spectacular but the dive is much nicer than the previous one. The dive is going well until we come around a small outcrop of the reef and one of the worse things that can happen on a dive happens.

I have had a dive many years ago where my air was used up with at least five minutes of decompression stop still required and that was not this scary. I have dived with five metre sharks within arm's reach and that was not this scary. No, this was the second worst thing that can happen on a dive. The worst thing I can think of is that you surface and the boat is gone. This wasn't that bad, but pretty dam close.

We have lost Darryl. I have lost dive buddies before, but if you ascend a bit to mid-water and do a 360° turn and you should see the bubbles. If not you go all the way to the top and then you should see your buddy doing the same. This is standard practice and all divers know this. Or should know this.

I ask the girl diving with me if she knows where Darryl is. She shows that she does not. I go up to five metres and do another 360°, but still see no bubbles. Dammit. This is not good. I go all the way to the top. The waves crash over me, as it is pretty choppy up here. I do yet another 360° and I can still not see him anywhere. I am about fifty metres away from the boat and cannot see Darryl anywhere. There are dozens of people around and he could be any one of those or none of them. There are divers getting onto the boat and other jumping in. There are snorkelers and then just people hanging over the edge of the boat.

Fuck!

The girl pops up next to me.

"What should we do?" she asks me. It is always interesting to see how people just feel that someone else is in charge and will know what to do. Some people just naturally look to others to lead. Moving that thought out of my mind I am now really scared something might have happened to Darryl.

"Well, we have to go to the boat immediately. If he is not on the boat, we have lost him and we'll need to alert the crew immediately." I say back to her between swallowing a mouth full of seawater. The surface is really rough and getting to the boat against the wind is going to be hard work.

"How much air do you have left?" I ask her. My thinking is that we will need to go back down to at least six metres and then work our way to the boat. There is less of a surge down there, so it will be much easier to cover the distance under water.

"Still quite a bit. I haven't really finished diving." she replies. I am almost pissed off.

"Ok, well, let's go back down and work our way over to the boat. If we run into other divers down there, you can join them and I will go to the boat." I say and don't wait for her to reply. I put the regulator back in my mouth, get my direction sorted and dive down. Once at six metres I start swimming towards where I believe the boat is. I have a look back and see that she had descended all the way to the bottom. She is a bit behind me, but basically tracking behind me. I keep the pace down enough so I do not lose her as well and then I see the anchor line up ahead. I dive down to her and show her the line and show that I am going up. She nods and follows. Looks like she decided to come up to the boat as well. I am caring less and less about what she is going to do. We have a potential crisis on our hands and I cannot care less if she has not had the best possible dive.

I come up and as I hand my mask up to the crew member I shout out to her.

"We lost our buddy!" She nods and asks his name and safety number. Each person is assigned a safety number as they come on board. They walk around the whole day asking you for your safety number to make sure you are onboard.

I really do not know what his safety number is, but that's a great idea. We can check if he has registered back onboard. If he is onboard we will know soon and if not, we will need to get back out there and start looking for him. Before I can get out I see Darryl standing next to her.

"Fuck dude! What the fuck? You can't just leave like that. Shit!" I am really pissed off. There are few things that can make a person as angry as being scared.

"Sorry dude. I became sea sick under water. I tried to go down again, but just kept throwing up. I needed to get out and could not get to you. I am sorry."

I shake off the anger. We got lucky. It could have been so much worse.

I take my kit off and am almost immediately hit by a strong wave of seasickness. The water is really choppy and the wind had picked up, throwing the boat around. I go get another ginger beer and sit outside waiting for the last few divers and snorkelers to get back onboard. Once everyone is confirmed onboard, the boat starts heading back to Cairns.

The ride back makes everyone feel better and soon most people are back on their feet. There are some who rises only now and they had been downs since we left the harbour. They must be feeling that this was money well spent. Shame.

When we get into the harbour the water settles down and the last few minutes is like drifting on a lake. Cairns is stunning from the water side. It is very green and the city has quite a nice skyline. Getting off the boat I was sure that we would see some people drop to the ground and kiss it, but nothing that dramatic happens. People who looked like corpses a few minutes ago are now walking on feeling back to normal and very hungry. It is a strange thing seasickness.

We go back to the hotel to take a shower and put on something else and then we decide to go get an early dinner. There are few things that can make you as tired as scuba diving. And also hungry. We go to an Indian restaurant and I ask the waiter to make the Butter chicken dish really hot. He says that's fine and will make it nice and hot, but it is pretty mild when I get it. Man, I hate it is curry is not hot enough. That being said, the flavour is good and the meal is a great success. I can feel the direct link between my heavy tummy and my struggling eyelids. We pay and ride back to the hotel. I keep my helmet face open so the cool evening air can keep me awake. Then back at the hotel I am on a one way road to bed. What an amazing day and tomorrow we go riding again I think as I float away on meds and good thoughts.

Day 21
Thursday 28 April 2011
From: Cairns
To: Mareeba – Atherton – Gordonvale – Cairns
Distance travelled: 288 kilometres

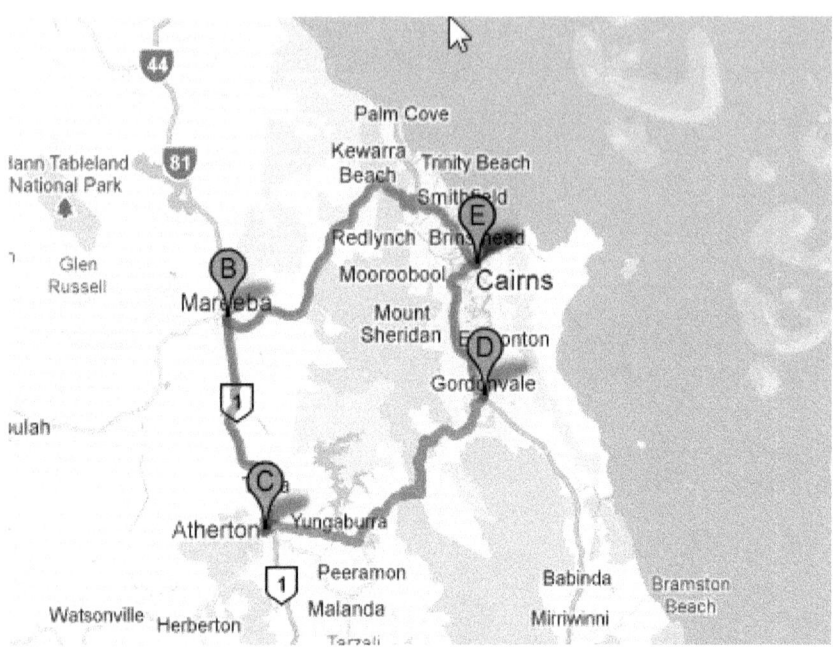

After yesterday where we spent only about fifteen minutes in total on the bikes and the day before where we spent almost no time on the bikes either, I am pretty happy to get up this morning knowing we are going for a ride. Our plan is to do a round trip where we will head inland over the mountain range around Cairns and spend some time stopping and having a look at what is out there.

We decide to get up early, so we are up and out by 7:15 a.m. It is later than we got going when we had long days to ride, but today's ride is not major. I had a pretty bad night's sleep with my sore rib and I pull over at the very first shop I see that is open. I need to get something in my tummy to be able to swallow some pills. This rib is really a pain in the ass. Or pain in the side, if you want to be technical about it.

I buy a couple of muffins and a chocolate milkshake and scoff that down and then swallow a couple of Voltarens. That should kick in within a few minutes and I will be able to save my teeth from the grinding destruction every time I go over a bump in the road.

We head out of Cairns riding north, but only till we just exit the city, then we turn off the northbound highway which we will ride out on tomorrow. For today we are heading west and immediately we enter a pass and start the long winding road upwards onto the mountain range. The road is pretty busy, as it is one of the main routes from Cairns to the inland towns.

As we get to the top of the hill, there is a turn-off to the left to "Barron Falls". Darryl is leading but I flash my lights at him and show him I want to stop there when he rides past it. He was watching his mirror, so I think he wanted to stop there as well and just saw it too late. He turns back and we ride down the small, single lane road into the forest. When we get to the parking area, there are no other cars. Clearly we chose a good day to do this.

It is a one kilometre walk to the falls and back, so we take off our jackets, grab the cameras and head into the forest. The walkway has been built to lead you through a nice windy path, allowing us to see the vines, expecting Tarzan to swing past any second. The plant life here is stunning and the rain forest buzzes around us. Except for the mozzies and bugs of the forest, I cannot hear anything else. I love it.

Then there is the deep bass vibration of the waterfall. Millions of litres of water rushing over the lip of the escarpment, crashing a hundred meters below in the large dark pool of water. As all waterfalls normally are, it is breathtaking. Darryl takes a bunch of photos and I also mange to snap a few on my point and shoot camera.

We walk back to the bikes and are both glad we stopped here. We have a look at the map and see that we now need to head off towards Mareeba. The ride there is stunning and with it being a little bit later now, the traffic is also thinned out a bit.

Arriving in Mareeba it is just another small town, but I notice that the small towns in Queensland are much different from the small towns in the Northern Territory. Up there in the north, the small towns are dirty, dusty places that you would not send your worst enemy to live. Once outside the towns it is stunning though.

The small towns in Queensland are actually quite nice. I like the really small town more than the bigger towns. Cairns, which is a cute is also very nice and I would recommend it a place to visit.

Mareeba is mostly a town that exists because of the wonderful produce from the area. The place is well known for the avocados, lychees, nuts, pineapples and sugarcane.

We grab a coffee and sipping it while waiting for the dark bean of motivation to cool down enough to drink, I feel really great. Back on the bikes after a couple of days of almost no riding, a slight sugar rush still from the muffins and milkshake I had for breakfast and the pills dulling the pain. Darryl says he is going to need some breakfast, so orders some eggs, toast and beacon. I don't need more food at this stage, so just stick to my coffee.

After the breakfast we head south towards Atherton. Reminds me of the English batsmen Atherton. The man was one of the most frustrating batsmen. We needed just his wicket to win a test match and the legend that is Allen Donald was bowling really well, but he dug in and took ball after ball on the body, but survived and drew the match. You have to respect that.

After Atherton we turn towards Yungaburra. Again it is a really nice little town and we stop at the information kiosk. We are looking for recommendations of where to go riding. There is a very nice old lady at the kiosk who tells us how to get to the lakes, which is one of the things we wanted to see in this area. Luckily we asked as it is not as simple as we thought to navigate to the lakes. She shows us on a map how to get there and after thanking her we head that way. The ride there is mind boggling once we get onto the Gilles highway. It is a small windy road through thick forests, where the trees forms a natural tunnel over the road.

Then we get to the lake which is quiet and peaceful. Standing here next to this remote lake, after such a long time on holiday and relaxing, it is difficult to think that in a few days I will be back at it at work and this trip only a memory. The in-control and relaxed feeling I have now will be slowly battered to pieces and I will one day sit at my desk working my ass off and hopefully be able to think back to this moment and get inspiration from it.

I take a few photos of the lake, but like in most cases where you are taking pictures of nature, the photo can never do justice to the scene. Darryl would be doing a better job at it with his professional camera and his eye for seeing the good photos. I decide, I will do what I can with my helmet camera and record the ride back to the main highway. That scene with the trees forming the canopy over the road is calling out to be recorded.

With Darryl focussing on the photos he is taking and me focussing on the film footage of the ride back to the highway, we talk like real men. Which means we both say something, both believe we heard and understood what the other one said and both confirm what we heard back and pretend to have listen to the confirmation. In other words, we have no idea what just happened and go off on our own tangents.

"Ok, so we are heading back the way we came? I will wait for you up ahead." I call out to Darryl.

In his mind he hears" Ok, so we will head on the way we came. I will wait for you up ahead."

Very close, but if you look at it carefully it means the exact opposite.

"Sure, I will see you up ahead." He calls back and then focuses on taking the next picture.

I hook up my helmet camera and wait for the other car to pass and then turn back and ride back the way we came. I am not going fast at all, giving Darryl ample time to catch up. It also allows me to stand up on the pegs to allow for a picture where all you will be able to see will be the road and the forest.

It is about twelve kilometres back to the main road and when I get to the main road and Darryl has still not caught up I am slightly confused. I had gone no more than eighty kilometres an hour, so he should have been here by now. Darryl rarely goes that slowly and I did not think he was far from finished with his photos.

I pull over next to the road and wait. After five minutes of waiting, I am starting to get grumpy. Have I mentioned that I have decided not to smoke any cigarettes today? It is all in preparation of stopping smoking completely once we leave Australia. No? Well, for anyone who has not been within the first twelve hours of not smoking, I can tell you your sense of humour failures are quick to happen, unreasonable and intense. Within seconds I am fuming and growling. What the hell is he doing? Why is he taking so long? If he fell off I am going to kick his ass before helping him!

I start laughing at myself almost immediately after being angry, realising how silly I am being. Then I get angry at myself for being so eager to record the ride that I did not make sure where we are going and waiting for Darryl. Then I laugh at myself for the rapid mood swings.

I feel sorry for pregnant women who have their hormones jumping trampoline inside of them. It must be awful feeling like this for such an extended period of time! I get my cell phone out to call Darryl to ask him where he is. But of course there is no signal here which means I will have to ride back and hopefully he has also noticed we have missed each other. The old law-of-the-bush rule for if you lose someone is to return to the last point where you were together. I hope there is some bushman in Darryl. I know he doesn't hunt, so I am doubtful.

I ride back through the forest and when I get to the lake where we last saw each other, he is not there. A couple is smooching on the grass and I realise I have to either buy some popcorn and settle down to watch them go at it, or leave now. I try to call Darryl again and even though I have a weak signal now, is seems he does not. I do have a voice mail though and it is Darryl telling me that he is going to the other lake and will meet me there.

I switch on my GPS and look for the other lake. There are a number of them, so I select the closest one and let the GPS tell me where to go. I am eventually leaving the forest and then with a few houses off to the right, the GPS tells me to turn right. I head that way and then get directed onto a small dirt road leading to a small pond behind one of the houses. This crazy ass GPS recons this is the lake I would be looking for.

It is at this stage where I decide to not fight against it right now and this is not the point where I should be making a stand. I take out a cigarette and smoke the anger away. Good, now I feel better. I even get to laugh about the GSP's idea of a lake. I look at the GPS again, but frankly there are so many lakes around here with this pond in the backyard being the biggest that I have no idea of where Darryl had gone. I decide that I have had enough. I change my destination to Gordonvalle, which is back on the other side of the mountain. As I get back to the main road, I stop and now I have reception so I call Darryl again. His phone is off, or he does not have reception right now. I leave him a message that I am heading to Gordonsvalle and then turn that way.

The ride out there is stunning. Soft rain and heavy fog settles in and going over the mountain's twisty roads with the thick forests is so beautiful. It is also quite nice to just be on my own for a bit. My speed is pulled down a bit by the traffic and the road works, but the scenery demands slow speed anyway, as it is worth having a look around. The road works is everywhere. Every few kilometres there would be a piece of road they are working on, or let's be honest, a piece of road where they have put hundreds of traffic cones out and left.

Eventually I get to one of the places where they are actually working. They have setup one of those traffic lights to control the traffic while they have closed one of the lanes. I use the opportunity to pass the ten or so cars in front of me. I am a very strong advocate for never ever passing on a solid line, but with nothing coming from the front and all the cars standing still, I pass them while just slightly over in the oncoming lane and over the solid line. For me to mention this you can probably pick up this is a big deal for me. I feel guilty while doing it and as I get to the car right at the front it is a hearse. As I pass the driver's window he shakes his head waves and gives one of those little nods someone does when they try to tell you something.

"Lots of space in here boy!" is what I imagine that nod to say.

"EEEEEK!!!!" I would have replied if I could. Luckily the oncoming traffic comes past us then and when we get the green light I am out of there. I am going a bit more carefully now. That body wagon freaked me out a little bit. I am not a superstitious person, but also not brave enough to laugh at omens.

When I get to the other side of the hill I pull off at the petrol station at the town entrance. I get my phone out and call Darryl up. He had received my message and is in Gordonsvalle as well. I meet up with him and we grab some cake for lunch. The coffee is good, but the cake is not. If you are doing a round the world tour of the world's best cakes, you can scratch Gordonsvalle from your list. As we sit there outside the coffee shop, heavy rain falls and we decide to just hang back for a short while to let the rain pass. We smoke a cigarette and when the rain eases off we decide to ride onto the peninsula to a small town called Yarrabah.

On the way there, we seem to have caught up with the rain again. Instead of easing off, it is worsening and within seconds I am drenched. It is really coming down. It is warm rain though and when Darryl pulls over to hear if I am keen to go on or turn back I suggest we just keep going. We are wet already and will never get to chance to see Yarrabah again. Darryl seems happy with this idea, so we keep going and then we get to a very steep hill. The road signs warn that the hill is over 45 degrees at some places. Surely that can't be right? That's almost straight up? If that is right, we sure are going to have fun going over.

So the town of Yarrabah is a dry zone, so no alcohol allowed in the town. It is an Aboriginal town according to the information board we pass on the way over the hill. We ride in and the looks we are getting are not letting me feel very welcome. We pull over at the beach and dismount from the bikes. There are a few wrecks out in the bay and this makes for a good photo opportunity. We walk onto the beach and Darryl walks off to the one side. I take a picture of the one wreck and then decide to walk closer. There are rocks all the way to the boat so I should be able to get pretty close. I can see a path to pretty much right next to the boat. All I have to do is give a small jump over the first pool and then I am right on the first rock.

It is just a little jump, but with the boots and the bike pants I will have to really give it a good jump. I take a short step back and then give a quick jump onto the rock and then sink into the mud up to my knees. For a moment I feel myself losing my balance and if I fall over now I will be mud all the way from my head to my toes. For a second I not sure if I can get my balance back. Luckily I do, but now I need to get out of here as was starting to sink further. I waddle through the water I had just jumped over and now I stand on the beach and take stock of my situation. The "rocks" I tried to jump onto is actually mud. The whole bay is just mud.

Standing there with mud in my boots and inside my pants up to my knees, I hear a funny bird calling. It sounds almost like someone laughing. Turning back from the beach I can see a couple of aboriginal boys who are sharing an ice cream laughing at me. I wave at them and they wave back still laughing. At least I am entertaining. I turn to see Darryl taking a nice big step back to jump onto the rocks just up the beach from me. Even if I could call out in time and stop him, which there truly wasn't time for it, I didn't. I watched him fly through the air and land on the rock and sinks in to his knees. Now I was joining the boys laughing at him. I see him struggle out and then he sees me where I am rinsing my boots and pants under the tap on the end of the beach.

After cleaning up walking back to the bikes I see a large sign warning us, "Beware Saltwater Crocs". I have scuba dived with pretty big sharks before. I have played with a lion cub, almost the same size as myself, I have stood my ground with a rhino while on my own in the bush hunting, but none of these scare me as much as saltwater crocs. I have seen a program on these monsters and I tell you what. If I never see one of these in my life, that would be just fine with me. These things are the largest reptiles alive. They grow to up to six meters long. Just stop and think about that. Six meters! To put it in perspective, think about the front door on your house. Take it off the hinges and lay it flat on the ground. Now take two more doors and put it so they are all in a row length wise. That is six metres and the length of these monsters. They weigh up to a ton. Up to a ton! The record length.... 6.6 metres! So, they are large. So what? Cows are large as well and not scary. Well these things can swim at a speed of eight metres per second. Think about it, they can swim a full Olympic swimming pool in eleven seconds. Try get away from that! And they feed on anything they can find, including humans.

With my mind made up about the future of walking around on this beach, we get back on the bikes and ride back over the hill. It was so nice to get to a place like this, just a few kilometres out of Cairns, but it could just as well have been a world apart. We ride back and now decide that this should do it for the day and ride back to Cairns.

After taking a swim in the swimming pool at the hotel we decide that we will go get some Nandos for dinner tonight. A bit of peri-peri chicken sounds pretty good. We ride back into town and park next to the Nandos. We go inside and order the food and sit down to wait for it. It will be nice to eat here, as the food will be nice and hot and once we get back to the hotel, I know I will be asleep in no time. Within a few minutes, Darryl's quarter chicken arrives and he starts eating it. I must admit, it looks really good and my tummy screams out for food as well. I can feel my tummy starting to chew on my spine.

After twenty minutes and Darryl having finished his food, my food has still not arrived. I decide that I will not ask for it again from the dumbass waiter and walk into the kitchen and ask them. The manager is quite surprised and manages to inspire his team of chefs to rustle up a burger. When they bring my burger I tell Darryl that we can leave, I will eat the food at the hotel. We are quite tired and when we get back to the hotel we head to our rooms and when the food settle in my tummy I am already half asleep. Tomorrow will be our last day for riding, so I want to be rested for it.

Day 22
Friday 29 April 2011
From: Cairns
To: Port Douglas – Mossman – Cape Tribulation - Mareeba – Cairns
8Distance travelled: 348 kilometres

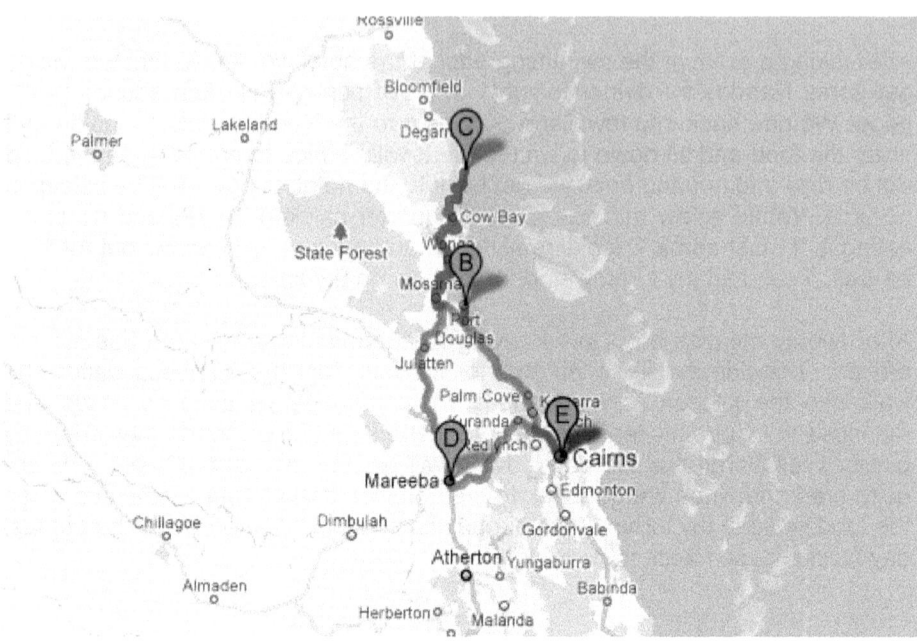

Not to start every chapter the same as all the others, but here we go. We get up early, but the difference today is that this is our last day's ride. The ride up to Post Douglas is rumoured to be very beautiful and looking outside I can see it is a very nice morning. It is nice and warm and no sign of the rain of yesterday. As we ride next to the coast, I can see the sea to the right between the trees every now and then. When we pass over a hill we pull over to have a look at the valley below. The view is breathtaking. This is truly one of the most beautiful places in the world.

When we get to Port Douglas I am very ready for a cup of coffee. I see a coffee shop next to the road and not being sure of what else is around I pull over. We order a coffee and when we sit outside, there is a man with a leave blower doing his thing. This brings me to one of the reasons why I believe mankind cannot survive and will self destruct. Here is actual proof of this fact. That man have become so bloody lazy to have a machine that does not only make an awful noise, but also pumps out exhaust fumes and all this to blow the six leaves from one side of the parking lot to the other and then to be swept up, just shows how terrible we are. Just sweep the bloody things up. Dammit, let me pick them up for you, just turn that noisy piece of shit off!! It will take you half the time and leave us to enjoy our coffees in peace you lazy bastard. The fact that he is at least twice my size stops me from actually saying everything, but I can tell you I did give him "The Look". Anyone who knows me and had to be on the receiving end of "The Look" knows what a terrifying experience this is. Somehow the man is not being affected or is immune against "The Look" and just keeps blow the six leaves around. I must be losing my superpower. I curve my left brow up further, cramps pull my left ear to the back and drool start dripping down my chin, yet he keeps blowing.

I have now found something I hate more than a lawnmower on a Saturday morning 7:00 a.m. I think I will be locked up for murder if my neighbour gets one of these!

"Nice choice of a place to have a coffee dude." Darryl comments and laughs when I start sputtering about the stupid man with the dumbass blower. He knows when to press my buttons and get me grumpy.

We get back on the road and now head to a place called the Daintree National Park. It is a very special area where the rainforest is being protected and quite a touristy place. We park in the large parking spaces, designed to hold tourists busses. We decide to take one parking each. The worrying thing is that there is space for eight of these babies. Can you imagine what this place must look like if the parking bays are all full? I think I would skip. I do get reminded about the busses pulling into Ayers Rock that morning, now so long ago. Luckily there are no large busses here today, just a camper fan and one other car.

We walk up to the shop where they have a little cafeteria and a souvenir shop where you can buy your fridge magnets, post cards, T-shirts cleverly saying "My parents went to the Daintree and all I got was this stupid t-shirt". HAHAHAHA. Where do they get this original material from?
The guy at the entrance to the walkway is quite excited about the place and takes us through a ten minute spiel about how great the walkway is, but when we get down to the entrance fee, he loses us. I must have seen it coming. It is one of those, "but wait, there's more!" sales pitches. They want $30 per person to walk through the forest. Ok, let me think about that for a second. Usually Darryl is the first one to walk away when people talk nonsense, but he is managing to keep listening to him. After the leave blower of earlier I am not as politically correct as Darryl so this time I am the one to walk away. I go order a juice while the man tells Darryl that for an extra five dollars you can get a radio that will give you commentary all the way through the walk. It picks up where

you are in the forest and gives you information about what you can see. I think at this point he had realized he was not getting this sale over the line as his enthusiasm has decreased and he did not object when Darryl said no.

Darryl also goes to get a juice and come and sat with me, where we can see the walkway leading off into the forest. It is very beautiful and if it was ten bucks I would have said it would be worth it. The lady who was behind the counter who served us our drinks must have felt sorry for us, as she brings over a couple of slices of caramel tart. She says we do not need to worry, we can have it for free. Again it occurs me just what we must look and smell like. I cannot remember ever getting free caramel slices while dressed in my suit at work....

But, I will not complain. The caramel slice is wonderful and very sweet. After we finished the tart I feel obligated to at least browse through the shop and look at the stuffed toys with interest and then placed it back on the shelves. When it seems we have spent enough time to at least have considered buying something, I wave goodbye and off we go to the bikes. We decide to go further along the little road into the forest, as there are signs claiming that there are more walkways further down the road. Within a few minutes we get to another walkway, which is completely open to the public. No caramel slices here though, but then again, I am still so sweet after the slice I did have that I am not put off by the lack of infrastructure.

We park the bikes and then go for the walk. It is a very nice walk and so many photo opportunities. I have a relatively nice camera. A Sony something or the other model that has a range of buttons I have no idea what they do. I usually just switch it between anti-shaking mode and the panoramic mode. I still need to figure out what the rest does. But moments like these when I get to places with spectacular beauty all around me, like this forest, long beaches, strip joint, etc. I get inspired to take professional photos. I will see a plant that had twisted around a tree with flowers perfectly lined up and then snap thirty photos, already seeing them published in some National Geographic magazine. The problem with that is I am not very good at it and don't know how to take good enough photos anyway. It is fun doing it anyway and with digital photos, I can just go ahead and delete them tonight if they suck, so I snap away throughout the walk.

The walk takes us via a long loop and after about an hour we are back at the motorbikes. I am glad we did get to walk in the Daintree forest, it is a very serene atmosphere. We have a quick look on the GPS and we now need to head on up further north. We are pretty close to Cow Bay and just before we get there, we will have to wait for the ferry that ferries traffic across to the remote northern areas of Queensland.

It takes us just a short few minutes of riding through dark green fields of sugar cane to get to the ferry. Riding up to the gate I see that it costs $28.00 to get a return trip on the ferry. The lady sitting in the booth smiles and opens her window. The smile disappears immediately. I am becoming real self conscious about my smell as the smile that replaces the friendly one she started off seems forced.

"No charge for you today. Just go on ahead to the chain and wait to be called onto the ferry." She says and before I have the opportunity to thank her she closes the window. I will have to rinse the jacket out before I think of getting onto the airplane with it on.

Not put off too much I ride up to the chain and then wait for Darryl. He comes and parks next to me.

"Did you pay for me?" he asks.

"No, she said there is no charge." I leave it at that.

"Sweet. She just waved me through." He replies.

The ferry is pretty much just a barge. It is pulled across the river on a thick cable to the other side which is only about eighty metres or so away. We ride onto the ferry and I use the time to take off my jacket. There is a forty kilometre per hour speed limit on the other side so we will be going pretty slowly. It is also very beautiful and we have nothing rushing us, so I am happy to ride without my jacket.

The scenery once on the other side is the most beautiful we have had for the whole trip. It is as if we had arrived in paradise. Thick forest all around us with the canopy hanging over the road creates the image of riding through a tunnel into another world. Then the road twists up over a hill and you can see forests to the one side as far as the eye can see and the Tasman sea on the other, blue with white sandy beaches. The slow pace allows for lots of time to look around and even though the road quality needs some of my attention, I am looking into the forest most of the time.

We come up to a place where there are a few cars parked next to the road and people looking off into the forest. I have done enough game drives in my time in Southern Africa to know when there is some wildlife next to the road. People just stop and point. I pull over as well as I have been hoping to see a Kuala. I stare into the trees, but can't see anything moving in there. I bend down and look into the car next to me, to see where they are looking. They seem to be looking at ground level. I look in the direction they were looking and just when I think they must be on drugs or something, it moves. It is a turkey on steroids. I kid you not, the thing must weigh three hundred kilograms and its head must be about the same height as mine! I will later find out that it is the Cassowary. Man, what a big bird. I would not like to be the one to have to catch that for the Christmas dinner. It is an endangered species, in fact the most endangered bird in Australia. If these things get angry, they can kill dogs and other small animals.

We carry on up the road and soon arrive at Cape Tribulation. This is pretty much the end of the road. From here of on it is unsealed road and we had decided not to do the off road riding. We see a parking area from where there is a foot path down to the beach. It looks like the bikes would fit through the gap, so off we go down the foot path. It is exhilarating to be riding on this small muddy foot path, but with the bikes unloaded, they are light and easy to control, so we soon get to the end of the footpath. From here it goes onto a wooden bridge, which will take us onto the beach. We decide not to try ride over the wooden bridge, the last thing we need now is to have one of the bikes fall through the wooden bridge into the swamp two metres below. I can imagine the total pain in the ass it will be to try get someone to help us get it out of there. We park on the grass next to the walk way and walk through to the beach. It is an amazing long, white, sandy beach with absolutely no one in sight. We decide it is time for a swim in the sea. Darryl had remembered to pack his swimming trunks, but me not being a morning person, I did not think of that. So, I will be swimming in my rocket ship underwear. Don't laugh, it is very comfortable underwear AND my wife had bought it for me, so it is cool. All cool people wear rocket ship underwear, or at least Superman underwear.

We walk down to the water line and the water is nice and warm. Unfortunately there is a bank of rocks and after going in about ten metre I decide to rather go back out and walk a piece down the beach. Forty meters to the right of where we are trying to go into the water there seemed to be no rocks. Darryl carries on and I walk down the beach and sure enough here is a spot where there are no rocks. I walk into the water and dive into the waves. The swim is great as the warm water is pleasant and there seems to be almost not undercurrent.

I decide that's enough after body surfing out half way to the beach and as I stand up, still in waste deep water, I see that I no longer had an empty beach to walk out onto. On the beach, just above the water line at the exact point where I will need to walk out, three girls had taken their seats for the show. I will not be able to go further to the side, as the rocks are pretty much right next to me already. I will have to walk right past them.

I decide that confidence will be the way to go and dive into the water and do my best James Bond exit where I break through the water and throw my head back so that the water loops over my head. I walk out with my shoulders calmly moving from side to side and the water running down my muscular stomach, which is being pulled in of course. I am just hoping the water wasn't too cold, but there is nothing I can do about that now. I walk out and up to the three girls, all being in their late teens and as I walk past them I nod and say,

"Good day ladies." In an octave lower pitch than my normal voice while running my hand through my hair.

They burst out laughing and I can't help but laugh as well. I walk on without looking back and when I get to where we had left our bike clothes, I grab my pants.

"Watch out. There were ants all over my pants." Darryl warns me. All I need now is for there to be hundreds of fire ants or something to be chewing on my balls. I shake out my pants and sure enough a bunch of ants are shaken off. I make sure there are none left and then put on my pants. I see there is a notice board next the entrance of the walk way where we had come through. This is not good. It warns that it is dangerous to swim here, as they have a lot of jelly fish that kills a lot of people here. Also, my old friend, the saltwater crocodile seems to be a regular visitor.

I decide to just forget I saw that and when dressed we go back over the wooden bridge back to the bikes. We ride back along the footpath and as we approach the entrance to the path a man comes running up to us screaming. What the hell? As we get closer to him I realise he is screaming at us. He is very unhappy about the fact that we had ridden down the footpath.

"There are no fucken bikes aloud on the footpath" he screams, spit flying from him mouth as I ride past him. I give him "The Look" back and just keep riding until we are back at the road. He is now about twenty metres behind us and had not given up. He is rushing up behind us.

Darryl asks if I am keen for lunch and I say I am, so Darryl turns to the right and then pulls over at the restaurant right there. I had hoped we could get away from the screaming man and find a place there to eat, but I guess this will have to do. I see in my mirror that he is still following us and still screaming. I am starting to get worried that the man might burst an artery in his head going on like that.

We park and get off and not for the first time the fact that we have not shaved and Darryl had shaved his head worked for us. We look pretty scruffy and I light up a cigarette while standing next to the bike. If the man wants to come over and discuss his concerns about the riding etiquette on footpaths, I would rather be here while he does, than to leave my helmet here on the bike and perhaps he starts screaming at my helmet.

He glares at us from the road and then turns back towards a small shop on the other side of the road. I guess he felt he had made his point and as we are clearly not on the footpath anymore, he doesn't have much to say anymore. When he is out of sight and the cigarette is done, we go inside to get some food. Must say, I am really hungry, so food would be great. The restaurant was recommended by his ex-girlfriend as a place to definitely stop and eat, so I am looking forward to it.

Unfortunately we are too early for lunch. It will be another hour before lunch is served, so we decide to just get a cooldrink and sit and drink that. I get a Coke Zero and we sit outside in their garden. The smoker's area is down next to the pool and we go sit there. A pretty good looking girl is lying next to the pool sun bathing and she does catch both of our eyes. We then sit down and talk about the guy that was so angry about us riding on the foot path.

While Darryl talks about how regulated it seems people live in Australia, where you shouldn't do anything unless expressly told you may, I notice something strange. Behind Darryl a guy is standing staring over the fence at the chick lying next to the pool. I agree she is good looking, but that is a bit creepy the way he is staring. I try to ignore him, but after two minutes of him still staring I am a bit unnerved. I think she must have felt him watching her and gets into the pool and has a swim. Then I noticed something even more bizarre. The guy was still staring at the same spot where she had been lying. Then his friend joins him and now I am truly baffled.

I get up and walk over to go and see what's happening and now it is my turn to feel embarrassed. He wasn't staring at the girl at all, it just looked that way from my angle. He is actually standing looking at a snake on the fence of the swimming pool area. It is about a metre long and working its way along the metal fence. It is stunning to see the way it is moving along the thin metal rods. Darryl grabs his camera from his bike to take a few pictures of it, but unfortunately by the time he is back, a young man with more alcohol in his blood stream than IQ in his head, has now decided to try catching the snake with a fly swat.

I think I have seen this on some TV show about people doing dumb things with animals. Playing with a snake is firstly dangerous as you are pissing off the snake and it will try to bite you or someone around you, or spit at you and the other thing is that snakes are actually very fragile and if you hurt its spine, it will die. Even small cuts in its skin can be deadly for snakes. I am no fan of snakes, but I believe that if I am in their environment, then I have no right to hurt it. If it comes into my home, it should be prepared to die though.

Anyway, this is my queue to exit, as I want nothing to do with the dumbass who is about to get bitten. Outside back in the parking lot, it seems the screamer had not come back. That's better, so we now turn back towards Cairns. The ride back is just as stunning as the ride this way and too soon we are back at the ferry. On the way over on the ferry we decide that we will ride over the hill and come back into Cairns on the same route we left it yesterday. It was so beautiful that it is worth a second look. And yet again it was amazing to come down the hill seeing Cairns stretched out and the picture perfect sea beyond.

Back at the hotel I go for yet another swim and we decide to chill out till evening when we will head into town and go and check out the night market.

The night market in Cairns is quite cool. In my mind's eye I saw a hustling and bustling market with fresh herbs and parakeets being sold. People screaming over each other, trying to sell you exotic spices, animals and jewellery. Unfortunately it is nothing like that. It is firstly all under roof attached to one of the shopping malls. Secondly they do not sell any exotics stuff, but basically kangaroo and Kuala soft toys, leather hats and all the other crap you can find in tourist shops, all under the one roof. We split up and my mission here is to get Elizna a present and of course to get my baby a present as well. I will need to find something to give her when she is born that will symbolise her dad riding around while she was growing in her mummy's tummy.

I find a shop that sells opal sourced from Coober Pedy, which catches my eye. That is perfect for a present for Elizna. Coober Pedy feels so long ago, but I can remember our dictators in hiding there and of course the Outback soapy that I saw take place outside the information building. I wonder what happened to Thulunka and her friends. I laugh thinking about it and all the bloody flies and the woman who is busy explaining to me where Coober Pedy is frowns. She must think I am laughing at her.

"Sorry. I wasn't laughing at you. So, you say these are from Coober Pedy. Have you been there?" I ask.

"No, never been out to the southern Outback. There's too many flies down there." The lady says and I then start telling her about us having just been there a couple of weeks ago.

"Really shocking what they are doing to the landscape there. It looks like they are digging up the whole place to find these rocks." She seems to be losing interest in my story, so I choose the one I want and pay for it. I still need to get something cute for the babe.

I find a shop that has pretty cute koalas, crocs and kangaroos of all shapes and sizes and I select a couple for her. I also get some bibs and then walk through the rest of the market. Eventually I had enough and head back out and give Darryl a call. He has gotten a few gifts as well and now we're heading back to the bikes.

As we walk past a shop selling didgeridoos, Darryl says he is interested to buy one. We stand outside trying to make the didge sing, but it sounds like elephants farting in a tunnel to be honest. The salesman comes outside and soon he is explaining what the different didgeridoos are and why they are different. He shows us what you should be doing with your lips and where I had been blowing into the pipe as if it is a trumpet, what you should be doing is doing the "bbbbbrrrrrrr" that little kids do with their lips when they play with their little toy cars. You do that, the pipe picks up the sound and echoes it correctly and viola, you have that didge sound.

I try it and within a couple of minutes I can at least do a few different sounds and feel pretty chuffed. Darryl decides to buy one and included in the deal he can come back tomorrow morning and get an hour session being shown how to use it. They will also mail it to him, so he doesn't have to struggle through customs with it when we fly. At a hefty rate of course, but nothing is free in the world.

The next shop towards where we parked the bikes also sells didgeridoos. To be fair, just about every shop in this area sells didgeridoos, but this one will send your didgeridoo to your preferred address for free. I have a good laugh at Darryl while he grumbles about the price he had to pay for delivery a few seconds ago.

We head back to the hotel and that is pretty much the day. I know I am going to bed tonight to then start the last day of the trip tomorrow. It's like really dark chocolate. Very bitter, yet it is chocolate.

Day 23
Saturday 30 April 2011
Off Day – Stayed in Cairns
Distance travelled: 18 kilometres

This is our last day in Australia and of this trip. We have nothing planned for today, except to rest out and prepare myself for re-entering the normal civilised world where we have to shave, dress in suits and do productive work. No more all day bike rides, no more afternoon beers and no more all day bike rides. I am going to miss getting on the BMW GS1200 every morning.

Mentally I feel really well rested, the riding and spending all those hours alone in my helmet has done wonders to my state of mind and after the last few days of taking it easy my body is also starting to feel rested. Today will be the last effort to make sure that when I get back home I am ready for it.

Waking up with the sun already up is a normal holiday feeling for me, even though we were up before the sun pretty much every morning on this trip. First things first, I go for a swim in the pool. The air is warm and so is the water so the swim is amazing. I drift with my ears just under the water line, starring straight up in the sky at the few clouds drifting past. It is difficult to think that in twenty four hours from now I will be in freezing, wet weather back in New Zealand. Elizna had warned me that it has been really cold the last few days, so I better enjoy this heat now.

Darryl comes down for a swim as well. Then he says he is heading off to town to go and do his Didge lesson. I will also go into town, as I have to mail the satellite phone back to the company we rented it from. Luckily we did not need it during the trip, but it was always good to know that it was there if something should go wrong. It is definitely something to keep in mind in places like this, that there is no mobile phone reception for long periods.

So, we decide we will go into town, have breakfast and then Darryl can go his way and I can go get rid of the phone. We ride back into the centre of the city and find a cafe that is serving breakfast. We gobble down our usual beacon, eggs, toast, hash brown and coffee. After breakfast I walk out and now have to look for the post office. I walk down the main road and can't find it. There was a sign pointing this way right next to the cafe where we had our breakfast, but the only thing I have managed to find is a post box. This will not do. I go into the pharmacy where I got the Voltarens a few days ago and ask them where the post office is.

"It is down to the left and all the way to the end of the inner city. About six blocks away. But they are closed over the weekends." She warns me.

"Closed? You gotta be kidding me." I reply.

"Yeah, I also had to get used to it when I moved here. Back in New Zealand the post office is open on the weekends." She says and now I have to make a plan.

We are leaving Australia tomorrow and yes, it is Saturday today, and so even if we did have time tomorrow, the post office would be closed tomorrow as well. We are flying pretty early, so would not have made a difference. The other challenge will be to get hold of the people from whom we rented the phone. It is weekend, so most probably not at the office. I will need to get back to the hotel to see what I can arrange. Now I feel stupid for not sending it back as soon as we arrived in Cairns.

I ride back to the hotel and call them up. The phone answers and then cuts out, with the very friendly lady from TelstraClear telling me that I have used up all my credit. GRRRRRR!

I go to the pay phones and when the Indian lady finished up on the phone I use the opportunity to use up all my coins. I manage to get hold of the man I rented the phone from and he is not much help. He has no idea what I should do now.

"How about I leave the phone with the hotel and ask them to mail it on Monday?" I suggest. It is no use just saying the post office is closed and then stop thinking. We need to come up with something.

"I don't know. What if it gets lost?" he asks.

"Well, I guess the chances of it getting lost are about the same as it is if I send it. I will make sure that I know whom I gave the phone to here at the hotel and make sure it is some type of manager. Then I will send you the name. Will that be ok?" I suggest

"Mmmh. I don't really know." This is where my patience runs out.

"Ok, well I give you ten minutes to think of a better idea. If you have not phoned me back by then, I will take it that we do not have a better idea and give it to the hotel." I say and before he has the opportunity to respond I say goodbye and hang up.

That felt good.

I ask for the manager at the reception desk and explain the situation.

"...so if you can just mail it out with your normal mail on Monday that would be great."

"I don't know." He responds to my utmost frustration.

"Come on mate. All you have to do is make sure this gets mailed on Monday. It is already paid for." I ask while counting to ten in my mind.

"Our mail only goes out on Tuesdays." He replies. The worrying thing about talking to this man is that his hand keeps coming up to his face with his finger seemingly on its way to his nose, then he stops just in time and drops his hand. It is quite distracting as I have a TAB betting odds going on if he is actually going to get to his nose or not instead of trying to talk to the man properly.

"Ok, thanks mate. I really appreciate it. I will tell them that you will send it on Tuesday then." I say as if we had just agreed to it and put the phone of the counter and walked away. I really hope it will reach them, but what choice do I have?

I go and email the rental company providing them with the details of when I handed over the phone, to whom and when they agreed to mail it.

Now it is time to relax. I get my book and order a beer and then just sit next to the pool. I am a magnet for the warmth.

As days always go when you have something you are not keen to do, it creeps up to you and too soon I have to go upstairs and get the panniers and top box. We now have to take the bikes in to the place where we drop them off. I dump everything from the panniers and top box onto the spare bed and carry the boxes down to the bike. Darryl is also there busy loading up the boxes. Not much to say.

Riding there I think back of the day we got to Melbourne and the excitement of getting to the bikes and riding out on that large highway. It feels so long ago, was that really just three weeks ago? I have formed a very close bond with the bike and am thoroughly impressed with the BMW. It handed very well, except for the few slips we had in South Australia while riding in all that rain. We had no mechanical issues and even though I was a bit worried about the height/weight factor, it only once really caused me a problem to get the bike back upright once. I laugh inside my helmet thinking of me standing next to the road being attacked by the flies and not getting the bike upright. Man I miss the ride through the centre.

We make a couple of wrong turns, by accident I promise. I was not trying to drag it out, but then we pull into the house where we leave the bikes. A lump forms in my throat, but then we have to do the paper work and we have the opportunity to tell him about the trip. He has a quick look at the bikes to make sure they are not damaged and looking at the back tyre of the bikes, we can see that we did a lot of kilometres and a lot of the kilometres we did were on strait roads. It is run down to almost no thread left on the tyres and it has run down flat in the middle. When we got the bikes, these were brand new.

After the bikes are signed over to him, it is time for us to leave. He offers to drive us back to the hotel, which he then does. And as he drives away, we now have only the afternoon, a quick sleep and then the flight left of this trip.
The rest of the day is depressing. I already miss the bike and after having a couple of beers and dinner I go to bed and watch a movie before falling asleep. The only thing keeping me happy at this moment is that tomorrow I fly back to my wife and cats.

Day 24
Sunday 1 May 2011
From: Cairns
To: Wellington
Total distance travelled by motorcycle for trip: 9639 kilometres

All great adventures and stories, no matter how great or important, must wind down to an end. This story has now also reached that point where the story has been told and the end has been reached.

What else can I tell you? Well, I can tell you about getting up early yet again, even though there is no adventurous riding after getting up. Yes, I did make my final cup of coffee and was still feeling proud that I could.

I could tell you about smoking my last cigarette and quitting for good.

I could tell you about flying back to New Zealand and the shocking freezing cold weather we got when we walked out of the Wellington airport.

I can tell you about ending up just short of ten thousand kilometres riding and how that makes your ass feel.

And I could tell you about the adventure of going through the pregnancy and the birth of my daughter.

But, I think the story has been told now and all I really have left to say is thanks for joining me on this journey and I hope you laughed a few time and managed to get some kind of idea of what it was like going through the journey.

Are there any further trips on the horizon? Who knows? We have secretly been discussing options like Alaska to New York or California. We also mentioned Scandinavia, but right now I am not sure if this was it, or if there will be further adventures like this. I am now going to be a family man, so future trips would probably be in a camper van with the bicycles on the back, waving at the dudes racing past on their bikes.

However, there will always be a part of me still riding up and down Stuart Highway, which I will miss for the rest of my life. The scorpion rider will always be there and always love that thing called riding.

Thank you and good night Seattle.

This is Deon signing off and wishing you good mental health.

www.ingramcontent.com/pod-product-compliance
Lightning Source LLC
Chambersburg PA
CBHW061633040426
42446CB00010B/1398